More Praise for

FLUKE

'In truth we are subject to a ceaseless barrage of unpredictable, but life-changing, events. Marshalling a series of provocative examples, Brian Klaas paints a convincing picture of the central role of randomness, and why there can nevertheless be a bit of order amid the chaos'

Sean Carroll, author of *The Biggest Ideas in the Universe: Space, Time, and Motion*

'At this book's fascinating core is the idea that all of our actions count because of the web of connectivity that envelops us. Brian Klaas is masterful in surfacing stories of history upended on a whim'

Jonah Berger, *New York Times* bestselling author of *Contagious*

'Klaas calls attention to the way chance redirects our lives and spins us into new orbits, showing how we can be energized by all of the jostling . . . A must read!'

Maya Shankar, founder of the White House Social and Behavior Sciences Team and creator of A Slight Change of Plans podcast

FLUKE

FLUKE

CHANCE, CHAOS, AND
WHY *EVERYTHING* WE DO MATTERS

BRIAN KLAAS

JOHN MURRAY

First published in Great Britain in 2024 by John Murray (Publishers)

1

Copyright © Brian Klaas 2024

The right of Brian Klaas to be identified as the Author of the Work has been asserted by him in accordance with the Copyright, Designs and Patents Act 1988.

Text design by Hope Herr-Cardillo

A CIP catalogue record for this title is available from the British Library

Hardback ISBN 9781399804516
Trade Paperback ISBN 9781399804523
ebook ISBN 9781399804547

Typeset in Minion Pro

Printed and bound in Great Britain by Clays Ltd, Elcograf S.p.A.

John Murray policy is to use papers that are natural, renewable and recyclable products and made from wood grown in sustainable forests. The logging and manufacturing processes are expected to conform to the environmental regulations of the country of origin.

Carmelite House
50 Victoria Embankment
London EC4Y 0DZ

www.johnmurraypress.co.uk

John Murray Press, part of Hodder & Stoughton Limited
An Hachette UK company

When we try to pick out anything by itself, we find it hitched to everything else in the Universe.

—John Muir

CONTENTS

CHAPTER 1

INTRODUCTION

If you could rewind your life to the very beginning and then press play, would everything turn out the same?

On October 30, 1926, Mr. and Mrs. H. L. Stimson stepped off a steam train in Kyoto, Japan, and checked into room number 56 at the nearby Miyako Hotel. Once settled, they strolled through the former imperial capital, soaking up the city's autumnal explosion of color, as the Japanese maples turned crimson and the ginkgo trees burst into a golden shade of yellow, their trunks rising above a bed of lush green moss. They visited Kyoto's pristine gardens, tucked into the mudstone hills that frame the city. They marveled at its historic temples, the rich heritage of a bygone shogunate embedded in each timber. Six days later, Mr. and Mrs. Stimson packed up, paid their bill, and left.

But this was no ordinary tourist visit. The Stimson name in the ledger at the Miyako Hotel would become a historical record, a relic marking a chain of events in which one man played God, sparing one hundred thousand lives while condemning a similar number to death elsewhere. It was, perhaps, the most consequential sightseeing trip in human history.

Nineteen years later, far from the Japanese maples, in the sagebrush-dotted hills of New Mexico, an unlikely group of physicists and generals gathered at a top-secret location code-named Site Y. It was May 10, 1945, three days after the Nazis had surrendered. The focus now shifted to the

Pacific, where a bloody war of attrition seemed to have no end in sight. However, in this remote outpost of New Mexico, the scientists and soldiers saw a potential savior: a new weapon of unimaginable destruction that they called the Gadget.

No successful test had yet been carried out to demonstrate the weapon's full potential, but everyone at Site Y sensed they were getting close. In preparation, thirteen men were asked to join the Target Committee, an elite group that would decide how to introduce the Gadget to the world. Which city should be destroyed? They agreed targeting Tokyo wasn't a good idea, as heavy bombing had already devastated the new capital. After weighing up the alternatives, they agreed on a target. The first bomb would be dropped on Kyoto.

Kyoto was home to new wartime factories, including one that could churn out four hundred aircraft engines per month. Furthermore, leveling a former capital would deal a crushing blow to Japan's morale. The Target Committee also noted a small, but perhaps crucial, point: Kyoto was an intellectual hub with an educated population, home to the prestigious Kyoto University. Those who survived would, the committee supposed, recognize that this weapon represented a new era in human history—and that the war had already been lost. The Target Committee agreed: Kyoto must be destroyed.

The committee also agreed on three backup targets: Hiroshima, Yokohama, and Kokura. The target list was sent to President Truman. All they needed to do was wait for the bomb to be ready.

The Atomic Age dawned on July 16, 1945, with a successful test explosion in the vast emptiness of rural New Mexico. The Target Committee's decisions were no longer theoretical. Military strategists consulted detailed maps of Kyoto and decided on ground zero for the explosion: the city's railway yards. The intended blast site was only half a mile away from the Miyako Hotel, where Mr. and Mrs. H. L. Stimson had stayed two decades earlier.

INTRODUCTION

On August 6, 1945, the bomb code-named Little Boy fell from the sky not on Kyoto, but on Hiroshima, dropped from the *Enola Gay*. As many as 140,000 people were killed, most of them civilians. Three days later, on August 9, *Bockscar* dropped Fat Man on Nagasaki, adding roughly 80,000 casualties to the horrifying death toll.

But why was Kyoto spared? And why was Nagasaki—a city that hadn't even been considered a top-tier bombing target—destroyed? Remarkably, the lives of roughly two hundred thousand people teetered between life and death because of a tourist couple and a cloud.

By 1945, Mr. H. (Henry) L. Stimson had become America's secretary of war, the top civilian overseeing wartime operations. As a man without a uniform, Stimson felt it was his job to develop strategic goals, not to micromanage generals on how best to achieve them. But that all changed when the Target Committee picked Kyoto for destruction.

Stimson sprang into action. In a meeting with the head of the Manhattan Project, Stimson put his foot down: "I don't want Kyoto bombed." In a discussion with the commander of the U.S. armed forces, Stimson insisted that there was "one city that they must not bomb without my permission and that was Kyoto." Yet, despite his insistence, Kyoto kept reappearing on the targeting list. It ticked all the boxes, the generals insisted. It needed to be bombed. Why, they wondered, was Stimson hell-bent on protecting a nerve center of the Japanese war machine?

The generals didn't know about the Miyako Hotel, the majestic Japanese maples, or the golden ginkgo trees.

Stimson, unwavering, went straight to the top. He met with President Truman twice in late July 1945, each time outlining his vehement opposition to destroying Kyoto. Truman finally relented. Kyoto was taken out of consideration. The final targeting list contained four cities: Hiroshima, Kokura, Niigata, and a late addition, Nagasaki. Stimson had saved what the generals called his "pet city." The first bomb was dropped on Hiroshima instead.

The second bomb was to be dropped on the city of Kokura. But as the B-29 bomber approached the city, cloud cover made it difficult to see the ground below. The clouds were unexpected. A team of army meteorologists had predicted clear skies. The pilot circled, hoping the clouds would clear. When they didn't, the crew decided to attack a secondary target rather than risking a botched drop. As they approached Nagasaki, that city was also obscured by cloud cover. With fuel running low, they made one last pass, and the clouds parted at the last possible minute. The bomb fell at 11:02 a.m. on August 9, 1945. Nagasaki's civilians were doubly unlucky: the city was a last-minute addition to the backup targeting list, and it was leveled because of a fleeting window of poor weather over another city. If the bomber had taken off a few minutes earlier or a few minutes later, countless residents of Kokura might have been incinerated instead. To this day, the Japanese refer to "Kokura's luck" whenever someone unknowingly escapes from disaster.

———

Clouds spared one city, while one couple's vacation decades earlier saved another. The story of Kyoto and Kokura poses an immediate challenge to our convenient, simplified assumptions of cause and effect following a rational, ordered progression. We like to imagine that we can understand, predict, and control the world. We want a rational explanation to make sense of the chaos of life. The world isn't supposed to be a place where hundreds of thousands of people live or die from decades-old nostalgia for one couple's pleasant vacation, or because clouds flitted across the sky at just the right moment.

Children incessantly ask the most important question there is: "Why?" And from a very young age, I, like you, learned that causes and effects follow straightforward patterns—from X to Y. It's a useful, stripped-down version of reality with precisely one cause and one effect. It helps us navigate a more complex world, distilling everything that happens into clear-cut relationships that we can understand, then tame. Touching a hot stove causes pain. Smoking causes cancer. Clouds cause rain.

But in Japan, many decades ago, clouds were the immediate cause of something other than rain: mass death in one city rather than another. More peculiar still, that mass death can only be explained through the combination of a near-infinite array of arbitrary factors that had to connect together in just the right way to lead to the mushroom clouds over Hiroshima and Nagasaki: the rise of Emperor Hirohito, Einstein being born rather than somebody else, uranium being forged by geological forces millions of years earlier, countless soldiers on foreign battlefields, brilliant scientists, the Battle of Midway, on and on, until finally the devastation hinged on one pivotal vacation and one pivotal cloud. If anything about the countless preceding factors had been slightly changed, everything could have been different.

Whenever we revisit the dog-eared pages within our personal histories, we've all experienced Kokura's luck (though, hopefully, on a less consequential scale). When we consider the what-if moments, it's obvious that arbitrary, tiny changes and seemingly random, happenstance events can divert our career paths, rearrange our relationships, and transform how we see the world. To explain how we came to be who we are, we recognize pivot points that so often were out of our control. But what we ignore are the invisible pivots, the moments that we will never realize were consequential, the near misses and near hits that are unknown to us because we have never seen, and will never see, our alternative possible lives. We can't know what matters most because we can't see how it might have been.

If hundreds of thousands of people could live or die based on one couple's vacation choice decades earlier, which seemingly trivial choices or accidents could end up drastically changing the course of your life, even far into the future? Could being late to a meeting or missing an exit off the highway not just change your life, but alter the course of history? And if that happened, would you even realize it? Or would you remain blind to the radically different possible world you unknowingly left behind?

There's a strange disconnect in how we think about the past compared to our present. When we imagine being able to travel back in time, the warning is the same: make sure you don't touch *anything*. A microscopic change to the past could fundamentally alter the world. You could even accidentally delete yourself from the future. But when it comes to the present, we never think like that. Nobody tiptoes around with extreme care to make sure not to squish the wrong bug. Few panic about an irrevocably changed future after missing the bus. Instead, we imagine the little stuff doesn't matter much because everything just gets washed out in the end. But if every detail of the past created our present, then *every* moment of our present is creating our future, too.

In 1941, four years before the atomic bombs were dropped, the Argentine author Jorge Luis Borges wrote a short story titled "The Garden of Forking Paths." The central metaphor of the story is that humans are wandering through a garden in which the paths available to us are constantly shifting. We can survey the future and see infinite possible worlds, but in any given moment we must nonetheless decide where to take our next step. When we do, the possible paths before us change, forking endlessly, opening up new possible futures and closing others down. Every step is important.

But the most astonishing revelation is that our paths are not determined solely by us. Instead, the garden we live in has grown and been tended by everything and everyone that came before us. The paths open to us are the offshoots of past histories, paved by the past steps others have taken. More disorienting still, it is not just our steps that matter because the paths through our garden are also being constantly moved by the decisions of living people that we will neither see nor meet. In the image Borges paints for us, the paths we decide between are relentlessly redirected, our trajectories diverted, by the peculiar details of other lives we never notice, those hidden Kyoto and Kokura moments that determine the contours of our existence.

Yet, when we try to explain the world—to explain who we are, how we got here, and why the world works the way it does—we ignore the flukes. The squished bugs, the missed buses, all of it we dismiss as meaningless. We willfully ignore a bewildering truth: but for a few small changes, our lives and our societies could be profoundly different. Instead, we return again and again to the stripped-down, storybook version of reality, as we seek new knowledge of straightforward causes and effects. X causes Y, and X is always a major factor, never a minor or random or accidental tweak. Everything can be measured, plotted onto a graph, and controlled with just the right intervention or "nudge." We are seduced by pundits and data analysts, soothsayers who are often wrong, but rarely uncertain. When given the choice between complex uncertainty and comforting—but wrong—certainty, we too often choose comfort. Perhaps the world isn't so simple. Can we ever understand a world so altered by apparent flukes?

—

On June 15, 1905, Clara Magdalen Jansen killed all four of her children, Mary Claire, Frederick, John, and Theodore, in a little farmhouse in Jamestown, Wisconsin. She cleaned their bodies up, tucked them into bed, then took her own life. Her husband, Paul, came home from work to find his entire family under the covers of their little beds, dead, in what must have been one of the most horrific and traumatic experiences a human being can suffer.

There is a concept in philosophy known as *amor fati*, or love of one's fate. We must accept that our lives are the culmination of everything that came before us. You may not know the names of all eight of your great-grandparents off the top of your head, but when you look in the mirror, you are looking at generational composites of their eyes, their noses, their lips, an altered but recognizable etching from a forgotten past. When we meet someone new, we can be certain of one fact: none of their direct ancestors died before having children. It's a cliché, but true, to say that you wouldn't exist if your parents had not met in just the same, exact way. Even if the timing had been slightly different, a different person would have been born.

But that's also true for your grandparents, and your great-grandparents, and your great-great-grandparents, stretching back millennia. Your life depends on the courting of countless people in the Middle Ages, the survival of your distant Ice Age ancestors against the stalking whims of a saber-toothed tiger, and, if you go back even further, the mating preferences of chimpanzees more than 6 million years ago. Trace the human lineage back hundreds of millions of years and all our fates hinge on a single wormlike creature that, thankfully for us, avoided being squished. If those precise chains of creatures and couples hadn't survived, lived, and loved just the way that they did, other people might exist, but *you* wouldn't. We are the surviving barbs of a chain-link past, and if that past had been even marginally different, we would not be here.

The Paul who came home to that little farmhouse in Wisconsin was my great-grandfather, Paul F. Klaas. My middle name is Paul, a family name enshrined by him. I'm not related to his first wife, Clara, because she tragically severed her branch of the family tree just over a century ago. Paul got remarried, to my great-grandmother.

When I was twenty years old, my dad sat me down, showed me a 1905 newspaper clipping with the headline "Terrible Act of Insane Woman," and revealed the most disturbing chapter in our family's modern history. He showed me a photo of that Klaas family gravestone in Wisconsin, all the little kids on one side, Clara on the other, their deaths listed on the same date. It shocked me. But what shocked me even more was the realization that if Clara hadn't killed herself and murdered her children, I wouldn't exist. My life was only made possible by a gruesome mass murder. Those four innocent children died, and now I am alive, and you are reading my thoughts. *Amor fati* means accepting that truth, even embracing it, recognizing that we are the offshoots of a sometimes wonderful, sometimes deeply flawed past, and that the triumphs and the tragedies of the lives that came before us are the reason we're here. We owe our existences to kindness and cruelty, good and evil, love and hate. It can't be otherwise because, if it were, we would not be us.

"We are going to die, and that makes us the lucky ones," Richard Dawkins once observed. "Most people are never going to die because they are never going to be born. The potential people who could have been here in my place but who will in fact never see the light of day outnumber the sand grains of Arabia." These are the limitless possible futures, full of possible people, that Dawkins called "unborn ghosts." Their ranks are infinite; we are finite. With the tiniest adjustments, different people would be born, leading different lives, in a different world. Our existence is bewilderingly fragile, built upon the shakiest of foundations.

Why do we pretend otherwise? These basic truths about the fragility of our existence defy our most deeply held intuitions about how the world works. We instinctively believe that big events have big, straightforward causes, not small, accidental ones. As a social scientist, that's what I was taught to search for: the X that causes Y. Then, several years ago, I traveled to Zambia, in southern Africa, to study why a coup d'état attempt had failed. Was it because the political system was sufficiently stable? Or, perhaps, because of a lack of popular support for the putsch? I set off to discover the *real* reason.

The Zambian coup plot had been simple, but clever: the ringleader sent troops to kidnap the army commander. The plan was to force that general, at gunpoint, to announce the coup on the radio. With orders seemingly coming from the military brass, the plotters hoped the rest of the soldiers in the barracks would join the coup, and the government would collapse.

But when I interviewed soldiers who participated in the kidnapping attempt, everything I had been taught in tidy models of reality fell apart. As the soldiers ran into the house, the army commander leaped up from his bed, ran out the back door, and began climbing up the back of his compound's wall. One of the men I interviewed told me that he reached up to capture the general, grabbing his pant leg between his fingers. The army commander pulled himself up. The soldier tried to pull him down. As if in a slow-motion film, the fabric of the general's pant leg slipped through the soldier's fingertips, allowing the commander to clamber over the wall and escape. In a split second, the coup plot failed. If the soldier had been a millisecond quicker, his grip a tiny bit stronger, the regime would likely have collapsed. Democracy survived, quite literally, by a thread.

In his 1922 play, *Back to Methuselah*, George Bernard Shaw writes, "Some men see things as they are and ask, 'Why?' I dream things that never were and ask, 'Why not?'" How are we to make sense of a world in which our existence is predicated on a near-infinite number of past events that might have turned out differently? How are we to understand ourselves or our societies when one person's life is contingent on other people's deaths, as mine is, or where democracy survives by the thread of a pant leg? We can imagine alternate worlds as we contemplate a universe of infinite possibility. But we only have one world to observe, so we can't know what would've happened if small changes were made to the past. What if the Stimsons had missed their train to Kyoto in 1926 and had vacationed in Osaka instead? What if the bomber targeting

Kokura had taken off a few minutes later and the clouds had parted? What if my great-grandfather had come home early on that tragic day? The world would be different. But how?

I am a (disillusioned) social scientist. Disillusioned because I've long had a nagging feeling that the world doesn't work the way that we pretend it does. The more I grappled with the complexity of reality, the more I suspected that we have all been living a comforting lie, from the stories we tell about ourselves to the myths we use to explain history and social change. I began to wonder whether the history of humanity is just an endless, but futile, struggle to impose order, certainty, and rationality onto a world defined by disorder, chance, and chaos. But I also began to flirt with an alluring thought: that we could find new meaning in that chaos, learning to celebrate a messy, uncertain reality, by accepting that we, and everything around us, are all just flukes, spit out by a universe that can't be tamed.

Such intellectual heresy ran against everything I had been taught, from Sunday school to grad school. Everything happens for a reason; you just need to find out what it is. If you want to understand social change, just read more history books and social science papers. To learn the story of our species and how we came to be us, dive into some biology and familiarize yourself with Darwin. To grapple with the unknowable mysteries of life, spend time with the titans of philosophy, or if you're a believer, turn to religion. And if you want to understand the intricate mechanisms of the universe, learn physics.

But what if such enduring human mysteries are all part of the same big question?

Specifically, it's the biggest puzzle humanity must grapple with: *Why do things happen?* The more I read, year after year, the more I realized that there are no ready-made solutions to that enormous puzzle just waiting to be plucked from political science theories, philosophy tomes, economic equations, evolutionary biology studies, geology research, anthropology articles, physics proofs, psychology experiments, or neuroscience lectures. Instead, I began to recognize that each of these disparate realms of human knowledge offers a piece that, when combined, can help us get closer to solving this bewildering puzzle. The challenge of this book is to try to join many of those pieces together, to yield a new, coherent picture that reframes our sense of who we are and how our world works.

When enough puzzle pieces snap together, a fresh image emerges. As we see it come into focus, there's hope that we can replace the comforting lies we tell ourselves with something that approaches a more accurate truth, even if it means that we must flip our entire, deeply ingrained worldview on its head. A fair warning: some of you may find that flip disorienting. But we already live in disorienting times—of conspiratorial politics and pandemics, economic shocks, climate change, and fresh society-bending magic, produced by the wizardry of artificial intelligence. In a world of rapid change, many of us feel lost in a sea of uncertainty. But when lost at sea, clinging to comforting lies will only help us sink. The best life raft may just be the truth.

We live in a more interesting and complex world than we are led to believe. If we gaze a little closer, then the storybook reality of neat, tidy connections might just give way to a reality defined much more by chance and chaos, an arbitrarily intertwined world in which every moment, no matter how small, can count.

In the coming pages, I aim to dispel some of the more damaging myths we pretend are true while exploring three facets of the human experience that can help us understand ourselves: *how our species came to be the way it is and why that matters to us; how our own entangled lives are diverted endlessly by arbitrary and accidental events beyond our control;* and *why we too often misunderstand the dynamics of modern society.* As I'll demonstrate, even the tiniest flukes can matter. As the late philosopher Hannah Arendt once put it, "The smallest act in the most limited circumstances bears the seed of boundlessness, because one deed, and sometimes one word, suffices to change every constellation."

—

Some of you may already be objecting to these bold claims and lofty quotes. If the storybook version of reality is a lie, and chance and chaos drive change more than we imagine, then why is there so much apparent order in our lives, in history, and in the universe? It's true: many facets of our lives are stable, dictated by regularities and comforting routine. Perhaps I'm overstating the case, and but for a few strange stories such as the one from Kyoto, most random encounters and happenstance events are merely inconsequential curiosities that don't matter.

For decades, the field of evolutionary biology has been divided by these two contrasting ways of viewing the world. One camp sees life as following a constrained, stable trajectory. Another isn't so sure, pointing to a perpetually branching tree of life, eternally diverted by chance and chaos. To frame this debate, biologists pose the question using opposing terms: Is the world *contingent* or *convergent*? The central question is whether evolution proceeds in predictable ways, regardless of freak events and random fluctuations, or if those contingencies can lead evolution down diverging paths. As we'll see, those terms don't just help us understand Darwinian theory and the beaks of finches in the Galápagos. They also provide a useful way of understanding why our own lives—and our societies—take unexpected turns.

Imagine our lives are like a film and you could rewind back to yesterday. Then, when you reach the start of your day, you change one small detail, such as whether you stopped to have coffee before you rushed out the door. If your day stayed mostly the same whether or not you paused to have your coffee, then that would be a convergent event. The details didn't matter much. What happened was bound to happen regardless. The train of your life left the station a few minutes later but followed the same track. However, if you stopped to have coffee and everything about your future life unfolded differently, then that would be a contingent event because so much hinged on one small detail.

The natural world seems to seesaw between contingency and convergence. Sixty-six million years ago, an asteroid nine miles wide struck Earth with the force of 10 billion Hiroshima bombs. It crashed into gypsum-rich rock beneath the shallow sea of the Yucatán Peninsula. When the asteroid hit the gypsum, the explosion unleashed huge clouds of poisonous sulfur into the atmosphere. Vast amounts of pulverized rock were also thrown up into the atmosphere, creating intense friction that culminated in an "infrared pulse." The surface of the planet surged by 500°F, cooking dinosaurs at the same temperature as a broiled chicken.

The heat was so great after the impact that the survivors mostly fit into one of two groups: those who could burrow underground, or those that lived in the seas. When we look at animals alive today, from jungles to deserts, or, indeed, when we look in the mirror, we're seeing the offshoots of these asteroid survivors, an arbitrary branch of life largely descended from resourceful diggers.

Change one detail, and we can imagine a completely different world. If the asteroid had hit a moment earlier or later, it would have hit deep ocean instead of shallow seas, releasing far less toxic gas, and killing many fewer species. If the asteroid had been delayed by just one minute, it might have missed Earth entirely. Even more mind-boggling, Harvard astrophysicist Lisa Randall has proposed that the asteroid came from oscillations in the sun's orbit as it passes through dark matter. Those small gravitational disturbances, she argues, flung the asteroid from the distant Oort cloud toward our planet. But for one small vibration in an unfathomably distant reach of deep space, dinosaurs might have survived—and humans might never have existed. That's contingency.

Now, consider our eyes instead. We've evolved extraordinarily complex, specialized rod and cone cells in our retinas that allow us to sense light, which our brains can process and translate into vivid images of the world. Those abilities are crucial to our survival. But for most of Earth's history, animals didn't have eyes. That was, until a random mutation accidentally created a clump of light-sensitive cells. Those fortunate creatures could tell when they were in brighter or darker spaces, which helped them survive. Over time, this survival advantage was reinforced through evolution by natural selection. Eventually, we ended up with sophisticated eyes, derived from a mutation to a snippet of DNA called the PAX6 gene. At first glance, that random PAX6 mutation seems like another contingent event: our distant ancestors got lucky. Millions of years later, we can watch Netflix.

But when researchers began sequencing the genomes of creatures that are astonishingly different from us, such as squid and octopus, they discovered something remarkable. Octopus and squid eyes are extremely similar to our eyes. It turns out that octopus and squid eyes emerged independently from a separate but similar mutation of the PAX6 gene. Lightning struck twice in the same gene. Our evolutionary track and the evolutionary track of octopuses and squid diverged roughly 600 million years ago, but we ended up with more or less the same kind of eye. The implication isn't that both humans and squids both beat the odds and won the species lottery. Rather, the lesson is that nature sometimes converges toward the same effective solution when presented with the same problem—because only so many solutions will work. That's a crucial insight because it suggests that the bumps produced by small, seemingly chance events sometimes get smoothed out in the end. If octopus eyes and human eyes end up mostly doing the same thing, maybe tiny changes don't matter so much. Contingency might change how the discovery happens, but the outcome is similar. It's as though hitting the snooze button in the morning might delay your journey, but not change your life path. You get to the same destination no matter what. That's convergence.

Convergence is the "everything happens for a reason" school of evolutionary biology. Contingency is the "stuff happens" theory.

These frameworks are useful for understanding ourselves. If our lives are driven by contingencies, then small fluctuations play a huge role in everything from our career trajectories to whom we marry and the children we have. But if convergence rules, then apparently random or chance events are more likely to be mere curiosities that don't radically change our lives. We could ignore the flukes.

For centuries, the dominant worldview in science and society has been defined by an unshakable faith in convergence. Newton's laws weren't supposed to be broken. Adam Smith wrote of an "invisible hand" that guides our behavior. Biologists initially resisted Charles Darwin's theories because they put too much emphasis on random chance and too little emphasis on elegant order. Uncertainty has long been shunned, shoved aside by rational-choice theories and clockwork models. Small variations are dismissed as "noise" that should be ignored, so we can focus on the real "signal." Even our famous quotes are infused with the neat logic of convergence. "The arc of the moral universe is long, but it bends toward justice." What it doesn't ever do, we are told, is bend at random.

Several decades ago, a heretic of evolutionary theory named Motoo Kimura challenged that conventional wisdom, insisting that small, arbitrary, and random fluctuations matter more than we think. As a child growing up in the 1920s, Kimura didn't seem destined for a life of academic study. He loathed going to school because he was taught in a system in which conformity and deference to accepted knowledge was required. Students who experimented with new ideas were disciplined. Knowledge meant order and certainty, transmitted down from authority. Kimura was naturally curious, but his school was no place for an inquisitive mind. Finally, in 1937, one teacher encouraged Kimura's curiosity. Kimura discovered a hidden academic passion: botany. He vowed to devote his life to learning the secrets of plants.

Then, in 1939, Kimura and his entire family were sickened by food poisoning. His brother died. Kimura was stuck at home, recovering. Unable to study plants, he began to read about mathematics, inheritance, and chromosomes. His obsession with plants morphed into an obsession with understanding how change can be scripted into our genes. Kimura's career trajectory—and later the field of evolutionary biology—pivoted on a rotten meal.

As a budding evolutionary theorist, Kimura pored over the molecular building blocks of life. The closer he looked, the more he began to suspect that genetic mutations occurred without much rhyme or reason. Many were neither helpful nor harmful. Instead, he discovered that they were often random and meaningless, neutral changes. Whenever a mutation occurred, Kimura's predecessors searched for an explanation, a reason, something that made sense. Kimura just shrugged. Some things happen without reasons. Some things just are.

Kimura's discoveries reshaped the field of evolutionary biology, bringing fresh insights that have influenced several generations of scholars. But his ideas are broader than that. Kimura's thinking, as we will see, can help us better understand the complexity of our world and the flukes within it. Perhaps not everything happens for a reason. And maybe, in an intertwined world, the smallest changes can produce the biggest effects.

Kimura was also a living, breathing illustration of his own ideas, a walking advertisement for how arbitrary, interconnected changes can create contingency. In 1944, Kimura had set off for university, hoping to avoid being conscripted into Japanese military service. In August 1945, he was a student at Kyoto University. If Mr. and Mrs. H. L. Stimson had missed their train in 1926 and vacationed in Osaka instead, Motoo Kimura and his ideas would likely have been obliterated in a blinding flash of atomic light.

CHAPTER 2

CHANGING ANYTHING CHANGES EVERYTHING

The delusion of individualism in an entangled existence

Few have had quite so dramatic an escape as Motoo Kimura narrowly avoiding death by atomic bomb. But everyone can pinpoint a moment that, in hindsight, was a fluke that changed his or her life. Perhaps it was a more traditional pivot, such as a chance encounter with your future spouse, or taking a class in high school that diverted your career plans to a new passion. Or maybe it was a near miss, such as a swerve of the steering wheel that kept you alive, or having a generous offer rejected on a house or an apartment only to find something far better that you now call home. These moments stand out because they're obviously consequential. We contemplate what could have been. It's clear there was an alternative path. But for one small change, spouses never meet, passions remain undiscovered, near misses become fatal hits.

But these seem to be the outliers, the moments we marvel at precisely because they are so rare and unusual. We feel as though we construct our lives not with chance, but with the building blocks of large, hopefully wise, choices—choices that we feel we, alone, control. We may seek advice for which path to choose, but we would not seek advice for that which we can't control. (Nobody buys a self-help book for how to avoid extinction from the next cataclysmic asteroid impact.) When we make big, life-altering decisions, it's obvious to us that we're changing our trajectories. Picking the right college. Working hard at our first job to set our career on the right track. Choosing the right person for a shared life. Focus on getting the big things right, we're told, and everything will be all right. Watch just about any inspirational TED Talk or read just about any self-help book, and you will be told that you, alone, are the solution that you seek. Those messages are popular because most of us view our lives through an individualist prism. Our life stories are not crowdsourced. Our major decisions define our path, which means *we* control our path. To understand that path, worship at the Altar of Me.

Every so often, though, we see a fleeting, perplexing glimpse of our path colliding with someone else's in a way that seems out of our control. We call those moments luck, or coincidence, or fate. But we classify them as aberrations. When the world functions "normally," life seems to have a predictable, well-ordered regularity, a regularity that we convince ourselves we can mostly direct, masters of our own destinies. Then, whenever we're confronted by strange coincidences or chance diversions that seem to challenge that confident certainty, we shrug at the brief respite from normality and move on, preparing ourselves to make the next big call that shapes our future. It's a style of thinking so ubiquitous and commonplace that it's uncontested. That's just how the world works.

There's just one problem: it's a lie. It's *the* lie that defines our times. We might call it the *delusion of individualism*. We cling to this delusion, the way a man overboard clings to floating debris. But every so often, a story comes along that makes clear how absurd it is to think of ourselves as separate or separable from everyone and everything else.

In the summer of 2022, a routine tragedy took place off the coast of Greece. A tourist named Ivan from North Macedonia was swept out to sea. His friends rushed to alert the coast guard, but the searches came up empty. Ivan was declared lost at sea, presumed dead. Then, eighteen hours later, Ivan was found. Miraculously, he was alive. It seemed impossible. But just before he slipped below the waves to drown, Ivan had spotted a small soccer ball, floating on the surface in the distance. He swam over to it with his last ounce of strength. He clung to it through the night and was rescued. The ball saved his life.

When Ivan's tale of survival made the Greek news, a mother of two boys reacted with shock. She recognized the ball Ivan was holding. Her two boys were playing with that exact ball ten days earlier when one of them accidentally kicked it into the sea. The ball had bobbed across the waves for eighty miles, until it converged with a drowning swimmer at precisely the right moment. The boys had thought little of the lost ball. They shrugged and bought a new one. Only later did they realize that without their accidental kick, Ivan would now be dead.

The real story of our lives is often written in the margins. Small details matter, and even the apparently insignificant choices of people we will never meet can seal our own fates—though most of us will never see that quite so clearly as Ivan did. The crucial mistake is to pretend Ivan is an outlier, a break from the normal way the world works. He's not. Rather, Ivan just accidentally caught a clear glimpse of what's happening around us constantly in our entangled existence, all while we ignore it because we're blinkered by a delusional worldview that assumes we're independent units solely in charge of our own lives.

The tapestry of life is woven with a magical sort of thread, one that grows longer the more you unspool it. Every present moment is created with seemingly unrelated strands that stretch far into the distant past. Whenever you tug on one thread, you'll always meet unexpected resistance because each is connected to every other part of the tapestry. The truth is, as Martin Luther King Jr. wrote in his letter from a Birmingham jail, "We are caught in an inescapable network of mutuality, tied in a single garment of destiny."

—

In 1814, a French polymath named Pierre-Simon Laplace was grappling with the enduring mysteries of such an intertwined existence. Why are we so bad at predicting our futures? Why do events so often surprise us? Is it possible to understand why the world changes, so we can better control it?

Laplace's mathematical genius stood on the shoulders of Isaac Newton, a man who must have seemed superhuman to his scientific contemporaries. Before Newton, the world was a wild enigma, impossible to decipher, closely guarding her secrets. Newton cracked the code and discovered many of those secrets, which he wrote as "laws" that explained the regular and predictable behavior of bodies in motion. Newton's laws created a profound shift, not just in our understanding of the universe, but also in our philosophical perspective toward it. In the ancient past, change and calamity were ascribed to the machinations of the gods. Ships were wrecked and towers crumbled because men had angered the immortals or failed to pay them sufficient tribute. Newton sent such interventionist deities into retirement. No longer did we need god(s) to explain every minute change in our lives or in the natural world. We just needed a supernatural power to explain where the laws that govern the universe came from in the first place. God may have created the clock, but Newton's laws kept it ticking.

That gave Laplace an idea. If we live in a clocklike universe governed by rigid laws, then understanding the mechanisms of the clock should allow us to predict the future with complete accuracy. A fuzzy world could be brought into sharp focus. We could see the future as clearly as we see the present. We just needed the right tools. After all, before the scientific revolution, accurately predicting the motion of billiard balls on a table would have seemed like wizardry. With Newton's laws, the equations of mathematics and physics gave you the power to do magic, to see the future. Could the whole universe be transformed into something that's entirely predictable?

Laplace surmised that every event, every gust of wind, every molecule, is governed by a rigid set of scientific rules: Newton's unbending laws of nature. Therefore, if you wanted to predict whether someone playing billiards would sink a ball into the corner pocket, you'd need to understand the principles of Newtonian physics, the weight of the ball, the force and the angle used to strike the ball, but you'd also need to know the seemingly insignificant details: the temperature in the room, whether a breeze was coming in from an open door, or whether traces of chalk residue were left on the cue stick. But *if* you had all the necessary information—down to the level of the atoms in the ball and the air molecules floating around the room—Laplace figured that you'd have perfect accuracy at predicting where the billiard ball would end up. Then, he proposed a radical thought: What if humans are just like billiard balls, too, our lives knocking together, but following the same laws of nature?

Drawing on that logic, Laplace came up with an intriguing thought experiment. Imagine you had a supernatural creature—now referred to as Laplace's demon—with omniscient intelligence. It would have no power to change anything, but it could know, with absolute precision, every detail about every single atom in the universe, from the molecular building blocks for each grain of sand on Bondi Beach to the chemical composition of each bacterium in the darkest recesses of an armadillo's gut in Paraguay. If that being existed, Laplace suggested, "for such an intellect nothing would be uncertain and the future just like the past would be present before its eyes." In other words, with perfect information, the demon would see reality across time and space like a solved jigsaw puzzle, so it would understand why everything was happening and could therefore know what would happen next. The drifting soccer ball surprised Ivan, but Laplace's demon—who could see clearly how everything fit together in the past, present, and future—would know the ball was coming when Ivan started to panic. For the demon, the world would hold no mysteries.

Other scientists and philosophers reject the clockwork world of Laplace's demon. It's not that we lack understanding or the right tools to measure a clockwork universe, they argue, but rather that the mysteries of the universe are unknowable. Our lives could be different. The future will always be enigmatic, no matter the technology, no matter the omniscient demons we can imagine. It's not that we don't know. It's that we can't know.

So, which is it? Do we live in a clockwork universe, or an uncertain one?

Sixty years ago, a man named Edward Norton Lorenz brought us closer to the answer. Since his childhood, Lorenz had taken an interest in the weather. But he'd set that interest aside as he went off to study mathematics at Dartmouth and later to pursue a doctorate at Harvard. Then, at the height of his studies, World War II broke out. Uncle Sam needed everyone, including budding mathematicians. By chance, Lorenz caught a glimpse of a recruitment flyer for the army's weather-forecasting unit. Remembering his childhood fascination, Lorenz signed up. He received advanced training in meteorological systems at MIT and was then shipped off to Saipan and Okinawa, where he was in charge of the "upper air section" of forecasting cloud cover for bombing runs against Japan. (It's likely he was a key figure in the weather forecasting when Kokura got lucky with unpredicted cloud cover.)

Even with the best minds and the best equipment, meteorology in the 1940s was guesswork. After the war, Lorenz took the lessons he'd learned from those unpredictable weather systems in the Pacific and decided to test larger truths about why things happen. In the 1960s, computers were still in their infancy, so it was impossible to simulate real-world weather systems. Nonetheless, Lorenz created a simplified miniature world on his LGP-30 computer. Instead of the millions of different variables that affect weather systems in the real world, his computerized model had just twelve simple variables, such as temperature and wind speed. In that primitive digital universe, Lorenz played the role of Laplace's demon: he could always know the exact measurements of everything in his imaginary world. Could he, like the demon, use that precise knowledge to see into the future?

One day, Lorenz decided to rerun a simulation. To save time, he decided to restart midway through, plugging in the data points from that earlier snapshot. He figured that so long as he set the wind speed and temperature at the same levels, the weather patterns would be repeated, just as they were before. Same conditions, same outcomes.

Instead, something strange happened. Even though Lorenz set everything up as it had been before, the weather that emerged in his rerun simulation was different in every way. There must have been some mistake, he figured. No other explanation made sense. But then, after a lot of scowling over the data to make sense of it, Lorenz realized what had happened. His computer printouts rounded data to three decimal places. If, for example, the exact wind speed was 3.506127 miles per hour, the printout would display it as 3.506 miles per hour. When he plugged those slightly truncated values from the printouts back into the simulation, he was always off by a tiny amount (in this case, just 0.000127 miles per hour). Such seemingly meaningless alterations, such tiny rounding errors, were producing major changes.

That led Lorenz to a realization that cracked the foundations of how we understand the world. Even in a clockwork universe with controlled conditions, minuscule changes can make an enormous difference. Just by raising the temperature one-millionth of a degree or lowering atmospheric pressure by a trillionth of a bar, the weather two months later could morph from a clear blue sky into a torrential downpour, even a hurricane. Lorenz's findings created the concept of *the butterfly effect*, the notion that a butterfly flapping its wings in Brazil could trigger a tornado in Texas.

Lorenz had inadvertently given birth to *chaos theory*. The lesson was clear: if Laplace's demon could exist, its measurements would need to be flawless. If the creature was off by even one atom, its predictions would, over time, become wildly wrong. We now know that many systems are chaotic—so sensitive to the minutiae of their initial conditions that, even though they follow a clockwork logic, they're impossible to predict. Still to this day, with the best supercomputers at our disposal, our weather forecasts are unreliable—and meteorologists rarely even bother trying to predict more than a week or two into the future. Microscopic differences can lead to big changes. Sherlock Holmes once quipped, "It has long been an axiom of mine that the little things are infinitely the most important." Chaos theory proved Holmes right.

Because small changes can make such a big difference, the universe will always *appear* uncertain, even random, to us. No matter the technological leaps we make, humans will never become Laplace's demon. If there is a clockwork universe ticking away behind everything we see and experience, we will never fully understand it.

Chaos theory meant that even those predictable billiard balls had to be reclassified as unpredictable. Even the slightly different pull created by the gravitational mass of human bodies standing near a billiard table would make the movement of a ball impossible to predict after it bounced off other balls six or seven times, which is why even a perfect bank shot can't be planned beyond a few collisions. If that's true at such small scales, imagine what it's like for the uncountable trillions upon trillions of atomic billiard balls that compose the world. The tiniest fluctuations matter. Confidence in a predictable future, therefore, is the providence of charlatans and fools. Or, as the theologian Pema Chödrön put it, "If you're invested in security and certainty, you are on the wrong planet."

Chaos theory changed how we understand the world. But Lorenz's discovery also leads to some unsettling questions about our own existence. If an infinitesimal change in wind speed can create storms a few months later, what about your decision to leap out of bed on a Tuesday morning rather than hitting the snooze button? Are our lives ruled by insignificant choices and seemingly random bits of misfortune or luck? And here's the perplexing bit: if Henry Stimson's vacation plans in 1926 can affect which one hundred thousand people live or die two decades later, thousands of miles away, then perhaps it's not just *our* snooze buttons we have to worry about. The snooze buttons and seemingly insignificant choices of 8 billion other people also sway our life trajectories, even if we never perceive it.

If you squint at reality for more than a moment, you'll realize that we're inextricably linked to one another across time and space. In an intertwined world such as ours, *everything* we do matters because our ripples can produce storms—or calm them—in the lives of others. That means that we control far less of our world than we think we do, because earth-shattering events can develop based on strange, unexpected interactions that are nearly impossible to predict. It feels more comforting to pretend the opposite: that we, as individuals, are in charge of an ordered, separable world. So, pretend we do.

Whatever the reasons for why we tend to discount the total unity of our world and instead divide everything into neat boxes, interconnectedness *is* reality. It drives everything. Ours is an intertwined world. Once you accept that entangled existence, it becomes clear that chance, chaos, and arbitrary accidents play an outsize role in why things happen. In an intertwined world, flukes matter. There can be no true split between "the signal" and "the noise." There is no noise. The noise of one person's life is the signal for another, even when we can't detect it.

That same dynamic is true for me, descended from the husband of a mentally ill murderess, and it's true for you, though, I hope, in a less macabre way. Every development in life pivots on small, contingent details, ad infinitum. We'd like to pretend it isn't true, but reality doesn't care what we think. We forever surf on the ripples of others.

Off the coast of Greece, Ivan experienced that truth quite literally. We mostly ignore it.

What's true for individuals is also true for societies. What accounts for what Nassim Nicholas Taleb calls Black Swans—large, unexpected, consequential events that wallop us in our complacency? In recent centuries, the world has become more intertwined, not less. This isn't a novel observation, but it does mean that small changes, accidents, and flukes can culminate in Black Swans more than ever before. One volcano erupting in Iceland can strand millions of people. One ship stuck in the Suez Canal can cause supply-chain disruptions in dozens of countries. One person getting infected with a novel virus in a city in China can shut down everything, everywhere, all at once. Ours is a hyperconnected world.

Our world is not just intertwined, but ever-changing, even if we can't sense it. While you're reading this, you're changing. You're aging (a minuscule amount, thankfully), but the neural networks in your brain are also imperceptibly changing as you perceive each word. Crucially, even when we're seemingly not doing anything of note, events are taking place outside your immediate surroundings that will change your life in the future, though you won't realize it yet. Heraclitus, the ancient Greek philosopher, rightly pointed out, "No man ever steps in the same river twice. For it's not the same river and he's not the same man." To that, Cratylus, a student of Heraclitus, added that we are not mere passive observers. When you step in a river, *you* change it. Nothing is static. Even microscopic changes add up over time.

Scientists, particularly those who study complex systems, have long known this truth. In a chaotic system, such as the ones Lorenz discovered, a small change in any subset of the system creates unpredictable effects throughout everything else. It's impossible for those scientists to miss the obvious point that nothing is truly independent. Everything is part of a unified whole.

A small group of humans have experienced this truth in a more visceral way than the rest of us: those who have seen the entirety of Earth all at once, set against the stygian blackness of space. That view moves people, resetting worldviews in an instant. But those lucky few astronauts who have glimpsed that full-planet view weren't exactly sentimental free spirits, easily swayed by beauty. Instead, when the American space program began, NASA searched for potential recruits by looking for rational and robotic pragmatists, those least likely to be moved by emotion or awe. NASA worried that those with the dispositions of philosophers and poets might crash an aircraft at a crucial moment, overcome by the experience.

Despite the astronauts being chosen based on their comparatively cold, unfeeling temperaments, those who have seen blue-green Earth in its entirety have become overwhelmed by a perspective-shattering epiphany. "It was the most beautiful, heart-catching sight of my life," said Frank Borman, who commanded the Apollo 8 mission. Edgar Mitchell, the pilot of Apollo 14, agreed, noting that the experience provided him an "ecstasy of unity" and made him recognize the unbroken connection of existence. In gazing out that tiny window, it occurred to him "that the molecules of my body and the molecules of the spacecraft itself were manufactured long ago in the furnace of one of the ancient stars that burned in the heavens about me." This reckoning with oneness is so common and profound for those who see Earth from the outside that it has a name: the overview effect.

We remain stuck with a limited field of view. Expand that view, as the astronauts did gazing out of their spacecrafts, and it immediately becomes clear that individualism is a mirage. Connection defines us.

At first, an intertwined world seems terrifying. Nobody wants to be told they're not in control, or that a stranger's decision half a world away, or a long-forgotten decision decades in the past, could kill us or cause our economy to collapse into a crippling recession. Like it or not, that's how the world works. Even decisions by those who are long dead continue to matter. You wouldn't be reading this sentence if four children hadn't been murdered in Wisconsin in 1905.

That reality, for better and for worse, isn't terrifying, but wondrous, giving every moment of life potentially hidden meaning. It flips the individualist worldview on its head. Rather than being in control of our individual destinies when we make big decisions, even our smallest decisions matter, forever altering the world. There is scientific truth in the opening lines to William Blake's poem "Auguries of Innocence": "To see a World in a Grain of Sand / And a Heaven in a Wild Flower / Hold Infinity in the palm of your hand / And Eternity in an hour."

It's time to adjust our lenses of how we see ourselves within the world. Our chaotic, intertwined existence reveals a potent, astonishing fact:

We control nothing, but influence everything.

———

Few recognize this astonishing fact because we're bombarded with messages that tell us the opposite: individualist, not intertwined. The myth of a controllable world that each of us can tame is ubiquitous, particularly in modern Western society. Everything about modern culture makes us feel like the main character, bending the world to our whims. Entitled adults live stream minor grievances. Three times as many children now aspire to be YouTube stars than astronauts. The American dream is the delusion of individualism on steroids. Everything is up to us! If that were true, then we could write off the fluctuations and ripples produced by other people's decisions across time and space. But then, every so often, life's hidden connections bludgeon us over the head with a story such as that of Ivan and the soccer ball. For a brief moment, there's a jarring snag in the myth of individualism. But then we just shrug, move on, and keep living the lie.

Western modernity, the dominant system of thoughts and beliefs in our world, has produced simplified myths to explain how change happens in our lives and in our societies. The conventional wisdom of separated individuals acting purposively and independently has become so pervasive that saying something like "Actually, we're all completely intertwined in a unified causal web of existence" makes one sound like a New Age guru with a self-help book, rather than someone proclaiming an observable, empirical fact. (Within science, it's often the theoretical physicists who embrace and spread this message the most.)

Our modern misconceptions trim the vast complexity of reality down, allowing us to cram its maddening messiness into tidy little boxes that feel more manageable. Those boxes replace uncertainty with certainty, chaos with order, disordered complexity with elegant simplicity, and an intertwined, accidental world with one governed by (mostly) rational individuals making independent choices. Those boxes comfort us. Humans like straightforward stories, in which X causes Y, not in which a thousand disparate factors combine to cause Y. We focus on big, singular changes to explain big events, ignoring the small grains of sand that pile up and create avalanches. We even put the vastness of nature into its own little separate box, treating it as a place we go to for a hike rather than seeing ourselves and nature as inseparable parts of one unified whole.

Our language reflects these misconceptions. As the writer and philosopher Alan Watts noted, when we speak of our birth, we often say that we came *into* the universe when plainly we came *out* of it, an aggregation of atoms that happen to be rearranged, happily and temporarily, into a human being. Everywhere you look, flawed assumptions abound, flowing out of this deceptive paradigm—especially the lie that the tiny fluctuations of life can safely be ignored. Our Western culture, which prioritizes individualism more than all other human societies in history, has made it easy to ignore the astounding connections that bind us together.

Not everyone, past or present, has bought into the delusion of

31

individualism. There is a fundamental division in philosophy, between the *atomistic* and the *relational* view of the world. The atomistic view holds that our individual nature is separable, the same way that one can describe any material in the universe by subdividing it into constituent atoms. Study the components, not how they interact. As the philosopher Elizabeth Wolgast put it, in atomistic thought "the individuals who make up a society are interchangeable like molecules in a bucket of water—society a mere aggregate of individuals." Western philosophical traditions tend to emphasize atomism.

Eastern philosophy tends to be dominated by relational thinking. The connections between components within the system, rather than just the components themselves, are most important. The relational view holds that individuals can only be understood as part of something larger, that our identities are defined socially and contextually within nature as part of a wider whole. In a relational mindset, we define our identities in reference to others, whether it's as a spouse, a mother, or an accountant. Even if we think of ourselves in atomistic terms, our lives are relationally defined. The connections and relationships between individuals constitute society. Nobody introduces themselves as "a human" at a cocktail party.

Where did this divide between Eastern and Western thinking come from? Some have argued it could partly be due to an accident of zoological history. In the book of Genesis, God proclaims, "Let us make man in our image, after our likeness: and let them have dominion over the fish of the sea, and over the fowl of the air, and over the cattle, and over all the earth, and over every creeping thing that creepeth upon the earth." In this vision of a world humans are distinct from the rest of the natural world. That felt true for the inhabitants of the Middle East and Europe around the time of the birth of Christianity. Camels, cows, goats, mice, and dogs composed much of the encountered animal kingdom, a living menagerie of beings that are quite unlike us.

In many Eastern cultures, by contrast, ancient religions tended to emphasize our unity with the natural world. One theory suggests that was partly because people lived among monkeys and apes. We recognized ourselves in them. As the biologist Roland Ennos points out, the word *orangutan* even means "man of the forest." Hinduism has Hanumen, a monkey god. In China, the Chu kingdom revered gibbons. In these familiar primates, the theory suggests, it became impossible to ignore that we were part of nature—and nature was part of us.

Regardless of its origins, the relational and atomistic divide is mirrored in religion. Hindus refer to the *Brahman*, the concept of total unity for all that exists in the universe, in contrast to the *atman*, or individual soul, which only has the illusion of independence from the whole. In Advaita Vedanta traditions of Hindu thought, true liberation can only occur when one recognizes the illusion of the self. Hindus therefore explicitly label individualism as a delusion. Relatedly, Buddhists seek to attain a sense of "nonself," the inversion of an individualist worldview. Many indigenous cultures echo these sentiments of intertwined rather than individual. For example, the Rarámuri people, who live in the highlands of the Sierra Madre, use a concept called Iwfgara to describe "the total interconnectedness and integration of all life."

Christians used to think more along these lines, too. Early European Christians saw God not as separate from nature, but as part of it—"present everywhere in everything." As Karen Armstrong, author of *A History of God*, explains, that meant that God was not a being, but being itself. By the Enlightenment, the conception of the divine had changed. God had been transformed into a separate agent, which Newton saw as an individual who was "very well skilled in Mechanicks and Geometry."

Today, modern Christianity tends to prioritize the role of a unique self, both in individual moral responsibility and in prayers asking for divine intervention from a singular God who acts and is depicted as an individual. In some strains of modern Protestantism, particularly in the

United States, "prosperity theology" has even taken root, in which an individual's faith, donations to religious causes, and positive thinking will directly be rewarded by God. Wealth is on a divine menu, but it's up to you, and you alone, to order it.

For many post-Enlightenment Christians, the scripts of our lives are written above us by a sole supernatural author, rather than all around us through a more diffuse divine presence. If Ivan avoided drowning, it wasn't because we live in an enmeshed world of intertwined threads that happened to produce a lifesaving knot, but because God, an individual deity, sent the soccer ball to save him as part of a hidden, larger plan. It's a crucial shift in interpretation and meaning, reinforcing a conception of a world that is shaped by intentional, separable personal decisions. American cultural identity has been particularly influenced by this outlook, as the "Protestant work ethic" suggests that anyone can demonstrate their godliness through their commitment to hard work—a view of eternal salvation that is individualist, through and through.

Over time, individualism has been reinforced because in modernity we've also lost our sense of connection to the natural world. We now see ourselves as above, rather than part of, everything and everyone around us. Hunter-gatherers were far more ignorant than we are of science and technology, but most ordinary people in the distant past had closer connections to nature and her secrets. They couldn't speak across oceans or travel into the heavens, but their lives were dependent on a general understanding of the world. We, by contrast, have deep, but narrow, expertise. Despite thousands of years of innovations and breathtaking scientific advances, you'd be more likely to survive if you were marooned on a tropical island with a tradesman or farmer from ancient Rome or medieval England than with most modern professionals. ("But I am proficient in Word *and* Excel," you protest.)

Modern humans master a tiny slice of the world. But by coordinating our efforts and putting those slices together, we've unlocked potential that was previously unimaginable. That was the great triumph of *reductionism*, in which it's assumed that complex phenomena can be best understood by breaking them down into their individual parts. Understand the parts, understand the system. But the more you focus on systems as separable parts, the easier it is to ignore intertwined connections. Reductionism has proven astonishingly useful. It has helped us forge breathtaking scientific progress. But we've focused so much on what is useful that we've forgotten what is true. Connections matter as much as, if not more than, components. The more modern science puts individualism under the microscope, the less it stands up to scrutiny.

Even the scientific concept of what it means to speak of "an individual" is being revised. Some systems biologists, recognizing the interconnected, interdependent nature of our existence, have stopped referring to humans as individuals and have started referring to each person as a *holobiont*, which includes a core host (in our case, a human) as well as the zoo of organisms living in or around us. It may sound strange, but we are not just ourselves, but are rather a collection of human cells combined with our associated microorganisms, including fungi, bacteria, archaea, and viruses. The best estimates suggest we have roughly 1.3 bacterial cells inside us for every human cell. As the biologist Merlin Sheldrake put it, "There are more bacteria in your gut than stars in our galaxy." Fresh evidence is emerging that viruses affect our biological clocks, parasites alter our thoughts, and our microbiome can cause mood disorders.* Scientifically, we have never been singular, though that has been impossible to know until quite recently.

---

* The toxoplasma parasite, for example, affects the behavior of infected animals so much that wolves who have the parasite become bolder and end up being more likely to become the leader of the wolf pack. The same parasite is often found in cats, meaning that humans who own cats are more likely to be infected, with some studies suggesting that it alters human behavior significantly. Roughly one in four humans is currently infected with toxoplasma.

The individualist mindset, of independent, authoritative control over a tamable world, makes less sense if we know that our thoughts are partly influenced by the tiny, invisible organisms that live within us. Bewildering, but true.

This way of thinking flies against every intuition we have. But the late Derek Parfit, one of the most original philosophers of modern times, conjured up a mind-bending scenario that exposes the flawed assumptions we hold about easily demarcated individuals. Imagine you have the world's smallest pair of tweezers, so minute and precise that it can clasp just one human cell at a time. You enter an operating room alongside, let's say, Madonna. You sit down in a chair on the left side of the room. She sits on the right side. Then, painstakingly, a philosophical surgeon begins to swap one cell at a time between the two of you, over and over, trillions of times, until entire percentages of your bodies have been replaced.

It's easy to understand the extremes of this thought experiment. Swap one cell and you're still "you." On the other extreme, if the tweezers swapped every cell in your respective bodies, it would be absurd to say that "you" were still sitting in the chair where you started. After all, a person looking and feeling exactly like yourself would now be sitting in the other chair. But here's the baffling question: At what exact point do you stop being you? Are you still "you" when 30 percent of your cells have been replaced? How about 50.1 percent? There's no clear answer.*

Gaze a little closer at the dominant individualist paradigm, and you'll see that it's a flawed concept, clinging to a worldview that cracks under even the lightest interrogation. Thankfully, coming to terms with the delusion of individualism allows us to glimpse some comforting

---

* This thought experiment has parallels with the Ship of Theseus discussed by Plutarch in the second century AD, considering whether a ship that has all its components replaced, like for like, one by one, is still the same ship.

revelations about how we really fit into the world. Parfit, wrestling with his own thought experiments, concluded that a recognition of an interconnected existence is profoundly liberating, even uplifting.

"My life seemed like a glass tunnel, through which I was moving faster every year, and at the end of which there was darkness. . . . When I changed my view, the walls of my glass tunnel disappeared. I now live in the open air. There is still a difference between my life and the lives of other people. But the difference is less. Other people are closer. I am less concerned about the rest of my own life, and more concerned about the lives of others." Understanding the relational, intertwined nature of reality changes—for the better—how we experience the world.

Many counterintuitive conclusions flow from recognizing our chaotic, enmeshed reality. We will explore them together, on a journey to solve some of the biggest puzzles we face about why things happen. Along the way, we may end up thinking differently about our origins, our societies, our lives—and even the nature of change itself.

We will tackle six big questions:

1. Does everything happen for a reason, or does stuff . . . just happen?

2. Why do tiny changes sometimes produce huge impacts?

3. Why do we cling to a storybook version of reality even if it's not true?

4. Can't we just tame flukes with better data and more sophisticated probability models?

5. Where do flukes come from—and why do they blindside us?

6. Can we live better, happier lives if we embrace the chaos of our world?

Cumulatively, the answers to these questions combine to produce a striking conclusion: that small, contingent, even accidental changes—flukes—are far more important than we tend to believe. All of us bob, like a drifting soccer ball, on a sea of uncertainty, even when it appears to us that we're swimming in a straight line. That means we live in a world that is far more accidental and arbitrary than we want to pretend. As we'll see, such mystifying fragility stretches back to the very beginning—all the way back, 2 billion years ago, to the greatest fluke of all time.

CHAPTER 3

EVERYTHING DOESN'T HAPPEN FOR A REASON

*Why contingency reigns supreme in a
world driven by chance and chaos*

In the closing passages of *On the Origin of Species*, Charles Darwin marveled at the astonishing explosion of complex life, progressing over endless eons, to us, as we moved "from so simple a beginning" to "endless forms most beautiful." And the beginning *was* simple. For much of Earth's history, life stalled, stuck as single-celled organisms. To develop those "endless forms most beautiful"—orchids and octopuses, magpies and magnolias, hyenas and humans—we needed to get lucky. And not just run-of-the-mill luck. We needed the kind of luck that only strikes every few billion years.

Until about 2 billion years ago, all living things on Earth were uncomplicated, tiny prokaryotes, single cells without a nucleus, such as bacteria and their cousins, archaea. Then, for reasons unknown, a single bacterium bumped into a prokaryotic cell and ended up inside it. That bacterium eventually evolved into a mitochondrion, the powerhouse of our cells.* In that instant, everything changed. Every future species

---

* The biologist Lynn Margulis proposed this idea in 1966 at age twenty-eight

of complex life—from trees to grass and snails to humans—owes its existence to this unexpected microbial merger. It's unsettling that the entirety of the human saga can be traced back to a microscopic accident. It happened just once, 2 billion years ago—and never again since. It is, perhaps, the greatest fluke of all time.

When you trace the history of our species, similarly astonishing stories abound. They make clear that our existence and the way we now live is accidental, arbitrary, and therefore precarious. Scientists even recently discovered that the reason we don't lay eggs may be traced back to a shrewlike creature's getting infected with a retrovirus around 100 million years ago, leading to the evolution of placenta and, eventually, live births. The stories of our lives have countless authors, human and not, in an interwoven collaboration stretching across vast distances and deep into the past. But for one small seemingly random accident in the long-forgotten mists of time, none of us would exist.

Such awe-inspiring fragility from the long stretch of our evolution-ary past may seem far removed from our modern lives, but our social world is transformed—moment to moment and year to year—by the arbitrary. Because our world is intertwined, where changing anything changes everything, apparently meaningless adjustments can manifest in the most bizarre and unexpected ways.

—

For my research, I've traveled to Madagascar regularly since 2011. A few years ago, I noticed a new delicacy in food stalls on the side of the road: marmorkrebs, or the marbled crayfish. They first arrived on the

---

and was widely mocked for it. She submitted her idea to over a dozen journals and was repeatedly rejected because it sounded absurd. Her theory was later proven correct. It's now considered one of the most important discoveries of the twentieth century.

red-earthed island off the coast of East Africa about fifteen years ago, but in the last decade, they've taken over. They're everywhere. Yet, there's a mystery: Where did they come from?

Scientists aren't certain, but the main working hypothesis is that the new species emerged, believe it or not, after a single female crayfish underwent a freak mutation in an aquarium in a German pet shop in 1995. For reasons that remain mysterious, that pet shop crayfish changed in bewildering ways. Rather than possessing the standard two sets of chromosomes, she had three. She didn't need a male crayfish to get pregnant, either. This mutant marmorkreb could suddenly clone herself asexually, laying genetically identical eggs. Every subsequent marmorkreb was female—a genetic replica from the original mutant mother. Because of that strange ability to reproduce solo, the introduction of just one marmorkreb can cause a population explosion—as it did in Madagascar.

Marmorkrebs are an invasive species, with a penchant for devouring rice fields. But in their cloned millions, they've provided unexpected benefits, too. Much of Madagascar's population is malnourished, deficient in expensive proteins. The abundant supply of crayfish is now providing a cheap, steady supply of delicious nutrition. And it seems that the marmorkrebs prey on freshwater snails that are carriers of schistosomiasis, a parasitic disease that afflicts millions on the island. Madagascar's rice crops have been devastated, but 30 million people have a new source of nourishment and millions of children are less likely to die from parasites—all because of a single genetic mutation, in a single mutant crayfish, that likely arose in a single German pet shop one day in 1995.

It gets weirder. When researchers took two genetically identical marmorkrebs and placed them in identical controlled environments, something astonishing happened. Despite being genetic copies of each other and being raised in the same environments, their offspring were bizarrely divergent. As the writer Michael Blastland notes, one daughter specimen grew twenty times larger than another. Across the group, individuals had variations in their organs. Their behavior varied in profound ways. One individual died after 437 days. Another survived for more than twice that life span. Nothing genetic or environmental could explain these vast discrepancies. So, what accounts for them? Nobody knows. It may have something to do with the growing field of epigenetics, but scientists are baffled.

Random fluctuations can spread out across time and space to cause unexpected opportunities or calamitous disaster—or both.* Millions of lives in Madagascar were changed by a mutation in one faraway, long-dead German crayfish. There was no grand plan behind it. It was just an accident, produced by a random genetic mistake—and the effects of that accident were amplified through our intertwined existence. Facing such unfathomable contingency, sometimes the best we can do is shrug and follow the explanation of the unexplainable offered by Scottish biologist D'Arcy Thompson: "Everything is what it is because it got that way."

However, we are told, over and over, "Everything happens for a reason." Such reassuring mythmaking causes us to make cognitive mistakes, misjudging reality as we try to cram it into an ordered pattern that makes sense. For example, we tend to systematically downplay the role of *luck*—the word we use to describe the random and the accidental intersecting with our lives. Consider the widespread—but mistaken—

---

* When I mention "random" events, I always mean *apparently random*—events that seem random to us due to our ignorance. A dice roll produces an unpredictable outcome that appears random to us, but it isn't random—each roll of the dice is a deterministic event that follows the laws of physics. Apparently random events still have definite causes, though they're not part of some larger hidden purpose. (As far as modern science can tell, the only phenomena in the universe that may be genuinely random are quantum effects at the atomic and subatomic levels.)

belief that the global superrich must have earned their wealth due to their genius. But look a little closer, and that myth soon crumbles.

Most human traits, including intelligence, skills, and hard work, are normally distributed, following a Gaussian, or bell-shaped, curve, a bit like an inverted U. Wealth, by contrast, isn't normally distributed. It follows a power law or a Pareto distribution, with a tiny group of people controlling huge swaths of global wealth. While you'll never find an adult who is five times shorter or five times taller than you, today's richest person is more than a million times richer than the average American. So, someone who is marginally smarter than you could become a million times richer, rather than marginally richer. This is the world of what is sometimes called fat tails, which Nassim Nicholas Taleb brings to life in *The Black Swan*.

But what if such extreme wealth is due not to talent, but to random factors that we'd usually call luck? In one recent study, physicists teamed up with an economist and used computer modeling to develop a fake society with a realistic distribution of talent among competing individuals. In their fake world, talent mattered, but so did luck. Then, when they ran the simulation over and over, they found that the richest person was never the most talented. Instead, it was almost always someone close to average.

Why was that? In a world of 8 billion people, most lie in the middle level of talent, the largest area of the Bell curve. Now, think of luck like a lightning bolt: it strikes haphazardly. Due to their sheer numbers, luck is overwhelmingly likely to strike someone from the vast billions of middle-level talent, not the tiny sliver of übertalented geniuses. As the researchers sum it up, "Our results highlight the risks of the paradigm that we call 'naive meritocracy' . . . because it underestimates the role of randomness among the determinants of success." Some billionaires may be talented. All have been lucky. And luck is, by definition, the product of chance. Taleb, Duncan Watts, and Robert Frank have each shown how we tend to infer reasons backward when success is produced, with what they call the "narrative fallacy" or, more commonly, "hindsight bias." The notion that billionaires must be talented is one such fallacy.

Yet, if luck plays such an important role in success, that should affect how we think about fortune and misfortune. If you believe you live in a meritocratic world, in which success is doled out to the most talented individuals rather than partly by accident or chance, then it makes sense to claim full credit for each success and blame yourself for every defeat. But if you accept that apparent randomness and accidents drive significant swaths of change in our lives—and they do—then that will change your outlook on life. When you lose at roulette, you don't kick yourself for being a useless failure. Instead, you accept the arbitrary outcome and move on. Recognizing that often meaningless, accidental outcomes emerge from an intertwined, complex world is empowering and liberating. We should all take a bit less credit for our triumphs and a bit less blame for our failures.

We're particularly prone to inventing and clinging to false explanations in the face of seemingly random misfortune. We can't easily accept randomness as an explanation for why we get cancer or end up in a car accident. Bad news requires something behind it that makes sense. It's impossible to move on from misfortune without figuring out the *real* reason for your suffering. It becomes a quest for an elusive meaning in what may have been a meaningless calamity. "Everything happens for a reason" is a coping mechanism most often heard when jobs are lost, when we're blindsided by breakups, or when people die. While it can help us make sense out of the senseless, comforted by the myth of a neat, ordered plan for everything, the saying isn't true. It's a useful, reassuring fiction. Some things—even important and maddening and horrific things—just happen. That's the inevitable result of an interconnected chaotic world. Accidents, mistakes, and, above all, arbitrary neutral changes create species, shape societies, and divert our lives.

Conversely, research has shown that people will happily accept randomness or chance as satisfactory explanations when they experience an unexpected positive, such as winning the lottery. In those moments of surprising joy, we are like a dog attending its own birthday party, unsure why chicken and cheese are suddenly and inexplicably abundant, but happy to gobble them down unquestioningly.

Yet when we try to explain anything important, randomness and chance fly right back out the window. Consider how we try to make sense of variation between humans. We almost always end up relying on a simplistic dichotomy: it must be due to some combination of nature (genes) and nurture (our environment, upbringing, and experiences). But a third possibility is often ignored. What if, as with the mysterious marmorkrebs, some variation between us is just accidental or arbitrary?

Behavioral geneticists have concluded that roughly half the variation between us is due to our DNA. That leaves another half that's developmental dark matter, the inexplicable minutiae of life. Damien Morris, a behavioral geneticist at King's College London, argues that our life paths can sometimes be subject to seemingly random chance, which he illustrates with a story of identical twins in a classroom. "One stares out the window and is distracted by a bird flying by, just as the other twin is enraptured by the teacher's account of a particular poem and it forms a lifelong love of poetry." Their college majors and career paths later diverge, all because of a bird flitting past a window.

That conjecture is being scientifically validated. It's becoming clear that seemingly random fluctuations begin during brain development before birth, and those small changes can play a profound role in our life trajectories. Researchers conducted experiments in which they compared the behavior of genetically identical fruit flies raised in the same environment. There was still considerable inexplicable variation in non-inherited traits. These differences seem to be due to tiny, apparently random discrepancies in their neural wiring, small fluctuations during development that created a lifelong imprint. Our brains have similar architecture to those of flies, so while it's unethical to conduct similar experiments on humans, there's good reason to believe that our wiring also follows haphazard but consequential variations even before we're born. No matter how much we pretend otherwise, we are sometimes puppets of the accidental.

Many people object to this way of seeing the world, insisting that such ideas are nice for philosophers to ponder, but that it's just "noise." Perhaps those seemingly random fluctuations just get washed out over time. Surely change happens according to structured patterns and order. So, let's finally answer that core puzzle once and for all: Is our world contingent or convergent? Does everything happen for a reason, or does stuff just happen?

—

In Hindu mythology, Chinese mythology, and some Native American origin stories, the earth is said to be supported on the back of a giant turtle. According to a well-known parable, a boy who hears about this asks the obvious follow-up: "But what does that turtle stand on?" The first turtle stands atop a second turtle, he's told. "And what does the second turtle stand on?" the boy asks. The answer is swift and definite: "It's turtles all the way down."

"Turtles all the way down" has become a shorthand for an *infinite regress*, in which each explanation stands atop another, which stands atop another, on and on. That's how contingency works. In a contingent world, you're the culmination of a nearly infinite web of events, arranged with just the right strands and interlocking pattern to produce your existence. Change any strand, no matter how minuscule, and you disappear, joining the ranks of what Dawkins called the "unborn ghosts." But for a small tweak, everything could have been different. Contingency all the way down.

Many popular books imagine the what-ifs of human history. But there's a fundamental problem. We only have one Earth. We can't test hypotheses about other possible worlds. There's no mechanism for testing counterfactuals by replaying time, rerunning events with slight modifications to see whether, or how, history would unfold differently. We're stuck with speculation.

In 1998, a film called *Sliding Doors* imagined that we could see other possible worlds. The film begins as Helen, played by Gwyneth Paltrow, rushes to catch a train on the London Underground. She runs down the stairs but is temporarily blocked by a little girl, costing Helen a split second. As Helen reaches the train, the doors slam shut, and she's left on the platform. Then, the tape rewinds by about fifteen seconds and restarts. Everything seems the same, except this time the little girl's mother pulls her daughter out of the way. As a result, Helen squeezes onto the train just as the doors slide shut. The film traces Helen's life through both worlds, one in which she caught the train, the other in which she missed it. In some ways, Helen's life radically diverges. In other respects, Helen's life converges toward similar outcomes, though her path was altered. When you consider the film, it becomes obvious that this *is* how our lives work, but we almost never think about it, perhaps because it's overwhelming and maddening to recognize that *every* instant matters. And unlike for the filmmakers, there's no rewind button for us, so we can never know which of our *Sliding Doors* moments mattered most.

The study of evolutionary biology mirrors the concepts in *Sliding Doors*. Do species rise and fall in predictable patterns, whether they catch the evolutionary train or not? Or do tiny, seemingly insignificant changes and accidents alter trajectories and give rise to new traits, new behaviors, and new species? Evolutionary biology is a historical science that gives us an unparalleled way of thinking about and evaluating change more generally. It's therefore worthwhile for us to briefly journey into

Darwin's world, using lessons from other flora and fauna to understand how our lives and our societies change.

Darwin's core insight was that the natural world creates "selection pressures" that determine, on average, who survives and who dies. If a group of birds with broad beaks live on a rocky crag where food is only to be found in narrow fissures, they are more likely to die than those with narrower beaks that allow them to extract food from those gaps. Over time, the narrower beaks are "selected" because birds that have them are more likely to survive and produce offspring, while the others who can't feed themselves will die off. Generation after generation, the species adapts to its environment, and if a finch with a narrow, spear-like beak is someday born, it will beat out the others in the evolutionary sweepstakes. This continues until the environment changes, and the selection pressures for survival shift.

But for evolution to make sense, the earth needed to be old, giving species time to experiment and adapt. For centuries, the prevailing paradigm was that the earth was only about 5,850 years old. (In the 1600s, Bishop James Ussher concluded the earth was created around 6:00 p.m. on October 22, 4004 BC.) That wasn't nearly long enough for evolution to work its magic. If Rome wasn't built in a day, pigeons certainly couldn't have emerged in six. Then, as geologists began to discover that the earth was far more ancient than previously believed, evolutionary theory became plausible.

In his lifetime, Darwin couldn't understand the underlying mechanism: that a microscopic chemical recipe produces variation within and between species. Several decades after his death, however, the field of evolutionary biology became shaped by an idea called the modern synthesis. It's a simple but powerful model that is useful for understanding social and cultural change within humans as well as shifts within and between species. Organisms mutate and random variations accumulate, which creates the genetic building blocks for a trial-and-error approach to solving problems. (Today we know that seemingly random mutations occur when DNA gets copied, but Darwin died seventy-one years before the double helix was discovered.) Those mutations may create different beak types, some long and narrow, others short and broad. Then, natural selection does its handiwork. Organisms with more useful traits survive and pass their genes more, on average, to the next generation, while organisms with less useful traits die more frequently, on average, before they can reproduce.

Survivors determine the future. Ruthless, but effective.

But biologists are divided between those who depict evolutionary change as the smooth, predictable contours of convergence toward an inevitable outcome, and those who see the jagged, unpredictable march of change defined by contingency. (This divide mirrors similar splits within fields such as history, economics, political science, and sociology.) How suddenly does change happen? Scientists have a sense of humor with this debate. Those who argue that it's a slow and steady process are sometimes disparagingly referred to as representing "evolution by creeps." Those who suggest that evolution is largely stable until a sudden shift changes everything are mocked as representing "evolution by jerks."*

These debates matter for us, for what we might call the snooze-button effect. If the world is mostly convergent, then it won't matter if you get out of bed five minutes later than you were originally planning. But if the world is sometimes diverted by small, contingent events, then each tap of the snooze button could change everything.

The natural world provides evidence for both viewpoints. On the side of contingency are creatures such as the duck-billed platypus. It's a

---

* Scientists, including one intrepid pair of married evolutionary biologists from Princeton University named Rosemary and Peter Grant, have since directly documented evolution happening on astonishingly short time scales. The more formal name sometimes used for *evolution by jerks* is *punctuated equilibrium*.

species of what the biologist Jonathan Losos calls "evolutionary one-offs." The platypus, a venomous egg-laying mammal with the bill of a duck, the tail of a beaver, and the feet of an otter, basically sweats milk out of the pores on its stomach to feed its young. The creature is so unusual, so unlike anything else, that when the first specimen was shipped to Britain in 1799, a leading anatomist remarked, "It naturally excites the idea of some deceptive preparation by artificial means." He searched, in vain, for stitches sewing other animal carcasses together into some sort of duck-billed Frankenstein's monster. Another even hypothesized that it was the freak offspring of an evolutionary orgy, "a promiscuous intercourse between the different sexes of all these different animals." Quite the hypothesis.

Or, consider the binturong, a bearcat native to South and Southeast Asia. Its urine contains a chemical called 2-acetyl-1-pyrroline. That chemical compound gives cooked popcorn its enticing aroma. Binturongs tend to lather their urine liberally on their feet and tail, creating a scent trail, which is why those who walk through the habitat of the binturongs often get a whiff of a movie theater lobby in the jungle. Evolution, through contingent events, can be rather strange.

Crabs are to convergence what platypuses are to contingency. King crabs, porcelain crabs, and hermit crabs, for example, are not true crabs, but unrelated crustaceans. That's because evolution has, on at least five separate occasions, transformed animals into a crab-like body plan. It's so common that there is even a term for it: *carcinization*, which means "turning something into a crab-like form." (Some have suggested that the convergent force is so great that humans are bound to eventually end up scuttling around with pincers.) Similarly, the ability to fly has evolved in at least four separate branches of the tree of life—in insects, bats, birds, and pterosaurs. Nature converges on similar solutions to common problems.

Our world flits between contingency and convergence, providing the illusion of structure and order, until one tiny adjustment changes everything. With sophisticated DNA sequencing, Mark Pagel, an evolutionary biologist at the University of Reading, has found evidence that an astonishing 78 percent of new species were triggered by a single event. Nature makes a random mistake, or a contingent deviation, and, poof, you've got a new kind of beetle.

But why does that matter for us?

—

Our understanding of human history is a battle between contingency and convergence. Do stable, long-term trends drive change? Or does history pivot on the tiniest details? We're left to speculate between the two worldviews because we can't experimentally test the past.

But what if you *could* create multiple worlds? And what if, within them, you could not just control what happens inside, but also control time? Imagine the ability to play God, pressing pause at will, even rewinding and replaying key moments. That would give us a glimpse of the inner mysteries of cause and effect with unprecedented precision. We would finally know how change happens—and whether contingency or convergence reigns supreme. It's an intoxicating thought experiment. But could it happen?

A few decades ago, a scientist named Richard Lenski realized it was possible without science fiction. Lenski, who sports an impressive Darwin-style beard, had been working as an evolutionary biologist, conducting fieldwork in rural North Carolina to study the predatory southern ground beetle. He enjoyed the outdoors, but the work was slow, there were a lot of venomous snakes to contend with, his beetles often drowned in downpours, and most important, the complexity of the real world introduced so many variables that it was impossible to accurately test the ideas that most excited him. Lenski began to wonder if experiments on evolutionary change could be run, not in the untamable wilderness, but instead in the controlled environment of a scientific lab. In 1988, Lenski launched one of the longest-running and most important experiments in scientific history.

Lenski's experiment is elegant in its simplicity. Take twelve identical flasks, populate them with twelve identical strains of *E. coli* bacteria, feed them the exact same glucose broth, and let them get on evolving. Because *E. coli* reproduce rapidly, they pass through 6.64 generations per day. The average human generation lasts for 26.9 years, so one day in the world of these bacteria is roughly akin to 178 years of human time. It's hard to believe, but since 1988, Lenski has directly observed evolution over seventy thousand generations of *E. coli*, the human equivalent of 1.9 million years of change. In 2004, another remarkable scientist, Zachary Blount, joined Lenski's lab. Together, they have long overseen twelve microbial universes, each swirling around in a flask.

I visited them so I, too, could gaze into these controlled universes. Lenski and Blount's lab at Michigan State University is unremarkable. There are beakers, graduated cylinders, petri dishes, and white bottles of chemicals on packed shelves. Next to the door, Lenski points out a boxy incubator, set to 37°C, or 98.6°F, the same temperature as the human body. The incubator is humming as it slowly swirls and shakes a flask of microbes. Despite its sterile appearance, the lab offers clues that it's a place obsessed with the mysteries of evolution. A poster depicting Darwin's famous voyage is affixed to the wall. A framed painting of a fantasy creature, upright like a man, but with the tentacles of an octopus, is next to the light switch. Above it all is a banner with a phrase that inverts America's motto, *e pluribus unum*, or "out of many, one." In the Long-Term Evolution Experiment (LTEE), they follow a different mantra, an homage to evolutionary change: *ex una plures*—"out of one, many."

I met Zachary Blount, the man who adopted that motto and made that banner, in an Indian restaurant in a strip mall near his lab in East Lansing, Michigan. He was impossible to miss, with colorful striped socks rising high above his hiking boots. He's a self-described "twenty-first-century oddball" without a cell phone. Blount is most likely to be found either in a lab breaking the code of life's most closely guarded secrets or pondering those secrets while reading a thick history book at a wilderness campsite. He's fascinated by flukes in both microbial and human history—a "bacteria by day, Byzantine Empire by night" kind of guy. After spending four hours with him, I'm not sure I've ever met someone so curious about the world, or so thoughtfully productive at understanding it.

Blount describes the experiment with enthusiasm. Every day, the bacteria in each of the flasks grow in an identical broth of glucose, or sugar, and citrate, better known as the "acid that gives orange juice its tang." The tiny organisms swim in citrate, but can only eat glucose. Rather than having sex to reproduce, bacteria subdivide into two nearly identical daughter cells. Variation in the flasks, therefore, mostly comes from mutations, or little mistakes in DNA that occur during copying. The genius of the experiment is that from one common ancestor, twelve different populations are free to evolve in identical conditions. *Ex una plures.* The experiment has therefore eliminated sex, environmental change, and predators from the equation, allowing the scientists to observe evolution at its purest. Lenski and Blount can therefore test whether contingency or convergence rules. If change is driven by convergence, then the twelve flasks should only have minor variations even over long periods. They might take a dozen different paths, but they'll end up in roughly the same place. That would mean evolution's snooze button is largely meaningless. But if contingency dominates, the twelve populations should eventually diverge in substantial ways, as chance occurrences create microbial freaks, forever shifting evolution's path. One tap of the snooze button could change everything.

Lenski and Blount also have something that most scientists do not: a time machine. *E. coli* can be frozen without harming it, allowing freezers to act like a pause button. To press play, just thaw the bacteria back out. From the beginning, Lenski and his team froze all twelve lines of bacteria every five hundred generations, which meant they could replay any part of the experiment from any given snapshot in time. Want to create a bacterial replay starting from the day the Soviet Union collapsed or from September 11, 2001? No problem. In those twelve universes of broth, Lenski and Blount control time.

For more than a decade, the experiment seemed to be backing up the hypothesis of evolutionary convergence. The twelve cultures were different, as tiny changes were inevitable. But all twelve seemed to be mostly changing in similar ways. Each lineage of bacteria was getting incrementally better at eating glucose, becoming more "fit" in the Darwinian sense. There was a clear sense of order. The specific mutations didn't seem to matter much. It was as though all twelve were following the same railway track, all racing toward the same destination. The creeps, not the jerks, were being vindicated.

Then, on a frigid day in January 2003, a postdoctoral researcher, Tim Cooper, arrived at the lab to tend to the twelve populations, just as he'd done hundreds of times before. This time, something was different. Eleven populations looked normal, "like flasks of water with a drop or two of milk mixed in, only their slight cloudiness indicating the millions of resident bacteria." But the twelfth was wildly different. It was partially opaque, a cloudy mixture when it should have been mostly transparent and clear. "I thought it was a mistake," Cooper told me. "But I was pretty sure something interesting was going on."

Cooper called in Lenski.

"I thought it was lab error," Lenski told me. "Our motto in the lab to avoid contamination is 'when in doubt, throw it out.'" Lenski decided to restart that line of bacteria from the last frozen sample. Thankfully, with their microbial time machine, mistakes could easily be corrected.

A few weeks later, the same flask turned cloudy again. Clearly there had been no mistake. Something was going on. Perplexed, the scientists sequenced the DNA of the *E. coli* in that opaque flask and found something incredible. The bacteria had evolved the ability to eat the citrate they were swimming in, which shouldn't have been possible. In the twentieth century, there was just one documented case of *E. coli* that was able to digest citrate. That it had now occurred by happenstance was already an important discovery. But the story was about to get much more interesting.

To digest citrate, this "freak" line of bacteria had first undergone at least four *unrelated* mutations that provided no apparent benefit to the population—seemingly meaningless errors. But if those four mistakes had not all occurred, in that specific order, the fifth mutation, which gave them the ability to eat citrate, wouldn't have been possible. Five contingent mutations were stacked on top of each other, and they were utterly improbable, too. Contingency all the way down.

Just how contingent were they? To find out, Blount spent years studying the freak population. He unthawed samples of the mutant lineage at various points, using the frozen bacterial fossil record to test whether the ability to eat citrate would emerge again. After analyzing roughly 40 trillion cells over nearly three years of experiments, he replicated the citrate mutation just seventeen times. But if he went back far enough into the bacteria's evolutionary history, the citrate mutation *never* arose again. It was contingency, through and through. To this day, after seventy thousand generations—equivalent to 1.9 million human life years of evolution—only one lineage out of the twelve has developed the ability to digest citrate. For one line of bacteria, one tiny change meant that *everything* about their future changed, all because of a random mutation, made possible by four unrelated accidents. The other eleven bacterial universes are stuck eating glucose, blissfully unaware that they are swimming in, as Lenski puts it, a "lemony dessert."

Blount argues that the Long-Term Evolution Experiment provides a sophisticated logic for thinking about critical turning points in human society. Many historians, for example, say that D-Day was the key to the Allied victory in World War II. If one could experimentally test that claim, historians would follow the same research design as Lenski and Blount. Imagine you had one thousand identical Earths and could pause them at various points throughout the war. The logic would be that if the Allied victory became far more likely with worlds that started after D-Day, the historians could conclude that D-Day was *the* key turning point. But if the Allies won 75 percent of the time whether the world was thawed in June 1942 or June 1944, then it would be clear that the historians were wrong. D-Day didn't matter so much. The Allies were always likely to win.

Sadly, there's only one Earth, we can't rewind time, and these contingency versus convergence experiments remain possible only with microbes in a science lab. For the moment, though, it seems that Lenski and Blount—and a much larger team of researchers who have worked on the LTEE—have resolved the contingency versus convergence debate: *to us, the world appears convergent, until we realize, with a jolt, that it isn't.*

We're often blind to the possible jolts until they happen. We follow routines, the world ticks on day by day, and little changes don't seem to matter. The morning news comes on at seven like clockwork. The commute takes between twenty and twenty-five minutes. From our perspective, the creeps of convergence appear supreme.

But then, every so often, our lives—and our societies—drastically change from the jerks of contingent events. Sometimes, these shifts are the culmination of lots of little changes. They build up over time, until they reach a tipping point, and everything collapses. Other times, seemingly independent individual trajectories become causally interlinked, as we saw in chapter 2 with Ivan and the drifting soccer ball, a phenomenon known as Cournot contingency. Imagine a fly buzzing around for hours, exploring empty airspace, until suddenly it collides with the eye of a motorcyclist, who swerves, crashes, and dies. The trajectory of that fly mattered enormously to the life of the motorcyclist, but he was oblivious of the importance of that fly to the trajectory of his life—until it was too late.

In that way, we, like Helen in *Sliding Doors*, are often oblivious of how small, contingent changes change our lives and shift our societies. Some are random accidents, such as mutations in DNA. Others are deliberate, but minor, decisions we make. They're happening constantly. We tell ourselves that we're in control of our lives. The truth is that everything is constantly in flux, including ourselves. We live, as do *E. coli*, in a world defined by what we might call *contingent convergence*, which is broadly how change happens. There's order and structure, but the snooze-button effect is real. That leads to an unsettling, but also exhilarating, truth: *every moment matters*.

———

If contingent convergence reigns supreme, then why is the role of randomness so often ignored in evolutionary change? *Survival of the fittest*, a phrase that Darwin didn't invent and only later adopted, seems to suggest a relentless progression from worse to better. Natural selection is sometimes presented in a way that fits neatly with the convergent "everything happens for a reason" school of thought, in which it is assumed that evolution is so unforgiving that any evolved trait that currently exists must have been shaped by the wisdom of nature's hidden hand. Evolution works, as Richard Dawkins once put it, like "a miserly accountant, grudging the pennies, watching the clock, punishing the smallest extravagance. Unrelentingly and unceasingly." Evolution fastidiously corrects its errors in a ruthless, optimizing process. In that conception, there's not just order and structure, but also a clear goal: the world strives ever closer toward greater fitness.

Evolution can sometimes be a more random process. This is pretty obvious when you learn that the rise of mammals was only made possible by a giant space rock that walloped the planet and wiped out entire branches of the tree of life. Evolution also follows random change through *genetic drift*, in which genetic variation in a population shifts due to chance. But for various historical reasons, biologists who have emphasized the role of randomness and chance in evolution have been shunned within the field.* In popular discussions of evolution, we mostly hear about survival of the fittest, not survival of the luckiest.

Nonetheless, you are alive today because of some lucky individuals—evolution's lottery winners—from the distant past. We are the descendants of various *genetic bottlenecks*, which is a subset of genetic drift. Bottlenecks happen when genetic diversity plummets due to a sharp loss in the number of individuals alive in a species. For example, many people (myself included) have marveled at the northern elephant seals scattered across California's beaches. But during the 1800s, humans hunted that species nearly to extinction for their blubber oil, until as few as twenty breeding pairs remained alive. Today, every elephant seal is a

---

* The late John Tyler Bonner, a former professor of evolutionary biology at Princeton, made similarly blasphemous claims in a book called *Randomness in Evolution*, though mostly in reference to microorganisms. One of the blurbs on the book says Bonner "doesn't just approach heresy, it is heresy."

descendant of that small cluster. It isn't hard to see how much it matters which individual seals survived to regenerate the species.

Now, imagine something similar happening with humans, in which the entirety of our species was whittled down to just forty people, before exploding to 8 billion individuals. The exact composition of those forty people would define the species. If all forty came from, say, nurses and doctors at a children's hospital, future humans would turn out quite differently from what would happen if all forty were, God forbid, Kardashians. With such low numbers, every individual would reshape humanity. For better or worse, billions descended from a gene pool that began with one-fortieth Donald Trump would be rather different from the descendants of a gene pool that contained one-fortieth Malala Yousafzai instead.

This isn't hypothetical. Humans underwent a severe population bottleneck tens of thousands of years ago (possibly multiple times).[†] One study concluded that, at one point, as few as one thousand human breeding pairs existed. Other estimates don't go quite so low, but still suggest that there may have been around ten thousand humans left during various bottlenecks, which was itself an arbitrary subset of the potential human gene pool. From ten thousand to 8 billion, in an evolutionary blink. Human genetic diversity seems to have plummeted so much during that bottleneck that modern chimpanzees on either side of a river in Cameroon show more genetic variation between them than modern humans living thousands of miles apart on different continents.[‡]

---

† Some bottlenecks proposed by researchers who study human evolution, such as one associated with the Toba volcano, remain controversial. It's uncertain precisely how many bottlenecks occurred or how severe they were.

‡ Cheetahs experienced an even more severe bottleneck, giving them such low levels of genetic diversity that researchers can take skin from one cheetah and graft it onto another without any problems; the body effectively accepts it as its own tissue.

All of our lives, all of our histories, pivoted on those bottlenecks, an evolutionary accident of a tiny snapshot in the ancient past. Without it, you, and everyone you know, wouldn't exist.

Subsequent prehistoric migrations also meant that some much smaller, but still arbitrarily selected, populations "founded" different groups of humans that then developed independently in a geographically isolated area. These are called founder effects. For example, some genetic studies suggest that indigenous populations of the Americas may have been established by as few as between 70 and 250 individuals who crossed the land bridge from Asia. On the remote islands of Tristan de Cunha in the south Atlantic Ocean, roughly 150 of the 300 residents have asthma because the island was settled by just fifteen people (many of whom had asthma). Even the famous, now-extinct dodo emerged from a founder event, when a wayward group of Asian pigeons landed on Mauritius millions of years ago, put on some weight, and lost the ability to fly. No hidden purpose guided the asthmatic islanders or lost pigeons. They were just accidents.

These ideas are related to a concept called *survivorship bias*, in which we can only observe that which has survived. Much of our knowledge of cavemen comes from cave paintings. It's possible some didn't live in caves and painted more often on the bark of trees, so we should think of them as treemen. But the trees are long gone, so we can't say, while the cave paintings survived. Similarly, classical thought from Greece and Rome has profoundly shaped modernity, but our interpretation of it is influenced by an arbitrary factor: which ideas survived through manuscripts while others were lost to history. Some aspects of human history, as with nature, are irreducibly arbitrary.

Yet, the image of nature as a relentless optimizer persists. Daniel S. Milo, author of *Good Enough: The Tolerance for Mediocrity in Nature and Society*, takes issue with that viewpoint and convincingly argues that the world is full of "good enough" solutions, which others call a kludge approach. (A *kludge* is defined as "an ill-assorted collection of parts assembled to fulfill a particular purpose." As we age, we all find out that the human knee or the human lower back both mostly do their job well enough, but few would call them optimal.) Motoo Kimura, the accidental biologist we encountered previously who fortunately didn't get vaporized in Kyoto, was one of the few in his field to demonstrate how much evolutionary change was driven by meaningless accidents. His neutral molecular theory has shown that randomness drives considerable change at the molecular or genetic level. Yet few outside of evolutionary biology have ever heard of him or that crucial idea. With tiny changes, so much could turn out differently. It's not just true in evolution, but also in our lives and our societies. Everything *doesn't* happen for a reason.

——

Seemingly random fluctuations have unexpected upsides. Evolution provides us with a crucial lesson: undirected experimenting is essential. In an ever-changing environment, a trial-and-error approach allows us to find the best path forward. For with experimentation, we discover the unanticipated joy and wisdom of the flukes of life.

In February 2014, many workers on the London Underground, or Tube, went on strike. Tens of thousands of commuters were affected. It forced commuters to experiment with alternatives. Using anonymized data, economists from Oxford and Cambridge examined 200 million data points, both before and after the Tube strikes. Many people stuck to the route they were forced to use due to the strike. They had been unaware of a better or nicer pathway to work, and it took a minor diversion to push them out of their rut. After crunching the numbers, the economists came to a surprising conclusion. With hundreds of thousands of commuters discovering a more efficient route to work, the Tube strike had inadvertently provided a significant net benefit to London's economy.

Experimentation is also crucial for how we—and our animal counterparts—invent music. Songbirds, for example, learn through a combination of imitation and trial and error, testing notes until they find something that's pleasing, then refining it through small iterative changes. Humans do the same. Beethoven carried notebooks everywhere, jotting down little snippets of notes that would later grow into a symphony. And in 2021, a documentary featuring rare footage of the Beatles showed an astonishing scene in which Paul McCartney starts strumming on his guitar haphazardly, until a few notes strike his fancy. He plays with those notes, testing subtle variations. In four wondrous minutes, "Get Back," one of the greatest songs of all time, gets composed out of thin air, all through experimentation.

Too often, though, we only learn this lesson through forced changes, rather than through voluntary efforts to try something fresh. In January 1975, the renowned jazz pianist Keith Jarrett arrived at the opera house in Cologne, Germany, for a special performance. But due to a mix-up, Jarrett was forced to play a rickety, out-of-tune, old piano that was only supposed to be used for amateur practice. Jarrett had to adjust to the broken piano. He experimented, matching flawless talents with a flawed instrument. It was musical magic. The recording of that concert remains the bestselling solo jazz album in history.

In a contingent world, experimentation moves us forward. Tiny, undirected mutations added up to profound advantage for one lineage of *E. coli* in Michigan. Commuters in London found better ways to get to work. The Beatles plucked a hit song out of the ether. And a jazz pianist, forced out of his comfort zone, adapted—creating art of unexpected beauty. In a world driven by a sense that deliberate optimization is always the route to progress, sometimes the contingent accidents are the ones that most inspire and improve our lives.

But if contingency can sway anything, and contingent convergence rules our world, why do we focus so much on the convergence and so little on the contingency? And why do we so often write randomness out of our explanations for why things happen? The answer, as we shall now see, is that our brains have evolved to lie to us.

CHAPTER 4

WHY OUR BRAINS DISTORT REALITY

Why deception is useful inside a mind designed to understand simple patterns of cause and effect

Imagine two creatures: we might call them the Truth Creature and the Shortcut Creature. The Truth Creature sees everything *exactly* as it is, able to visually perceive every molecule of oxygen, every stream of ultraviolet light, each atom within every bacterium lurking under each toenail. Every possible fragment of visual information is perceived and processed by the Truth Creature's brain. Nothing goes unnoticed. By contrast, the Shortcut Creature can't see any of that detail, but instead only perceives and processes that which is most useful to it. All else is either ignored or is invisible to that creature's perceptions. As a result, the Shortcut Creature cannot sense most of reality.

Which creature would you rather be?

We are tempted to side with the truth. But that would be a fatal mistake. Shortcut Creatures always win. Thankfully, that's exactly what we are—a species that has evolved to perceive reality in a stripped-down, simplified form, so we can make sense of it to survive. That conjecture has been validated by something called the Fitness Beats Truth theorem, an idea proposed and tested by mathematicians and cognitive scientists—and popularized by Donald D. Hoffman at the University of California, Irvine. What they've discovered inverts our commonsense ideas about how the world works.

Most of us assume that truth is, by definition, useful. But consider it a bit more carefully, and it becomes clear that's not the case. We do not see reality, but rather a "manifest image" of it, a useful illusion that helps us navigate the world. Hoffman invokes the metaphor of a computer to make his point. The "true" mechanical operations of a computer are indecipherable to nonspecialists. Most of us couldn't get more than a sentence into trying to explain what's happening on a physical level when we double-click on an icon, clack away at our keyboard, or delete a file. Thankfully for us, technological conjurers have developed a completely inaccurate, but useful, illusion of how a computer operates that we can understand. We call it "the desktop" and we can move a cartoon cursor around it. But there is no desktop and no cursor inside the machine we're using. Instead, it's just a bunch of silicon, plastic, and copper that performs binary calculations. Alas, if we saw computers that way when we wrote an email, we'd never get anything done, mired in truth, lost in reality. Computing became far more useful to us precisely because it was transformed into a shortcut illusion—of a fake visual space, with files and cursors and icons. To Hoffman's point, I'd add that this analogy becomes even clearer when you think about early incarnations of personal computing, such as the MS-DOS operating system. That put us, the computer user, one step closer to reality—which was precisely why it was confusing. MS-DOS went extinct when something that was further from reality, but more useful, came along: a visual desktop.

The same dynamic operates constantly in nature—and it's the origin story of our minds. Our perceptions of reality are the contingent by-product of evolution by natural selection. Along the evolutionary track, our ancestors faced a forking path. One path led to truth, the other to usefulness. You can either be the Truth Creature or the Shortcut Creature, but not both. For evolution, what matters most is reproductive success. And as the Fitness Beats Truth theorem proves, when truth and usefulness are in conflict, the Shortcut strategy always eventually beats out the Truth strategy. The cognitive psychologist Steven Pinker put it like this: "We are organisms, not angels, and our minds are organs, not pipelines to the truth. Our minds evolved by natural selection to solve problems that were life-and-death matters to our ancestors, not to commune with correctness." Our perceptions have been forged over millions of years, fine-tuned to help us survive, nothing more, nothing less.

Neuroscience evidence is accumulating that one mechanism by which we get better at navigating the world is through "synaptic pruning." The brains of newborns are packed with 100 billion neurons. But you, I'm afraid to say, have a measly 86 billion (give or take a few billion). Toddlers have got you beat in synaptic density in their cerebral cortex, too, which is about 50 percent higher than what you're working with. The good news is that evolution, with synaptic pruning, has figured out a rather good trick for helping us make sense of the world. As Alison Barth, a neuroscientist at Carnegie Mellon University, explains, "Networks that are constructed through overabundance and then pruning are much more robust and efficient." Our brains use a winnowing process to help us retain connections that are most useful to us, calibrating our minds to match the world in which we live.

The same is true of our senses, though we never pause and consider that the way we view the world isn't as unbridled truth, but is rather filtered through evolved senses. We are incapable of perceiving plenty about reality because we don't have the organs to sense it—everything from ultraviolet and infrared light to atoms and quarks and amoebas. What you see is not what there is. But even for the information that we can perceive and process, we automatically ignore most of it. Our brains filter it out.

Walking through our world is an information explosion. We couldn't possibly pay attention to everything. If we did, it would overload us, blinding us to what's important. To cope, our brain has a laser-like focus on detecting helpful patterns and potentially threatening abnormalities, while discarding that which is less useful. As the philosopher Ludwig Wittgenstein observed, "We see emotion. . . . We do not see facial contortions and make the inference that he is feeling joy, grief, boredom. We describe a face immediately as sad, radiant, bored, even when we are unable to give any other description of the features." Such are the advantages of the Shortcut Creature.

To survive, we jettison the unnecessary detail. Don't believe me? Try drawing, as accurately as possible, something you've seen thousands of times, such as a five-dollar/pound/euro note, purely from memory. I assure you, it won't go well. Our brain automatically processes reality and retains little for future recall. We perceive and preserve just a tiny, useful slice.

The basic way we experience reality, then, is partly derived from arbitrary evolutionary accidents. Consider this: our vision, the window through which we see the world, could be extremely different but for a few haphazard changes. Would wars have unfolded the same way if we had the visual acuity of eagles, able to spot an enemy soldier two miles away? How would history have diverged if we could only see in black and white?

These aren't far-fetched thought experiments. Our perception of reality is just one possible way of seeing the world. With three types of photoreceptors in our eyes (red, green, and blue), we're known as trichromats. Most mammals, including our pet dogs, have only blue and green receptors, so they're dichromats, with similar color vision to humans that are red-green color-blind. Dolphins and whales are monochromats and can only see in black and white. Most birds, fish, and some insects and reptiles (including the dinosaurs), are tetrachromats because they can also see ultraviolet (UV) light. New World monkeys, such as spider monkeys, are weirder still. Generally, females are trichromatic, whereas males are dichromatic. (A strange world it would be if men and women perceived different colors.)

Due to the nature of the genes that produce our eyes, it's theoretically possible for humans to be born with four, rather than three, functioning color cone cells in their eyes—human tetrachromats. For much of her career, Dr. Gabriele Jordan of Newcastle University searched for one. After several false positives, Jordan finally found a genuine case. The woman, who understandably wanted to avoid reporters and podcast hosts regularly swooping into her life, is a doctor in northern England, known to science as cDa29. We see life in the rich panoply of roughly a million different colors. For cDa29, that figure is *100 million*, a splendor the rest of us can only imagine.

We like to think everything happens not just for a reason, but for *good* reasons. But the truth is that, but for a few small changes, we could've all ended up perceiving the world with eyes like cDa29's, or like whales stuck in black and white, or perhaps even like a peacock mantis shrimp, which has a whopping twelve color cone photoreceptors. If we had, *everything* in human history would've been altered. Counterfactual histories often imagine constrained what-ifs, picturing a world identical to ours in which one crucial choice or outcome has gone the other way. What if Hitler had gone to art school or Abraham Lincoln had survived? But think of the counterfactual history that would emerge if all humans, across hundreds of thousands of years, perceived reality differently. Our senses are a crucial, but hidden, variable of our species. As with so much in life, given a few little tweaks, it could've been otherwise.

Our senses emerged not randomly, but as the contingent, accidental outcome of a complex evolutionary history. So, why do humans have three color cones (red, green, blue) instead of two? Millions of years ago, primates split into two groups. Researchers noticed an intriguing correlation that divided the two groups: primates that lived in areas that had lots of reddish figs growing among bright green palms evolved to detect red against a green background, helping them survive. Primates that lived in areas without figs didn't—and remained red-green color-blind. We're the offshoots of the fig primates. Scientists may have proposed a plausible "reason" in the formal sense—that humans have three photoreceptors in our eyes *because* we are descended from ancestors who evolved to see figs better than rival species did. But how arbitrary is that? The answer to one of life's great mysteries is . . . figs?

Another trick of the Shortcut Creature is that human brains are pattern detection machines. From the beginning, the ancients connected the dots in the sky to form constellations, complete with stories and tales of celestial bravery.* Today, many neuroscientists regard our "superior pattern processing" as the feature that makes us fundamentally human, giving rise to exceptional intelligence, imagination, and invention. We have the neurological architecture to categorize, to infer cause and effect, and to spot patterns from a world that is exceptionally complex.

But our brains also evolved to be allergic to chance and chaos, wrongly detecting patterns and proposing false reasons for why things happen rather than accepting the accidental or the arbitrary as the correct explanation. The Shortcut Creature comes up with neat explanations in the face of apparent randomness. That causes us to wrongly dismiss flukes as unimportant. With cognitive processes that prioritize survival over

---

* The patterns of the constellations and the idea of making stories out of them are so universal that they recur across time and space. For example, Orion's Belt was known as Frigg's Distaff in pre-Christian Scandinavia; in New Zealand's indigenous Maori culture, the three stars are known as the "string of three" and they form part of a great sky canoe. Humans repeatedly latched on to the same patterns in the skies.

truth, our minds have evolved to simplify our understanding of cause and effect into a misleading, but useful, form. We tend to look for one cause for one effect; we tend to imagine a straightforward linear relationship between causes and effects (small causes produce small effects, while big causes produce big effects); and we tend to systematically discount the role of randomness and chance, inventing reasons even when reasons do not exist, averse to the uncertain and the unknown.

We've evolved to *overdetect* patterns. It's safer to mistakenly assume that a rustling noise is caused by a lurking predator than to ignore a lion by dismissing the rustling as a random bit of wind. To survive, our brains have become supersensitive to movement and to understanding intent. As the evolutionary philosopher Daniel Dennett argues, we're particularly attuned not just to movement but to the beliefs, desires, information, and goals of others. Or, as he puts it, "Who knows what?" and "Who wants what?" are questions that evolution has trained us to ask. Does this strange creature with fangs want to eat me, or is it merely curious? That's a rather important question. Those that got it wrong in the distant past were less likely to pass on their genes, thereby weeding them out of the future of humanity. In a world in which false positives are annoying but false negatives are deadly, neuroscientists and evolutionary biologists suggest that our brains have evolved to be hyper-attuned to pattern detection that could someday save our lives.

As pattern people, we crave reasons for why things happen—even when good reasons don't exist. In 1944, the psychologists Marianne Simmel and Fritz Heider of Smith College in Massachusetts discovered how deep this tendency runs with a simple animation of shapes moving haphazardly around a screen. In their study, thirty-five of the thirty-six participants who watched the animation described a larger triangle as a bully that was chasing the "valiant" and "spirited" smaller shapes. The participants' minds couldn't resist imbuing the shapes with causation, narrative, even personality.

But the flip side of that sensitive pattern detection is that we either ignore random events or pretend they're part of some hidden, ordered structure, as we draw neat lines through disordered scatterplots. Our species is a devoted disciple of the Cult of Because.

Nothing is more disconcerting to us than feeling like the victimized puppet of chance, nothing more unsettling than the notion that life and death come seemingly at random. But they often do. Hoping to make sense of the senseless is a long-standing ambition for us and our hominin relatives. Neanderthal graves from fifty thousand years ago have even shown possible signs of superstitious belief, as some burials have been found with grains of pollen scattered around the bones, or in one instance a variety of animal horns and the skull of a rhinoceros.

After the Enlightenment ushered in the Age of Reason, nonreligious superstitious beliefs have increasingly been subjected to ridicule in intellectual discourse. But they remain widespread, even in unexpected places. In a perhaps apocryphal story, a visitor to the house of the Nobel Prize–winning physicist Niels Bohr noticed a horseshoe hanging over the door. Astonished that one of the founding fathers of atomic theory and quantum physics would put his faith in superstitions, the visitor asked if Bohr actually believed the horseshoe would bring him luck. "Of course not," Bohr allegedly replied, "but I am told that they bring luck even to those who do not believe in them."

We will go to great lengths to invent explanations when none are readily available. For example, when World War I ended, the blood-soaked trenches were full not just of bodies, but of talismans. Sprigs of heather, heart-shaped amulets, and rabbit-feet were buried alongside makeshift graves. Troops from the mountains of the Austro-Hungarian Empire had sewed bat wings into their underwear to help them stay alive. Few dared to wear the boots of the dead, no matter how fine the leather.

Two decades later, world war returned, and superstition again surged. As doodlebug rockets began falling on London in 1944, residents began a frantic attempt to predict where the next cluster would land, complete with maps and rival superstitions. But when blast sites were analyzed after the war, their destruction followed a Poisson distribution, an almost perfectly random spread.

Superstition is the daughter of the unexplained and the apparently random. We invent it to deal with causal uncertainty, a disorienting feeling we experience when we don't know why something is happening and we feel like the playthings of chaos. Superstition is not, as many unfairly believe, the providence of simpletons. Instead, it is an understandable and nearly universal way that humans assert control when they feel that ordinary, rational methods of manipulating the world have become fruitless. In the words of Theodore Zeldin, superstition functions the same as the "modern car-driver, who does not know how his car works, but trusts it all the same, interested only in knowing which button to press." The lucky amulet may not work, but if bombs are raining from the skies, have you got any better ideas?

Randomness is also unsatisfying to us because we are, to borrow the phrase used by Jonathan Gottschall, a "storytelling animal." Our brains are designed for narratives. We tell ourselves stories, and all good stories have a clear cause and effect at their center. We don't sit on the edge of our seat waiting for a random-number generator to rattle off fresh digits.

E. M. Forster once wrote " 'The king died and then the queen died' is a story. 'The king died and then the queen died of grief' is a plot." The detective novelist P. D. James agreed, but suggested that the plot might be improved with the addendum "Everyone thought that the queen had died of grief until they discovered the puncture mark in her throat." The three sentences proceed in order from least to most memorable.

The first has no causation and is therefore just a list of unrelated facts, the sort of information we find most difficult to retain. The second invokes causation, but provides the reason for the queen's demise immediately, dampening our interest. The third, however, makes us wonder who put the puncture mark in the queen's throat, and that causal cliff-hanger is easily remembered. It's why mystery writers produce bestsellers and why true crime dominates podcast and documentary charts. We want to know who, but above all, we must know *why*.

In *Cat's Cradle*, Kurt Vonnegut parodies this human impulse while writing of a fictional religion called Bokononism. The religion speaks of an encounter between Man and God. "Man blinked. 'What is the purpose of all this?' he asked politely. 'Everything must have a purpose?' asked God. 'Certainly,' said man. 'Then I leave it to you to think of one for all this,' said God. And He went away."

If we don't know why, we pretend we do. Nowhere is this tendency to invent causes more apparent than with split-brain experiments. Every so often, someone with severe epilepsy undergoes a surgery that severs the corpus callosum, a thick tract of nerves that connects the right hemisphere of the brain with the left. Patients are still able to function, but information can't physically pass between the two distinct hemispheres of the brain—the channel has been cut. The left half of the brain specializes in language, so it's where we formulate narrative explanations for understanding the world. Bizarrely, experiments have shown that when information is given to the right half of the patient's brain, but not to the left, the patient's left hemisphere deals with the confusion by automatically inventing a plausible explanation. This gave rise to the neuroscience theory that the left hemisphere can be thought of as the Interpreter within our skulls. When there are no reasons, our brains make one up.

It's not just that we need reasons, but we need simple ones. In the neat and tidy world we crave, one cause produces one straightforward effect, in proportion to the magnitude of the cause. But that's not how the modern world works (more on that in the next chapter). When we make the cognitive mistake of slapping ordered reasons with a purpose onto disordered, even random processes, it's called teleological bias. That bias seems to be innate across cultures. For example, children in China as well as in the West are susceptible to believing intuitively that mountains were made for humans to climb them. Education erodes such cognitive biases, but teleological thinking persists. It's virtually impossible for thinkers who shape popular conceptions of change to argue that a specific event was driven by neutral events, by randomness, or by the chaotic or the contingent. When soldiers in trenches imbue randomness and uncertainty with simple, clear-cut cause-and-effect relationships that often turn out to be wrong, we call it superstition. But when we do something similar to explain change in our complex world, we call it something else: punditry and bad social science.

I speak from personal experience. I'm sometimes invited to appear on TV news shows. I do my best to answer the questions. But punditry has many unwritten rules. Novel "takes" get rewarded. Forcefully expressing confidence and certainty in a shaky opinion is better than timidity and uncertainty. *Because* is better than three unspeakable words: *I don't know*. An unwritten iron rule is that you can never, ever suggest that a major event occurred because, well, sometimes major events occur due to small, accidental perturbations in the extremely complex, intertwined system of 8 billion interacting humans that we call modern society. Or, more precisely, you can't say that if you want to retain the recurring privilege of appearing as one-eighth of a breathless octobox debating the news in forty-second sound bites on cable TV. This phenomenon is particularly prominent in market analysis, in which some stochastic (apparently random) fluctuations in stock prices are almost always explained as being the natural result of some unambiguous cause and effect. Whenever you hear "markets are reacting to" or "stocks dipped today because," your antenna for teleological bias should perk up on high alert.

Teleological bias is related to a phenomenon called apophenia, the inference of a relationship between two unrelated objects, or a mistaken inference of causality.* This manifests itself in sports, with the "hot hand fallacy," in which a basketball player making several shots in a row is considered unable to miss, even though the player's past shots have no bearing on future ones (other than perhaps as a confidence boost). The "gambler's fallacy" is similar, in which a string of winning bets makes someone overconfident, wrongly inferring a pattern out of a random outcome.

Conspiracy theories thrive on such cognitive biases, including *magnitude bias*. Following the simplistic linear worldview, big events *must* have big causes, not small, accidental, or random ones. Christopher French, who led the anomalistic psychology unit at Goldsmiths, University of London, told me that Princess Diana's death spurred so many conspiracy theories precisely because many people wouldn't tolerate the notion that such an important event could have been caused by mere human error and the mundane deadliness of a car traveling too fast. Something else had to be going on, the conspiracists figure, a secret pattern waiting to be detected. They're even willing to accept mutually contradictory explanations rather than rule out a larger, hidden explanation. Some conspiracists believe Diana is still alive *and* that she was killed by British security services. The logical impossibility of both being true is less of a problem to the conspiracists than the unsatisfying explanation that it was an accident.

---

* A particularly intriguing subset of these cognitive biases is pareidolia, in which we spot visual patterns, such as faces, in random images. In 1994, Diane Duyser of Florida saw the Virgin Mary in her grilled cheese sandwich and auctioned it off for $28,000 because others saw it, too.

Voltaire was inspired to write *Candide* after trying to make sense of the apparently random tragedy of the 1755 Lisbon earthquake, which, for no apparent reason, flattened the city, unleashed a tsunami, and killed twelve thousand people. In the book, the overly optimistic character, Dr. Pangloss, is teleological bias in human form, seeing reason and optimization everywhere he looks. Stones were put on the earth so that feudal lords could later create castles. Legs were designed so that eighteenth-century breeches would fit them perfectly. Our noses were etched onto our faces in precisely the right shape in anticipation of the invention of spectacles. Voltaire's character inspired a new word, *Panglossian*, which refers to a relentless optimism that the world we inhabit is the best possible world that could exist, marching endlessly toward progress, where everything is designed precisely for its function. This view is a natural bedfellow of the mantra that everything happens for a reason, all with a hidden purpose waiting to be discerned. "If you had not been put into the Inquisition," Dr. Pangloss proclaims, or "if you had not lost all your sheep from the fine country of El Dorado," then "you would not be here eating preserved citrons and pistachio-nuts."

Maybe so, but Dr. Pangloss makes a misdiagnosis—as many of us do—when he suggests that a linear trajectory of events has an end goal of progress. Hegel and Marx were wrong. nature and complex systems such as modern human society are not moving relentlessly toward some idealized end point. It sounds absurd when Dr. Pangloss trumpets that kind of thinking at its most extreme and outlandish, but similarly Panglossian thought still dominates huge swaths of modern society. We sometimes see patterns and meaningful relationships where none exist because that's better than seeing nothing. In the words of the late philosopher Susanne Langer, "Man can adapt himself somehow to anything his imagination can cope with; but he cannot deal with Chaos."

Every so often, then, the shortcuts fail us. For most of the time we've graced the planet, our evolved minds have done a great job at keeping us alive—and the survivors shaped our species. But when the world changes, the Shortcut Creature may find itself in peril. If old patterns give way to new ones, what was once a useful heuristic can abruptly become harmful. We can learn that lesson from two species that are rather unlike us, but are nonetheless directed around the world by brains, like ours, evolved to usefully deceive them. When the world changed, their internal deception proved fatal.

We briefly turn to sea turtles and jewel beetles. Both are, like us, Shortcut Creatures. Sea turtles use light as a shortcut: hatchlings head toward the brightest bit of the horizon, which is usually the moonlight reflected on the water of the ocean. This shortcut was reliable—until humans constructed beachfront hotels with bright spotlights. The turtles began to die off, struggling relentlessly to find water as they moved toward the light, away from the sea. (Many coastal areas have now passed light ordinances to prevent this sad fate.)

But the jewel beetle offers the most memorable example of a shortcut gone wrong. The male beetle can't see the "truth" of the much-larger female beetle's body, but instead searches for her distinct coloring, size, and dimpled shell pattern. That shortcut worked well, until an Australian beer company, by complete chance, created a virtual replica of a female jewel beetle's traits in its bottle design. The similarity was uncanny. Following the shortcut, the male beetles began trying to mate with discarded bottles, thereby failing to produce offspring. As scientists rather delicately described the phenomenon when they came across a discarded beer bottle on the roadside, the male beetles had mounted the beer bottle in droves, "genitalia everted—attempting to insert the aedeagus."

These mismatches from broken shortcuts are known as evolutionary traps. They arise when the old ways of survival become incompatible with a newer reality. Unfortunately, as we'll now see, humans trying to navigate the unimaginable complexity of modern society are now facing an evolutionary trap of our own because our minds didn't evolve to cope with a hyperconnected world that relentlessly converges toward a knife's edge, in which one tiny fluke can change everything in an instant. The Shortcut Creature doesn't do quite so well when navigating a new, more complex world.

CHAPTER 5

THE HUMAN SWARM

Why self-organized criticality creates Black Swans

In 1875, a plague of locusts the size of California swept across the United States, devouring everything in its path. The locusts spread across the fertile plains, up to Minnesota and down to Texas. An estimated 3.5 trillion insects formed a cloud eighteen hundred miles long. As the locusts approached, farmers were baffled by what they saw in the distance. To some, it looked like a ferocious hailstorm battering crops on the horizon. To others, it was a raging prairie fire, with smoke swirling in unusual patterns close to the ground. Then, as the insects got closer, the true horror became clear. It was the largest recorded swarm in human history.

Locust plagues ravaged America for several more years. The earth was "covered and hidden with a seething, crawling mass several inches in depth." Daylight was snuffed out, the darkness accompanied by the roar of "thousands of scissors cutting and snipping" in unison. The locusts ate everything. Barley, wheat, and cabbages disappeared in a gray flash. Peach trees had their bark stripped clean, with only pits left hanging from their branches. Vast cornfields "melted down as if each leaf were a spray of hoar frost in the rays of the noon-day sun." Men shot into the air out of desperation, but a bullet was no match against 3.5 trillion buzzing soldiers. Women threw clothes and blankets over their garden vegetables, only to watch as the locusts treated the fabrics as an amuse-bouche for the meal hidden below. The locusts even ate the wool straight off the backs of sheep. Farmers hastily invented makeshift "hopper-dozers," broad horse-drawn devices designed to trap the pests, smeared with kerosene or sticky molasses to thin the swarm. The governor of Minnesota proposed a bounty to be paid for locust embryos, crushed before they could take flight.* Everyone tried to predict where the locusts would go next, so people could prepare for the onslaught.

None of it worked.

The locusts ate America's breadbasket. In total, the swarms devoured three-quarters of the value of all farm products in the United States, the modern equivalent of $120 billion in damage. (A writer for the *New York Times* helpfully suggested that the lost crop yield could be replaced by the locusts themselves, their nutty flavor released when they were crisped on a grill, the insects served with honey, John the Baptist–style.) The locusts didn't even spare Laura Ingalls Wilder's little house on the prairie. She described the destruction in *On the Banks of Plum Creek*. As the locusts gobbled up her family's crops, she noted that they destroyed with purpose, marching onto the wheat field "like an army."

Locusts *do* march. That's the technical term used by scientists to describe their coordinated behavior in a swarm. While it is perhaps not the most flattering comparison, we humans can better understand ourselves by exploring our commonalities with plagues of locusts. Yes, both locusts and humans can consume and destroy on an awesome scale, but our shared rapaciousness isn't what we can learn from them. Instead, the individual and collective behavior of locusts in and out of swarms provides a useful analogy for modern human society, a

---

* That governor was John S. Pillsbury, the cofounder of the Pillsbury company, later to be represented by the Pillsbury Doughboy and the Jolly Green Giant.

domain engineered to be extraordinarily coordinated, regimented, and structured—but that is nonetheless more erratic and prone to random shocks than ever before in the history of our species. The patterns of the swarm can help us understand a social world that seems tremendously ordered, until suddenly everything changes in a flash. We live in a swarm that, to borrow a phrase from physics, teeters on the *edge of chaos*.

Locusts are a bit like Dr. Jekyll and Mr. Hyde. For much of their lives, they flit about in their solitary state, harmless grasshoppers moving somewhat at random, happily munching when they get hungry. If left to their own devices, they will avoid fellow locusts. But if locusts get forced together—often by food shortages—the crowding brings out their inner Mr. Hyde. They transition into their "gregarious" state, ditching their green-brown camouflage and morphing instead into a much brighter yellow, or even black. Despite the apparently friendly "gregarious" description, these are not guests you'd want at a dinner party, unless you like visitors who eat everything but your mortgage.

Scientists have long been perplexed by why swarms form. Recent research may have finally solved those puzzles—and it's all about density. When there are fewer than seventeen per square meter, each locust keeps to itself. The locusts' movements lack coordination or purpose. Predicting their path is impossible because it's so prone to fluctuations without clear patterns. It's almost complete disorder. Each locust is mostly unaffected by others. Isolation and independence, rather than connection and interdependence, define the life of a solitary locust.

When more locusts join the party, their behavior starts to shift. At medium densities, of an average of twenty-four to sixty-one locusts per square meter, they gather together in small groups. They move somewhat in unison, but these mini-swarms are independent. Each semiorganized cluster will move as one, but there is no coordinated motion *between* groups. They're more like cliques in a high school than an army. And like cliques, they can be quite erratic, rapidly changing direction in an instant, as though they're chasing one fad before darting toward another. Each locust can sway the clique, but it won't affect other cliques.

Locusts begin to march as a unified swarm at precisely 73.7 locusts per square meter (don't ask how or why the locusts settled on that specific density; nature guards many secrets). "It's a fairly firm tipping point," Jerome Buhl tells me, a professor at the University of Adelaide, who conducted the research. At such teeming concentrations, marching emerges. These dense swarms are, by far, the most stable and predictable form for the gregarious locusts. They move as a unified whole, an arrangement that is ruthlessly enforced. If a locust moves against the swarm, it will be eaten, a cannibalistic punishment that ensures the swarm stays together. And it does. The cloud marches as one.

Despite this ruthlessly enforced order, it's impossible to predict where the frenzied locusts will go next, a similar erraticism to what we often see with a flock of birds swooping in a murmuration across the sky or a school of fish flitting in and out of coral reefs. "In the context of our laboratory experiments," Buhl notes, "we have in fact shown that the direction changes are purely random and unpredictable." That's a bit of a problem if you're a government hoping to spray pesticides in the right place, or a nineteenth-century farmer trying to position your hopper-dozer where the locusts are likely to arrive next. This is what we might call the *paradox of the swarm*. Out of complete chaos, the locusts produce astonishing order. But wait long enough and the swarm's overall movement is complex and unpredictable. They march in unison, then suddenly switch direction without warning.

It's not a perfect analogy—we aren't insects—but humans have, over thousands of years, transitioned from societies that mirror the medium-density locusts to a high-density swarm. We evolved to live in small, isolated mini-swarms. Now, all of us live in an enormous one, more frenzied and fragile than ever before.

Fifty thousand years ago, for example, most humans lived in small, isolated bands. Every so often, they might encounter another band, but the interaction would be brief. Communities developed unique customs and culture. There was no significant cultural exchange or shared customs across large distances because even the most nomadic Stone Age hunter-gatherers in Britain would never encounter their counterparts in Asia or Africa. We were a bit like the locust cliques, semiorganized in small groups, but separate.

Chiefdoms and states were later formed, followed by sprawling empires. But humanity kept to this middle tier, in these societies of loose control, where physical proximity mattered most. It was a world defined by low connectivity and limited interdependence across space. A few powerful individuals, such as kings, religious leaders, and generals, could reshape society, but even they had limited reach and their influence was often temporary (recall the scene in *Monty Python and the Holy Grail* where a peasant meets Arthur, king of the Britons, but has never heard of Arthur, nor of the Britons). Ordinary people, such as peasants, could rarely reshape the collective group. That dynamic persisted for most of human history.

It's useful to think about these premodern lifestyles in terms of how stable, regular, and ordered life was from one year to the next. The past was largely defined by *local instability*. Day-to-day life was unpredictable. One day you could be healthy, the next day you could be dead, struck down by a mysterious plague. Childbirth was a death trap. Starvation was a constant threat, as crops might inexplicably fail, or animals that were once abundant were suddenly nowhere to be found. But our distant ancestors also experienced *global stability*. That didn't mean that the world never changed, but rather that, broadly speaking, society ticked along more or less in similar ways from one generation to the next. If your parents were agrarian peasants, you were likely to be an agrarian peasant. Unlike today, grandparents and grandchildren lived in the same kind of world. Parents taught children about technology, not the other way around. And in the Stone Age, technological revolutions came around every few thousand years, not every few months.

Modern society is fundamentally different. Like the locust army marching as one, there is now immense order and apparent regularity, even as the population soars and density hits unprecedented levels. There are 8 billion humans, but bring them together into civilization within a modern rule-based economy, and they start to exhibit extremely predictable patterns. We, unlike our ancestors, experience more *local stability*. One recent study using anonymized cell phone data found that it was possible to accurately predict where any given person would be about 93 percent of the time, as we are creatures of repetition and habit. Society exerts significant control over individual behavior—so much so that we can confidently hurtle down a narrow asphalt strip in giant hunks of metal traveling seventy miles per hour almost certain that everyone else will follow the same rules. Those who don't obey those rules, like the locusts who foolishly move against the swarm, are often killed.

Connections between populations are at their highest level, too, leading to the convergence of cultures and customs across the human swarm. Next time you get into an elevator, anywhere in the world, look around you. Everyone will be facing the door. No rule, no law, says you must. If you're in an elevator within an office building, many of the men will even be wearing similar attire whether you're in Manila or Manhattan, an astonishing fact given the vast cultural gulfs needed to be bridged by the stiff allure of the business suit.* Type a four-digit code into an ATM almost anywhere in the world, and, in an instant, money will be spit out, drawn from your local bank thousands of miles

---

* There is contingency in every detail of life if you know where to look. The emergence of the modern business suit can arguably be traced back to a single individual, Beau Brummell, a socialite in Regency-era England. When people refer to someone as a "beau," they're referring to Beau Brummell.

away. You can order the same McDonald's hamburger in 118 countries. Modern human society has an unprecedented regularity. We live in a world that is more ordered, regimented, and structured than ever before. It feels sturdy and predictable.

But now, as with the marching locusts, everything can change in an instant. Our lives are frequently disrupted by large social shocks such as financial crises, pandemics, and wars. We get blindsided by those large, unexpected consequential events—the Black Swans. That makes our existence more prone to *global instability*. These days, nobody—no matter how much of a recluse—is protected from the whims of contingency.

That's the paradox of the swarm. Human society has become simultaneously far more convergent toward ordered regularity (which makes it appear seductively predictable) and also far more contingent (which makes it fundamentally uncertain and chaotic). Modern humans live in the most ordered societies that have ever existed, but our world is also more prone to disarray and disorder than any other social environment in the history of humanity.

What's going on?

—

Our brains adapted to live within a simpler world. There have been roughly eight thousand generations of humans in the last two hundred thousand years. But there have only been about fifty-seven generations since the fall of Rome. That means our brains were overwhelmingly forged, through evolution, in a world that is quite unlike the one we now inhabit. In the past, we only needed to understand simple patterns: "a saber-toothed tiger causes painful death" was often sufficiently complex when it came to understanding causality. Our minds evolved to work well with straightforward models of cause and effect. Today, we might imagine such a direct relationship as Smoking → Ingestion of harmful chemicals → Damage to DNA → Elevated risk of lung cancer.*

Few complex social systems can be captured with that stripped-down version of reality, with simple unidirectional arrows moving from cause to effect in such a basic way. Today, the real world is chock-full of feedback loops, tipping points, reverse causality (in which an effect simultaneously produces a cause), and the endless array of seemingly insignificant ripples—flukes—that turn out to matter enormously. It doesn't always matter so much in our day-to-day lives; we can still navigate our environment effectively. But the problems start when we try to understand—and tame—a far more complex society. So, what are we to do, given that our minds evolved to understand a simpler social world?

The answer lies with a relatively new realm of knowledge called complexity science and complex-adaptive-systems research. Complexity science has grown out of several distinct fields of inquiry, from physics, mathematics, and chemistry to ecology and economics. It's concerned with states of the world that are between the two extremes of order and disorder, between pure randomness and stability, between control and anarchy. The mecca of complexity science is the Santa Fe Institute, a thriving research hub not far from where the atomic bomb was developed, in the sagebrush hills of New Mexico. Modern human society clearly is a complex adaptive system, though researchers who explicitly treat it that way unfortunately remain a tiny minority within mainstream economics, political science, sociology, and so on. But this isn't about interdisciplinary collaborations. Instead, it's an entirely different lens with which to view the world, making everything come into sharper focus.

---

* Modern research is bursting with these simplistic distillations of reality, which are often called directed acyclic graphs or DAGs. They can be useful in closed, stable systems but are often useless in modeling dynamic, chaotic systems (such as the ones we care about most in economics, ecology, politics, and so on).

Through the old lens, researchers presented models that largely relied on misleading linear systems with a single point of equilibrium, such as a supply-and-demand curve, where an equation gives a "right" answer as the price produces a single convergent point. The real economy isn't like that, but generation after generation of students produced these deceptive drawings to pass their exams. It distorted generations of thinking, as countless millions were taught to imagine a two-dimensional cookie-cutter world with rigidly defined rules and boundaries. Similarly, in the old, streamlined linear models for social change, any causal shift was deemed directly proportionate to the size of the effect. Small changes produce small effects, and big changes produce big effects. That, quite clearly, isn't true. The old lens also tended to involve three assumptions that seem, at first glance, to make intuitive sense:

1. Every effect that you can see also has a specific cause that you can see.

2. If you want to understand something, just understand its constituent parts.

3. If we understand patterns from the past, then we will better understand the future.

But in complex adaptive systems, such as modern human society, none of those three assumptions holds true. Minuscule causes often produce big effects. Effects almost always have multiple causes, which can't be easily disentangled. Understanding the constituent parts of a system isn't good enough. You need to understand how each component interacts with every other part, because complex systems are defined by intertwined relationships and ripples, not separable, individual pieces. And patterns from the past are not necessarily a useful guide to the future because the dynamics of a system can shift drastically over time—or hit tipping points that upend long-standing patterns of regularity. Our modern world is rather different from how we've long imagined it.

Let's clear up some terminology. A Swiss watch is complicated, but not complex. The watch has many intricate moving parts, each doing a different task, but it's not difficult to understand, nor is it difficult to predict how it will behave. Crucially, it's complicated but not complex because the individual components do not adapt to changes in another component. If the gear train in the watch breaks, it's not as though other parts will morph into something new, develop new functions, and take over the work of the gear train. The watch just breaks. Even at the extremes of human ingenuity, a space shuttle is complicated but not complex, which is why the *Challenger* could explode due to a single faulty O-ring. So, what makes something "complex"?

Complex systems, such as locust swarms or modern human society, involve *diverse*, *interacting*, and *interconnected* parts (or individuals) that *adapt* to one another.* The system, like our world, is in constant flux. If you change one aspect of the system, other parts spontaneously adjust, creating something altogether new. If one person pumps the brakes while driving, or if a person in a crowd stops to chat to someone else, people don't just carry on, following a fixed trajectory. They adapt and adjust. The entire flow of people or cars in the system can be drastically affected by a single small change.

As a result, complex adaptive systems are *path dependent*, a bit like the Garden of Forking Paths. If you take one path, it will affect which future paths are available to you, just as the arbitrary layout of the QWERTY keyboard long ago now means that we still type with that system. Even if a better keyboard layout is developed, it's too late—we've already made

---

* This definition comes from the complex-systems scholar Scott E. Page of the University of Michigan.

our choice. As a result, to understand a complex adaptive system, you must also understand its history.

As a system adapts, a precarious order emerges, just as it does in a locust swarm. However, the entire system is *decentralized* and *self-organized*. It's the aggregation of a nearly infinite number of adjustments and behaviors that determine how the system operates, not an overarching rule being imposed from above. Consider the stock market. Prices are not set from on high, and crashes do not get ordered by a central banker. There's neither predictable order, nor disordered chaos. Instead, the market lies somewhere between the two, with millions of interacting agents producing its behavior. It's a decentralized system that, like the swarm, can't be controlled.

The interactions of lots of diverse, interconnected agents or units that constantly adapt to one another can produce a phenomenon known as *emergence*. Emergence arises when individuals or components organize themselves in a way that produces something different from the sum of their parts, the way that locust swarms have fundamentally different characteristics from solo insects. (The human brain is sometimes said to be emergent, because no individual neuron can produce consciousness or complex thought, but together, the neurons are capable of astonishing feats.) Human society is also full of emergent characteristics.

With decentralized, self-organized emergence, complex adaptive systems produce regularities and patterns. That's partly because of a phenomenon that complex-systems scientists call *basins of attraction*. It's a straightforward phenomenon disguised in jargon. It means that, over time, a system will converge toward one, or many, particular outcomes. Picture a pendulum swinging. It doesn't matter where you start it swinging, it will eventually end up at rest at the lowest point in the middle, which is the basin of attraction in that extremely simple system. If we apply the logic to humans, the flow of traffic, the speed of cars, and the gap between them could be thought of as a basin of attraction.

Cars may start off driving at various speeds, but will tend to organize themselves at roughly the same speed, similarly spaced out, as they careen down a road. When basins of attraction exist, we're likely to see patterns appear, in similar ways, repeatedly.

In complex systems, basins of attraction can change over time, creating instability. If you apply the metaphor of basins of attraction to political parties, for example, we can use the idea to think of the U.S. political system as having two main basins of attraction for partisan identity: Republicans and Democrats. Every time a person becomes politically engaged, no matter the person's initial ideology, that individual is most likely to gravitate toward one of those two basins. But every so often, splits occur, such as when Donald Trump split the Republican Party in 2016 between Never Trumpers and MAGA Republicans, or when the traditional divides between Labour and the Tories in Britain gave way to new basins of attraction defined by Brexit.* Similarly, the Western world used to have one main basin of attraction for religion in medieval times, but the Protestant Reformation created a split and new basins of attraction, again ushering in volatility. When the number of basins of attraction increases abruptly, a system can become more prone to shocks.

Conversely, when society appears stable, that's often because the basins of attraction are stable and are operating according to their "normal" patterns. But here's the problem: modern society only produces the illusion of stability. We've engineered many complex systems with an unfortunate trait: they're designed to have basins of attraction that are on the precipice of a cliff, near tipping points, or what is sometimes known as the *edge of chaos*.

---

* These are loose analogies. All these concepts from chaos theory and complex systems are mathematically precise terms with more specific definitions in dynamical systems theory, so please forgive any imprecision, for the sake of ease of understanding. Attractors can exist in stable systems, too; and "strange attractors" exist in chaotic systems.

Imagine that human society is like an explorer, wandering around a rugged landscape. For much of human history, the wanderings were haphazard, ineffective, and inefficient, but less prone to shocks, as hunter-gatherers explored their terrain in reasonably simplistic social networks.

But in modern times, we are obsessed with efficiency, so society is like an explorer that has become a compulsive, obsessive mountain climber. Rather than wandering around somewhat at random, modern society optimizes, making a beeline for the top of the nearest peak, even if it's right on the edge of a precarious, crumbling cliff. As soon as the explorer gets to the summit, there is a rumble, then an avalanche, and everything comes crashing down. But after the explorer tumbles to the bottom, the obsession returns, and the explorer hikes straight back up the mountain, waiting for the next cascade of snow. Because of our relentless drive for ruthless, perfected optimization, most modern social systems have little slack—such as our economies and our politics—and the levels of interconnection are now so great that even minor perturbations can create major shocks. We, by design, race toward the cliff edge, but continue to be surprised when we fall off it.

Another way of thinking of this is to imagine a bowl made from paper with a marble placed inside. When the paper is in that bowl shape, small perturbations won't matter much. The marble will always come to rest at the lowest part of the bowl.† Now, imagine that the system changes over time, and you flatten the paper bowl out completely. Now, if you start the marble rolling, it might leave the paper altogether, ending up somewhere entirely new. Push it back in the other direction and it will return to rest on the paper. But what happens if you invert the bowl, even folding it into a vertical cone, with a sharp point at the

---

† This analogy of stability only works for human society on short time scales. Because the overall system is chaotic, even our most "bowl-like" societies will eventually succumb to chaotic dynamics over longer periods.

top? If you place the marble at the pinnacle, balancing precariously on the peak, then even the tiniest gust of wind—maybe even a single human breath—will cause the marble to cascade down, ending up much farther away from its original location. You can try to shoot the marble back at the cone, but it's extremely unlikely that it will come to rest again on the point of the cone. This is a useful way of thinking about our societies. Sometimes, they're more resilient—like the bowl. Other times, they're like the flattened bit of paper. But increasingly, we're optimizing so much that our social paper ends up as the cone with a sharp point, on the edge of chaos. A crisis can then emerge from the tiniest tremor.

Because complex systems are nonlinear, which means that the scale of change is not proportionate to the magnitude of the effect, small changes do sometimes produce a major, unpredictable event—the Black Swans that Taleb warned about. They are often the result of cascades, which are consequential but difficult to anticipate. And when the cascades happen, we often can't understand them—even with the benefit of hindsight.

In 1995, for example, gray wolves were reintroduced to Yellowstone National Park. It triggered an unexpected trophic cascade, in which the entire ecosystem adjusted abruptly due to this comparatively small change. Without wolves, elk in the park didn't need to move much to avoid predators, so they stayed put and munched on willow plants. When the wolves returned, the elk began to move more, eating a more diverse diet, allowing the willow plants to recover. That presented new opportunities for beavers, who had dwindled down to a single colony. Soon, with renewed willow, nine beaver colonies thrived. The rise in beavers changed the streams in the park, boosting the ecosystem for fish populations. The cascade went on and on, and nearly three decades later it's still only partly understood. And it all began with thirty-one wolves being released into the park in 1995.

In human terms, cascades take many forms. Plenty of people griped about the Catholic Church in medieval Europe, but when Martin Luther nailed his 95 Theses to the church door in Wittenberg in 1517, it sparked a religious revolution that would splinter one of the most powerful institutions in the world. Christendom, in that moment, was already on the verge of bifurcating—nearing a tipping point—and Luther's small act pushed the system over the edge. The ensuing cascade broke the dominance of Catholicism across much of Europe.

These days, we end up on the edge of chaos more easily—and it doesn't take centuries of pent-up resentment. Before the 2008–9 financial crisis, the mortgage industry moved toward the cliff in risky ways, offering generous mortgages to people who couldn't afford them. The market climbed ever higher, toward a new basin of attraction. Everything seemed to be going great. Then, suddenly, the financial system hit its tipping point. The avalanche wiped out countless livelihoods.

When complex systems are approaching the edge of chaos, primed to hit a tipping point, they can start to show warning signs. One red flag is a newly discovered phenomenon that scientists call *critical slowing down*. The "slowing down" refers to how long it takes a system to return to an equilibrium after a minor disturbance. When complex systems are robust, small changes might get absorbed, at least for a time, and the system will snap back to "normal" quickly. Such systems are said to be resilient. But when complex systems become fragile, small fluctuations can create extreme volatility, until one tiny change radically rearranges the entire system—and everything changes. This theory of critical slowing down was developed by ecologists who noticed that the number of tree-eating insects in a forest would suddenly and inexplicably explode in unpredictable ways, devastating the ecosystem. But just before these insect explosions, the numbers of insects in various parts of the forest would fluctuate dramatically, and the forest wouldn't return to its "normal" state. This slowing down of the snapback to stability, the ecologists suggest, could be nature's early-warning system. Sure enough, shortly after the ecologists detected population fluctuations, just one tiny change could unleash armies of insects that would devour the forest.

Why do such unpredictable cascades happen? The answer may lie with a phenomenon known as *self-organized criticality*. The name was coined in 1987 by Per Bak, a Danish physicist who showed how his concept applied to grains of sand in a sandpile. The grains slowly build up, one by one, in a stable pattern. Everything seems perfectly ordered, stable, and predictable as the pile grows steadily. That is, until the sandpile hits a critical state and one additional grain of sand triggers an enormous avalanche. In such a sandpile model, you would expect to see periods of stability followed by catastrophic cascades that occur with no warning. Because a single grain can create that avalanche, small changes can have a large, destabilizing impact on the system. As Victor Hugo wrote in *Les Misérables*, "How do we know that the creations of worlds are not determined by falling grains of sand?" Per Bak's answer was simple: we do know. Worlds can be determined not just by falling grains of sand, but by a single grain.

Like sandpiles towering too high, locust swarms exist in that "critical" state, meaning that they appear stable for a time, but are precarious and fragile. Researchers studying locusts have discovered that tiny perturbations to the movement of a few individual insects can create a cascading effect, abruptly redirecting the swarm on a new trajectory. If one or two insects are jostled out of place by even an inch or two, the entire group may switch direction with a whoosh. The motion of the swarm—billions of insects that may stretch for miles and miles—can radically change by a minor disturbance the size of a human hand. This leads to a mind-boggling conclusion: for farmers in 1870s America, or in modern Africa, their entire livelihoods could be saved or wiped out by the slightest flit of a single insect. In our intertwined world, self-organized criticality amplifies contingency.

However, no single locust can direct the swarm. An insect can't decide to move the swarm east or west because the outcome of any individual movement is unpredictable. As Scott Page rightly points out, *each individual controls almost nothing, but influences almost everything.* The same is true of us. Swarms and sandpiles are useful analogies that help us understand why we're so often lulled into a false sense of security. We delude ourselves into believing we're in control, until we are, yet again, thwacked by a devastating crisis, such as a financial crash, a disruptive new technology, a terrorist attack, or a pandemic. But rather than understanding those inevitable avalanches as the normal functioning of the system—a sandpile existence working exactly as it's designed—we mistakenly think of them as "shocks."

When we try to assert our control over complex systems, much can go wrong. China, under Mao Zedong, found this out the hard way. Mao didn't understand that nature's ecology is complex—untamable and sensitive to changes to even a few species. During the Four Pests campaign, China's dictator ordered citizens to kill rats, flies, mosquitoes, and sparrows. He hoped it would help eradicate human disease. But when the sparrows were wiped out, locusts no longer faced a natural predator. It contributed to unexpected ecological havoc, as the locusts took over. The ensuing famine left as many as 55 million people dead.

Academics disagree over whether modern human society meets the precise mathematical definitions for self-organized criticality, but it clearly provides a useful framework for understanding our world.* We've built a world that seems regular and controllable, so long as we pass the right laws and enact the correct monetary policy. When we're surprised

---

* For example, Jean Carlson, a physicist and pioneer of complex systems at UC Santa Barbara, has convincingly argued that many real-world systems are better described by a theory she has developed, called highly optimized tolerance, which may better predict the behavior of biological and man-made complex systems.

by a social shock, the lesson people tend to learn is that we just need to work harder to control the world better. If only we had better laws, better regulation, better forecasting data, Black Swans might become a scourge of the past. That's not true. The real lesson is that the modern world, like the locust swarm, is fundamentally uncontrollable and unpredictable. Our hubris deludes us. Modern society is a complex system, seemingly stable, teetering on the edge of chaos—until everything falls apart due to a small change, from the accidental to the infinitesimal.

—

Complex systems can help us better understand our history. The outbreak of World War I nicely illustrates the relationship between criticality and contingency. Historians have long debated the causes of the Great War. Prior to the outbreak of the war, major powers in Europe had formed a series of alliances. This created stability for a time because it carved out clear power structures on the Continent that could be seen as a deterrent to aggression. Then, France and Russia agreed on an alliance to counterbalance Germany. The sandpile grows. In response, Germany decided to develop stronger ties with the Austro-Hungarian Empire to counterbalance France and Russia. The sandpile grows. Britain worried about the new balance of power being created and aligned itself with France and Russia. The sandpile grows. In turn, Germany worried about "encirclement" from the three major powers that had lined up against it. The sandpile grows. All the powers began arming themselves to the teeth. The sandpile grows. By 1914, the sandpile was towering high, bringing the world to the precipice of a catastrophic avalanche. But would it be a minor avalanche, or a major one? That was unclear—and the answer would be determined by a contingent event, a terrible accident of history.

In November 1913, the heir presumptive to the Austro-Hungarian Empire, Archduke Franz Ferdinand, came to Britain to visit the Duke of Portland at Welbeck Abbey in Nottinghamshire. Deep snow covered the grounds of the palatial estate, but the duke and archduke nonetheless ventured out to hunt pheasants. During the shoot, several pheasants flew up into the air, startling the "loader," the servant tasked with loading the guns. He tripped and fell toward the snow. As he tumbled, both barrels of the gun in his hand discharged. The accidental shots narrowly missed Archduke Franz Ferdinand. If the loader had twitched slightly, causing the angle of the barrel to move by even a single degree, the archduke would likely have been killed.

Instead, the archduke survived, allowing him to travel to Sarajevo several months later. Once there, Franz Ferdinand traveled in a car made to scream luxury: an Austrian-built 1910 Gräf & Stift double phaeton, with the license plate A-III-118. As his motorcade snaked through the city, the archduke was unaware that he was being targeted for assassination. When the car passed by Nedeljko Čabrinović, he threw a bomb at the archduke. It bounced off the car and detonated, wounding around twenty people, but leaving its intended target unscathed.

That might have been the end of the story. But the archduke and his wife, Sophie, decided to visit the hospital to pay their respects to those wounded by a bomb that had been intended to kill them. No assassin could have prepared for this unplanned trip. However, as their motorcade progressed through the streets, they took a wrong turn. The driver reversed the car, then stalled it. In one of the most consequential pieces of bad luck in history, the car sputtered to a stop six feet away from Gavrilo Princip, another would-be assassin. In the chaos of the crowd, Princip pointed his gun toward the car and fired two shots. He got lucky. The bullets hit their targets. The archduke and his wife both died.

Their deaths unleashed a cascade that culminated in World War I. But the magnitude of the cascade was determined by the criticality within Europe. It was neither a contingent event nor a critical state alone that led to the war. Rather, the combination mattered. Historians are still divided over whether the war was inevitable, but it might plausibly have been avoided if a few small details had unfolded differently. That exact thought occurred to the Duke of Portland, who had witnessed the archduke narrowly avoid death by a hunting accident. In his memoirs, the duke wrote, "I have often wondered whether the Great War might not have been averted, or at least postponed, had the Archduke met his death then, and not at Sarajevo in the following year." Nobody knows. But the outbreak of World War I shows how a critical state can produce a major cascade from a single contingent event. If the angle of one man slipping on the snow had been slightly different, millions of people might not have died, history could forever have been altered, and the people alive now in the modern world might be drastically different.

This story has one more lesson to teach us. As noted, the license plate on the archduke's car read A-III-118, which could also be written as A-II-I1-18. Armistice Day, when the guns fell silent on the Western Front, was November 11, 1918, or A-11-11-18.

How amazing is that?

This is a test: Are you still falling into the trap of teleological thinking? The license plate is just a coincidence. The word for armistice in German is *Waffenstillstand*. It's a meaningless fluke, like so many others, churned out by a maddeningly complex world.

———

More than a century after World War I ended, big data, analytics, and machine learning have given us unprecedented precision in anticipating the average behavior of large groups of people within seemingly stable systems. For example, in England, the power grid is now managed to account for "TV pickups," in which millions of people watching a television event (such as a World Cup match) will, in unison, switch on their teakettles during halftime. The data-driven predictions for the needed power supply are often extremely, eerily precise. We're better than ever at anticipating coordinated behavior across millions of individuals. That has given us an inflated sense of mastery over our world, something I call *the illusion of control.*

That illusion is dangerous. It produces the kind of thinking that sees recessions and wars and pandemics as mere aberrations, outliers to be discarded and moved past so that we can get on with the business of "normal" order. Hundreds of grains of sand pile up without incident, so we imagine that dynamic will continue indefinitely. I call this the *mirage of regularity.* Then, we're blindsided by the avalanche. When the avalanche comes, we label it an external shock, rather than the inevitable culmination of events within a system that's on the edge of chaos. But it wasn't a bolt-from-the-blue shock: it was the inevitable outcome of our social sandpile. We are now extremely prone to catastrophic cascades triggered by small fluctuations. Yet, we keep piling our sandpiles higher and higher, tempting fate.

Modern society is now so intertwined that ordinary individuals, not just kings and popes and generals, can redirect the *entire* human swarm. Consider this question: Who has been the most influential person of the twenty-first century so far? Some might say Xi Jinping, or Vladimir Putin, or Donald Trump. I disagree. My nomination would be an unnamed person. The COVID-19 pandemic likely started with a single person, in a single event, in Wuhan, China.* The lives of literally billions of people were drastically changed, for years, by one virus

---

* The debate over the origin story of COVID-19 is beyond the scope of this book. Whether it started from a zoonotic infection or an accidental "lab leak," both explanations are contingent on a single act involving one person.

infecting one individual. Never in human history have the daily lives of so many people been so drastically affected, for so long, by one small, contingent event. Welcome to the swarm.

———

Why has modern society lurched toward criticality and become more contingent over time? There are many reasons, but I'll highlight just a few. First, because we've become obsessive optimizers, worshipping the false idol of ever more efficiency, modern social systems have little slack. When something goes wrong, as it inevitably does, the consequences are amplified due to connectedness and interdependence. A fully optimized system pushed to the edge of chaos is more likely to drift toward tipping points and cascades.

Conversely, when complex systems are designed for a little less optimization and a little more flexibility, they're more resilient. For example, after a massive 8.8 magnitude earthquake shook Chile in 2010, the power grid was only briefly knocked off-line because local systems were designed so that they could be "decoupled" from the national system. It slightly reduced the overall efficiency of the system, but it made it easy to stop the cascade and prevent nationwide blackouts lasting for weeks. (Plenty of lessons can be learned from this example for our own lives: build in a bit of slack and make it easy to compartmentalize potential damage should things go wrong.)

The world is also more likely to be in a state of criticality than ever before because of the internet, which has drastically increased connectivity in an already-intertwined world. Many communication technologies throughout history have been transformative. But the printing press, newspapers, radio transmissions, and TV broadcasts all expanded the number of people who could *consume* information. The internet is fundamentally different. It's a revolution that has, for the first time in history, created an explosion in who can *create* widely disseminated information. It's a fundamental shift: from *few-to-many* communication to *many-to-many* communication. Ideas, even false ones, spur action, and billions are now being exposed to new ideas at a rate that has never before existed. As the historian Felipe Fernández-Armesto writes, "Ideas are the main motors of change in human cultures and . . . the pace of change is a function of the mutual accessibility of ideas." That motor of change is now in overdrive.

Modern society is also becoming more contingent because our swarm is speeding up. Consider economic trading. Speculators can easily make money when they have an information advantage over their competitors, knowing a crucial piece of economic intelligence before their rivals. These days, high-frequency trading is done by computers. Speed advantages are measured in milliseconds. (For context, a hummingbird flaps its wings about once every eighteen milliseconds.) With great speed, financial systems more often drift toward dangerous criticality. That helps explain why on May 6, 2010, a *trillion* dollars of value on the stock market was wiped out in a few minutes, between 2:42 p.m. and 2:47 p.m. Just as one locust could redirect the swarm, this devastating cascade was triggered by a single rogue trader manipulating the markets, for fun, from his bedroom in London. For locusts, the *rate* of movement is largely static. We're a different kind of swarm—one that's become much more frenzied in modern life.

Complex-systems thinking can teach us important lessons. We fit our lives into informal social rules, patterns, and expectations, a bit like human basins of attraction. That creates the illusion of stability and regularity out of 8 billion wildly diverse, unique people. But we get into trouble when we allow ourselves to be fooled by the mirage of regularity, focusing only on the highly predictable and repeatable aspects of the world, while dismissing accidents, outliers, and chance fluctuations as merely white noise to be tuned out, rather than understanding what it really is: the buzz of complex life.

Over the past several chapters, we've seen how an intertwined world means that everything matters, as little ripples reshape lives and upend societies. Those ripples give rise to a world that is far more random and accidental than we tend to believe, undercutting the mantra that "everything happens for a reason." We've zoomed into bacterial evolution and zoomed out to warfare to recognize that contingency reigns supreme, rewriting lives, altering histories, even spawning new forms of life. We've also seen how our perceptions of reality have been fine-tuned to write out chance and contingency, with shortcuts that allow us to focus on simplified patterns of cause and effect. And now, we've seen how self-organized criticality—the human swarm—makes it more likely that ripples, accidents, and contingent events will culminate in big shocks or Black Swans. It all leads to a single, seemingly unsettling conclusion: we live in a world that is far more unstable and uncertain than we'd like to imagine.

But as I'll now try to convince you, uncertainty can have some hidden upsides.

CHAPTER 6

HERACLITUS RULES

The limits of probability in a complex, ever-changing world

Sentient beings, including humans, are prediction machines. Our survival depends on it. The decision to forage, fight, or take flight are all based on attempts to calculate the unknown. Even without numbers, sophisticated logic, or Nate Silver, animals make informed guesses about the future that are shaped by their experiences. So do we. Every experience in our lives becomes a neurological data point, processed by the pinkish-gray computer within our skulls. When something unexpected happens, networks of neurons adjust slightly. That's how we navigate the world. So, how do the prediction machines inside our heads cope with an unstable world—one in which a devastating cascade can be triggered by a single grain of sand?

Humans have long accepted some uncertainty beyond our control. Many civilizations, ancient and modern, have put their faith in all-knowing interventionist gods. Priests or oracles could tap into divine wisdom or attempt to sway the god(s) to help the righteous and punish the wicked, but it wasn't humanity's role to understand or forecast the future. Within that worldview, uncertainty isn't a feature of the world, but rather a flaw of human ignorance. The divine always knows. God doesn't concern himself with probabilities.

The best mere mortals could do was to channel divine wisdom, to catch a useful glimpse of the mysterious beyond. In ancient China, for example, the *I Ching* functioned as a divination machine, with yarrow stalks used to tap into a deeper, sturdier truth. But for much of human history, trying to overcome uncertainty with measurement or data was viewed as a hubristic fool's errand, a blasphemous attempt to mathematize God. For millennia, surprisingly few systematic attempts were made to precisely measure or quantify uncertainty and risk.

Perhaps that partly explains why the ancient Greeks, who worshipped a pantheon of gods, articulated extremely sophisticated thoughts about just about everything in the natural world, but failed to develop even the most basic math of probability. This knowledge gap was perplexing because the ancient Greeks relished games of chance. The anklebones and knucklebones of hooved animals (known as astragali) have been dated to as early as 5,000 BC in Greece, where they were used as a precursor to dice. People were contemplating odds, even if they didn't create a systematic logic for them. Similar games of chance also existed in other cultures throughout history. For example, the Arabic word for dice, *al-zahr*, is where we get the word *hazard*, a modern synonym for *risk*, and the Spanish word *azar*, which means "chance" or "randomness." The math lagged the games.

Then, the first usage of the Latin word *resicum*, which gave birth to our word *risk*, emerged from a notary contract in the Italian maritime republic of Genoa in 1156. It was used to proportionally award the spoils of risky shipping journeys across the Mediterranean, which would typically result in riches, but sometimes in ruin. However, to quantify risk—to measure it in a logical, precise way—mathematicians were needed. From the very beginning, their understanding of risk was partly flawed, as it took up Aristotle's position from the distant past: that deriving future probabilities simply required you to calculate "what happened for the most part" in the regular patterns of life. (As we shall see, this assumption—that the past is a reliable guide for the future—can be a catastrophic mistake in navigating a changing world.)

Probability theory, however, didn't get developed until much later. One reason for the delay was, fittingly, a contingent accident of history. Roman and Greek numerals were clunky to manipulate mathematically. (Try quickly subtracting MDCCCXLIII from MMXXIII.) The Arabic numeral system—the one we now use—didn't spread globally sooner because Europeans worried that Arabic numerals were too easy to forge on official documents. The number 1, for example, could easily be changed into a 4 or a 7. (The writer Peter Bernstein explains that this concern explains why many Europeans still write 7s with a second line through the upward stem.) Arabic numerals became dominant in Europe with the advent of printing presses, which made forgeries with a quill impossible. The articulation of probability theory in Europe was plausibly delayed by centuries because of an oversensitivity to forged documents.

Breakthroughs in early probability theory were driven by games of chance. Most notably, in 1654, Blaise Pascal and Pierre de Fermat proposed a solution to what is known as an interrupted game, in which two players start playing a game, but are forced to stop for some reason before either player has won. Before Pascal and Fermat, how to split the pot based on who was mathematically most likely to win was not clear-cut. In solving that conundrum, they unleashed rapid advancements in the nascent field of probability, bolstered by titans such as Gerolamo Cardano, the Chevalier de Méré, Jacob Bernoulli, Pierre-Simon Laplace (of Laplace's demon), and Thomas Bayes (who developed what we now call Bayesian inference or Bayesian statistics).

As the mathematical tools grew, a greater proportion of the world could be understood and calculated. Soon, a craze swept the intellectuals of European high society: to count everything. As Isaac Newton developed his mathematical physics, in which the world is shown to follow quantifiable patterns, thinkers were tempted by the prospect of solving the mysteries of human society using numbers and equations. In 1662, John Graunt produced a groundbreaking quantitative assessment of mortality in London, giving birth to the field of demography. In the early-to-mid-1800s, the French philosopher Auguste Comte gave rise to the field of sociology, derived heavily from an influential branch of thinking he founded called positivism and a new quantitative approach to rational decision-making. The Belgian astronomer, mathematician, sociologist, and statistician Adolphe Quetelet developed early social science that was obsessed with counting and quantifying. This was a period of radical new thought about how much of our social world could be transformed from uncertainty into certainty.

In the eighteenth century, however, the Scottish philosopher David Hume warned that probability was far from certainty, by articulating his famous "problem of induction." Hume's warning was astute: most of our understanding of cause and effect is based solely on experience, based on what happened in the past. There is no guarantee, Hume noted, that the future will be like the past. Or, as he more charmingly put it, "probability is founded on the presumption of a resemblance betwixt those objects, of which we have had experience, and those, of which we have had none." Probabilities can be useful. But the future could be different from past patterns—and if it is, it will blindside us. (As we shall see in a moment, Hume was right.)

Today, probability theory has become a sophisticated and lucrative branch of mathematics. Millions are employed in probabilistic forecasting. Billions use those forecasts to make better judgments and informed assessments about an unknowable future. Increasingly, everything is quantified, fed into reductionist regressions, ever-smarter algorithms, and the black box of sophisticated machine-learning models.

We've come a long way from throwing knucklebones. Today, we depend on more reliable oracles: science and statistics, the yarrow stalks replaced by empirical evidence and sprawling datasets. This momentous shift has unlocked vast human potential. But, as we will see, our faith in humanity's ability to become the master of uncertainty has gone a bit too far. We too often pretend that we can answer questions that we cannot. That overconfidence has meant that we write out chance, chaos, and contingent flukes because they don't fit into the neater world we like to imagine exists.

—

Why has this happened? Part of the explanation is that we are a cognitive victim of our astonishing successes. Scientists have become modern wizards. They can edit genes, discover seemingly invisible particles, even divert asteroids. Those breakthroughs have given us an understandable, but misguided, sense that we've figured out most of the mysteries of the world. Too many people believe human knowledge is on mop-up duty, cleaning up those pesky lingering unknowns that will soon be satisfactorily answered. There's no cure for cancer, but it's within reach; there's no man on Mars but there will be soon. The apparent all-knowingness of modern science seems to confer protection on the rest of us from the risks of contingency and chaos.

But much remains uncertain or unknown. Some of the universe's most unresolvable mysteries are its most basic and important ones. They remain clouded in the fog of absolute uncertainty—we just don't know. Nonetheless, we're bombarded with forecasts, from polls to economic predictions, an endless array of models. These have a certain hubris, as though we've tamed the world. If you believe that the world can be predicted, controlled, and manipulated to our liking, then it's easier to imagine that arbitrary, mysterious forces play a small role in our lives. If you think that way, the storybook version of our world seems reasonable. By contrast, if you have a sense that many of the biggest, most important mysteries remain unsolved, then there's more room to recognize that flukes matter. Yet most of us ignore the shrouds of fog we live within, keeping our gaze on what we can see and measure.

The greatest mystery of all is consciousness, and we don't understand it. Since 1994, the thorniest challenge has been called the *hard problem of consciousness*, the term coined by a titan of modern philosophy, David Chalmers. Humans have long been baffled by the so-called mind-body problem, the question of whether there is something fundamentally different between what we think of as our minds and the physical, chemical structures of the brain. If we happily accept that the lungs and liver are just organized chunks of tissue and cells containing chemicals, why should the brain be any different? But Chalmers highlighted something deeper. As the writer Oliver Burkeman summarized the conundrum, "How could the 1.4 kilogram lump of moist, pinkish-beige tissue inside your skull give rise to something as mysterious as the *experience* of being that pinkish-beige lump, and the body to which it is attached?" It's *the* question of being a human—and we don't have a clue.

Then, there are the fundamental laws of the universe. In 1874, a German genius who had just started university at age sixteen asked his academic mentor for guidance on what to study. Don't bother with theoretical physics, the mentor advised. "In this field, almost everything is already discovered, and all that remains is to fill a few holes." Thankfully, the student, a young Max Planck, ignored the advice and decided to try to fill in a few of those holes. In 1918, he won a Nobel Prize for developing the new theory of quantum physics, which upended everything we thought we knew about the ways of the universe.

At the smallest levels, matter behaves in ways that seem impossible. Conventional interpretations of quantum experiments imply that tiny particles can be in two places at once, a phenomenon called superposition. However, when we observe those particles, they collapse into a single position, suggesting that reality changes depending on whether someone's looking. Even more mind-boggling, some interpretations of quantum entanglement suggest that twinned particles separated by vast distances nonetheless affect one another instantly—not quickly, but instantly—when one particle is measured, something that Einstein disparagingly referred to as "spooky action at a distance." We don't have the vocabulary to explain these phenomena because the behavior of these particles is completely unlike anything we encounter in our directly observable world. Even our best scientists don't know what's going on, but it does seem as though the particles are somehow fully intertwined, by yet another of life's seemingly magical threads.

Perhaps most bizarre, some of the top scientists in quantum physics have come to believe the *many-worlds interpretation*, as a way of making sense of the core equation in the field—known as the Schrödinger equation. The interpretation, the brainchild of Princeton grad student Hugh Everett, emerged during an evening in which "all parties agree that copious amounts of sherry were consumed." According to the many-worlds interpretation, everything that could happen does happen, so the world is constantly branching into an infinite number of universes. The theory implies infinite copies of you exist, as well as infinite universes in which you never existed. It may sound like the pipe dream of a 1960s sci fi writer who picked up his pen after taking too much LSD, but it's also one of the most straightforward mathematical interpretations of the firmly validated equations that govern quantum mechanics—and some very smart, very accomplished physicists believe the many-worlds interpretation is true. Whether an uncountably large number of alternative versions of you in other universes exist seems like a rather important unanswered question.

Nobody really understands our world. And as the evolutionary biologist Zack Blount put it to me, perhaps that's unavoidable: "I'm not sure it's even possible to fully understand the universe, at least not for humans using brains that evolved to keep bipedal social apes alive long enough to reproduce." We live in a world that will always seem uncertain to us. The question, then, is, Can we at least understand ourselves?

———

In 2016, the *Economist* analyzed fifteen years' worth of economic forecasts from the International Monetary Fund (IMF), covering 189 countries. During that period, a country entered a recession 220 separate times, a crucial economic downturn with serious consequences for millions. The IMF produces forecasts twice a year, once in April, and once in October, after they've seen half the actual data for the year. How often do these forecasts correctly predict the onset of a recession? How often do our best minds get it right?

Out of 220 cases, the answer for the April forecasts was none. Zero. These forecasts never saw it coming. The October forecasts, which already had six months of real-world data laced with warning signs to work with, only got it right about half the time. The IMF forecasts were only slightly better compared to a static model that just predicts that every country in the world, from Afghanistan to Zimbabwe, will grow at a flat rate of 4 percent every year. In physics, theories are discarded if their predictions are off by a fraction. But when we study ourselves, we're sometimes working on theories that have *never* gotten it right, even on such basic questions as "Will that economy shrink next year?"

By contrast, in 2004, humans launched a spacecraft that traveled for ten years before softly touching down on a comet two and a half miles wide that was traveling at eighty-four thousand miles per hour. Every calculation had to be perfect—and it was. Conversely, trying to figure out, with certainty, whether Thailand's economy will grow or contract in the next six months or whether inflation in Britain will be above 5 percent three years from now, well, that's just not something we can do.

That's not to pick on social science. I am, after all, a (disillusioned) social scientist. Yet all social scientists know a secret that we rarely discuss openly: even our best minds don't *really* understand how our social world works. This is particularly true for rare, nonrepeatable, and contingent events, which are often the most important events to understand. Our intertwined social world is too complex for us to master, driven by feedback loops and tipping points, forces that are constantly changing, swayed by chance and chaos, accidents and flukes.

In the early twentieth century, a renegade economist named Frank Knight challenged the conventional economic wisdom, which relied on a series of simplistic assumptions. Knight persuasively articulated the difference between, in his terminology, uncertainty versus risk. (Risk in this context relates to volatility, not the risk of something bad happening.) Knight argued that risk, the more manageable of the two, occurs when a future outcome is unknown but the precise odds of something happening are known and are stable. We don't know what will happen, but we do know how or why it's happening. For example, tossing a six-sided die is a matter of risk rather than uncertainty. We don't know which exact number it will land on, but we do know that each number has a one-in-six chance of ending up on top. Risk can be tamed.

Uncertainty, by contrast, refers to situations in which a future outcome is unknown *and* the underlying mechanism producing that outcome is also unknown—and may even be constantly changing. We don't know what will happen and we don't have any way of assessing the likelihood that it will happen. We're completely in the dark. In this formulation, the IMF constantly fails to predict the onset of recessions because it is treating uncontrollable uncertainty as though it's resolvable risk. It's not, so the forecast fails.

Knight's dichotomy between uncertainty and risk is useful. To avoid catastrophic errors of judgment, it's crucial to separate what can and can't be known, as some realms are simply unknowable. To cope, many have turned not to the old superstitions of divination, but rather to the sometimes misleading comfort of probabilities. Much of the time, probabilities are properly applied and help us navigate risk by making wiser decisions. But if you venture into an unknowable, uncertain realm armed with your trusty probability to make decisions, you might be in for a nasty—and potentially catastrophic—shock. Don't mistake untamable chaos for tamable chance.

The economist and former governor of the Bank of England Mervyn King put it well in a recent interview: "We've all grown up with the idea that if you are intelligent, you think about uncertainty in terms of probabilities, and there are many people who will try to interpret any kind of future uncertainty in terms of some probability. I think this is a serious mistake and it detracts from good decision-making." Probabilities are a wonderful tool for tackling risk and should be embraced for those kinds of problems. In cases of unresolvable uncertainty, however, admitting "I don't know" is often better than using a false probability based on flawed assumptions to navigate an unknowable landscape.

Sometimes, however, we must choose, even when we're hopelessly uncertain. The world of questions can be split into two categories: those that must be answered and those that need not be. We might call these the "take your best shot" questions versus the "don't bother trying" questions. If you have a rare disease, doctors must decide how to treat it, even if they don't know what's causing it or what's likely to work. Saying "I don't know" isn't a viable option to deal with a mysterious form of cancer. Take your best shot.

However, no law, no moral imperative, states that we must forecast that economic growth in Burundi will be exactly 3.3 percent in five years, which is impossibly precise, certain to be wrong, and may cause us to make serious mistakes as fake certainty clouds our judgment. Saying "I don't know" doesn't mean that you must throw up your hands and do nothing. It just means avoiding making silly forecasts when it's not necessary. When it is necessary, it's important to at least acknowledge the unpartable mists of uncertainty and to incorporate an acceptance of chaotic dynamics into decision-making. Unfortunately, the exact opposite viewpoint tends to dominate our societies. Rather than rewarding intellectual humility, we too often mistakenly conflate (false) certainty with confidence and power. Too many people rise to the top following the strategy of always certain, but often wrong.

But if probabilities aren't helpful in situations of genuine uncertainty, why do we misuse probabilistic reasoning so often? The problems begin because we use that single word—*probability*—to mean countless different things. That confusion is compounded because once someone provides a specific number such as a "63.8 percent chance" to describe the likelihood of a future event, it's as though the quantification has transformed the person into a modern oracle, commanding knowledge that has magically become more legitimate or true because it has been produced by math (even if that math is based on severely flawed assumptions). It's harder to argue with a stated probability than with someone who just says "I believe" something will happen. But is that the right way to look at it?

We hear probabilistic statements constantly. But what does it actually mean to say that there's an 80 percent chance of rain today? The answer seems obvious until you try to explain it to someone else. Does it mean that, given the exact same initial physical conditions in the atmosphere, rain will occur 80 percent of the time (as though weather patterns are like rolling dice with static odds)? Does it mean that out of one hundred possible imagined worlds with similar conditions to today, rain should be expected to happen in eighty of them, but not twenty others? Does it mean that the evidence is uncertain in the weather model, but that the forecasters want you to know that they have an 80 percent confidence level in the prediction that it will rain?*

---

* Notably, some weather forecasting models deliberately bias the results in a way that is likely to yield fewer complaints. People are more likely to complain if the forecast says it will be sunny but it ends up raining, and less likely to

And what does it mean for a forecast to be right? Is the forecast wrong if it doesn't rain, since the probability of rain was above 50 percent? Surely, that can't be right, because 80 percent and 100 percent aren't the same thing. Or is the forecast correct if it rains eighty times out of one hundred whenever the forecast says there's an 80 percent chance of rain? In that case, you can only verify the accurate calibration of a forecast over lots and lots of repeated predictions. But who's to say that today's physical conditions are comparable to those in the future? After all, as chaos theory has demonstrated, tiny variations in physical systems that produce the weather can produce big changes. What if we're comparing apples to oranges?

These questions become even more difficult when the probability moves from weather patterns to a unique, non-repeatable event, such as an election. What does it mean when Nate Silver forecasted that Hillary Clinton had a 71.4 (not 71.3 or 71.5) percent chance of winning the 2016 presidential election? Does it mean that if you rerun the election over and over in the computer model, Clinton comes out on top 71.4 percent of the time? Okay, but there's just one election, with one outcome, and you can't run reality over and over, no matter how much we might wish to do so in hindsight. Or, does it mean that elections are like dice rolls, but rather than having a one-in-six chance, Hillary Clinton's die was weighted to show up with a win 71.4 percent of the time? When she lost, was the 71.4 percent forecast wrong, or was it just that the less probable outcome happened?

Clearly, we've got a problem. When we say, "There's an X percent probability that Y will happen," many unwritten, unspoken assumptions are baked into that statement that could mean wildly different things. To say "there's a 60 percent chance Confucius was a real person from

---

complain if the forecast says it will rain but it ends up sunny. To avoid getting complaints, some models deliberately seek to minimize the former kind of being wrong while being less worried about the latter type.

history" is probabilistic, but so is "there's a 50 percent chance that a coin will land heads in the next toss." Those are radically different kinds of claims, but both are lumped together under the label *probability*. To confuse matters further, an endless supply of words describe probabilities: *Bayesian*, *objective*, *subjective*, *epistemic*, *aleatory*, *frequentist*, *propensity*, *logical*, *inductive*, or *predictive inference*. To make matters worse, those labels mean different things to different people.

Let's try to clear up the confusion.

There are two main camps for probability statements. As the eminent philosopher of science Ian Hacking explains, many probabilities are part of either *frequency-type probability* or *belief-type probability*.

The frequency type is mostly based on how often an outcome will occur, particularly over the long run during repeated trials. For example, if you flip a coin one hundred times, you may get heads forty-three times and tails fifty-seven times. Two explanations for that outcome are possible. Maybe it's a biased coin that lands on tails more often. Alternatively, the coin might be a fair fifty-fifty coin, and there's just been slight variation within those one hundred tosses. Once one hundred coin flips become 100 million, it would become clear whether the coin was biased. If it is a fair coin, the overall proportion of heads and tails would converge toward a fifty-fifty ratio.

Belief-type probabilities are completely different. They are expressions of a degree of confidence that you have in a specific claim or future outcome, based on the available evidence. Confucius was either a real person or he wasn't, so any probabilistic statement about his existence is a belief-type probability. It's completely unlike a dice roll. It's not as though you can just keep running a computational model of history and see how many worlds Confucius exists in and how many he doesn't. Instead, it's just a best guess based on the evidence you have, put into numerical form. But those who make probability statements rarely explain whether their claim is a belief type or a frequency type, which leaves people understandably confused. That confusion creates an intellectual sleight of hand, and it often leaves people too willing to defer to the veneer of seemingly automatic wisdom that often accompanies numbers and statistics in modern society.

Probability can only be a useful guide in certain situations. When we're confronting a problem in a simple, closed system—such as a roll of the die, with six clearly defined possible outcomes—then probabilistic reasoning works flawlessly. But when we move probability into the realm of messy reality, in the complex adaptive systems we live within, well, things can go haywire pretty quickly. As John Kay and Mervyn King put it in their excellent book, *Radical Uncertainty*, probabilities can be best applied to situations in which "the possible outcomes are well defined, the underlying processes that give rise to them change little over time, and there is a wealth of [relevant] historic information." Unfortunately, for many of the most important problems we face, those assumptions don't apply. Probability doesn't work in chaos.

To see why, let's return to a problem concerning risk rather than uncertainty: coin flips. The underlying dynamics of cause and effect are stable across time and space. They are, to use the technical term, *stationary*. It doesn't matter whether the person flipping the coin is a soldier from the Qin dynasty in ancient China or a bartender in modern West Virginia. The overall proportions of heads and tails should each end up at roughly 50 percent. Furthermore, when we talk about the probability of a coin flip, we're talking about the *average* distribution of outcomes, rather than trying to forecast whether a *specific* toss will be heads or tails. We're also able to conduct coin tosses as many times as we'd like, so the phenomenon is *repeatable*. The coins themselves are also *comparable* or *exchangeable*—it doesn't matter whether I use my coin or yours, so long as they're both quarters or are part of a category of fair coins more generally. As a result of all these factors, the coin toss probability is *convergent*. The longer you do it, the closer you'll get to 50 percent for each outcome. The combination of these factors (stationary, average, repeatable, comparable, and convergent) makes coin tosses ideal for probabilistic analysis, in which past events are a nearly perfect predictor of future outcomes.

Now, let's consider another example, in which we're trying to figure out whether ibuprofen helps alleviate headache symptoms. It's more complicated than coin tosses, but the same principles apply. Unless the headaches are being caused by a new, unknown disease, it's safe to say that the mechanism by which ibuprofen may help alleviate headache symptoms isn't changing from day to day, so this is a *stationary* problem. We are also interested in *averages* because we're seeking a treatment that tends to work across all possible patients, not one that will work in every specific case. Headaches are, unfortunately, extremely *repeatable* both within individuals and with humans more generally. They are also mostly *comparable*, as it's a reasonable assumption that the chemical process that reduces my headache will likely reduce yours, too.

However, this only makes sense if we are using the right category. It may sound pedantic, but the language we use matters enormously for probabilities. Statistics are only as good as our linguistics. What if I use the word *headache* to refer to a migraine or a feeling of head pain produced by a brain tumor? Probability-based estimates rely on accurate categories, the notion that when I refer to a *headache* in different contexts, I'm comparing apples to apples rather than apples and oranges. If it is the right category, then, as with the coin flips, the problem of headaches and ibuprofen is *convergent*: even if there are discrepancies between us in age, gender, race, height, income, and so on, ibuprofen will probably still work. The same dynamics apply to a variety of fields, such as actuarial tables that try to determine insurance premiums, or sports leagues with the same rules and teams from one season to the next. Past patterns are a reliable predictor of the future, so probabilities are a safe bet. This is the *Land of Stationary Probabilities*, where Nate Silver feels most at home.

Now, let's move to thornier problems of uncertainty that arise from our complex, dynamic, contingent, intertwined world, prone to tipping points, feedback loops, and cascades caused by the tiniest changes. The economists Kay and King point to the illuminating example of Barack Obama's decision to order the special forces raid that killed Osama bin Laden on May 2, 2011. So much was unknown: Was bin Laden in the compound in Pakistan? Would the raid succeed in killing him with minimal loss of life if he was there? Would the Pakistani government attack or denounce the United States for violating its airspace?

Obama's advisers tried to give the president probabilistic estimates so he could make the right call. "There's a seventy percent chance he's there, Mr. President." These were subjective, belief-based expressions of confidence in the available evidence, not what most people think of when they hear the world *probability*. Bin Laden was either there, or he wasn't. It wasn't a coin-flip scenario, in which he'd be there in half the worlds and wouldn't be there in the other half. Nobody knew whether bin Laden was there. Nobody knew how Pakistan would react. Nobody knew what would happen. The decision needed to be made with unavoidable uncertainty.

Let's consider how the bin Laden raid differs from a coin toss. Rather than being a case of stationary causality, in this instance, the underlying dynamics that would determine the outcome of a potential special forces raid in Pakistan were *nonstationary*. Perhaps Pakistan might have responded badly to a similar raid in 2008, but not so badly in 2011. Perhaps the response would depend on how much sleep the Pakistani intelligence chief had the night before. Perhaps it would depend on the government in power, on the prime minister, on how the facts were presented to him, or even on the mood of the generals on duty. No static cause-and-effect relationship here could reliably be teased out. The outcome of the exact same raid might unfold radically differently if it had been tried on May 1 and not on May 2. The dynamics were variable and therefore unknowable.

Moreover, while one coin toss can be compared to another, Barack Obama wasn't interested in average outcomes across all past special forces raids. He cared whether this proposed raid would succeed, making him concerned with a *specific* outcome rather than an average one. That's because the raid wasn't repeatable. It was a *one-off*, very much unlike a coin flip. It was also *unique* rather than comparable or exchangeable. You could try to compare the bin Laden raid to previous ones by putting it into the category of other special forces raids, sure, but they were too different to be usefully compared. Information about previous operations could only tell you that the SEALs had a good track record and were competent (which was already obvious without conducting any calculations of probability). The success of a Navy SEAL Team Six raid three months earlier in Somalia wouldn't tell you much about whether this exact raid against bin Laden would succeed.* Finally, the raid was *contingent*, not convergent. Small mistakes or seemingly insignificant fluctuations could radically change the outcome. Together, those factors made for irreducible, or radical, uncertainty. Nobody knew how the raid would turn out. The past offered no reliable guide to the future. There were no oracles to consult, no matter how good they were at math. Obama had to make his decision in the face of uncertainty, not risk.

This is what I call the *Land of Heraclitean Uncertainty*. You'll recall that Heraclitus is the pre-Socratic philosopher who spoke of

---

* This problem, of trying to infer a specific, individual outcome from observed patterns across a general group of reasonably similar events, is known as the *ecological fallacy*. Even if smoking tends to cause lung cancer, it doesn't guarantee that if you smoke, you will get lung cancer. The dynamics in a specific case can only loosely be inferred from a pattern across a group.

the ever-changing river and the ever-changing man. Heraclitus was clearly right that change is constant. The world—indeed the entire universe—morphs from millisecond to millisecond. But sometimes, as we saw in the previous chapter, those changes reach tipping points, producing observably different mechanisms of cause and effect. We can never fully understand or predict when those abrupt shifts will occur. When uncertainty is produced because the world itself is changing, that's Heraclitean uncertainty, and probabilities quickly become useless, as past patterns can become meaningless in an instant.

Imagine it's 1995 and you've been asked to predict how many hours per day the average British person will spend using his or her telephone by the year 2020. You could study past patterns until the cows come home and use whatever forms of Bayesian logic you wanted, but it wouldn't likely have helped. In 1995, 1 out of every 130 people used the internet. The iPhone wouldn't be invented for another twelve years. It wouldn't matter whether you used a supercomputer with the most sophisticated formulas known to humanity, and it wouldn't matter whether your statistical models generated a probability using frequency-based or belief-based logic. Any probabilistic forecast in 1995 about phone usage in 2020 would have been wildly off. Why? Because the relationship between humans and phones fundamentally changed. Plus, a once-in-a-century pandemic kept people at home and bored. The world became different. A few prescient futurists in 1995 might have anticipated the rise of smartphones, but their insights would have come from understanding emerging technology, not from probabilistic reasoning based on patterns from history. When the world changes, the past can't always guide us. We get lost when we use probabilities in the Land of Heraclitean Uncertainty.

There are other forms of uncertainty. Let's briefly return to weather forecasting. Putting climate change to the side for a moment, it has mostly been reasonable to assume that the causal dynamics driving weather patterns were largely *stationary*—that past patterns could be used to predict future events. Weather forecasts are designed to be *specific*, predicting whether it will rain on a certain day, not whether it rains on the average March 1. They are also *repeatable* rather than being one-offs. And weather patterns are also *comparable* rather than being unique. It makes sense to compare thunderstorm cells across time and space, in a way that's different from comparing the bin Laden raid to another raid in Somalia. But now for the problem: weather patterns are *contingent*. As we know from Edward Lorenz, the meteorological founding father of chaos theory, initial conditions matter enormously, so weather patterns will diverge more and more over time based on the smallest imaginable changes. The weather an hour from now is manageable risk, but because the system is sensitive to tiny, unpredictable fluctuations, it quickly becomes more uncertain the longer you gaze into the future. Because we need specific predictions for weather forecasting to be useful, and because infinitesimal shifts in initial conditions create wildly different results, all bets are off after about ten days. Chaos theory takes over. We might call this *chaotic uncertainty*. With weather, we've recognized the limits of our understanding; nobody tries to forecast whether it will rain on someone's wedding day three months into the future. But with the Land of Heraclitean Uncertainty, which we frequently encounter, many people still foolishly try to pretend the limits of our knowledge can be ignored. They use probabilities to navigate radical uncertainty, as mismatched a tool as donning flippers and a snorkel while climbing a mountain.

Layered on top of these forms of uncertainty are other kinds that catch us by surprise because of what former U.S. secretary of defense Donald Rumsfeld called the "unknown unknowns." We often don't know what we don't know. We can't search for the right information because it often doesn't even occur to us that it might exist. Imagine you travel back in time, find a caveman, and ask him, "What are the odds that books will exist by the year 874?" It's a nonsensical question. Writing didn't yet exist, let alone books. There was no such thing as a modern calendar. The number 874 would be meaningless to the caveman.

It's impossible to calculate what you can't anticipate.

We are, too often, asked to make calculations where we are like the caveman in that situation, but just pretend we aren't. We imagine that we *can* calculate what we can't anticipate. This is a serious problem for modern data analysis because most research efforts only collect data for variables that are already considered important. But in a complex system, as we've seen, seemingly insignificant details matter. Those aren't included in the data, which is one reason why we keep getting it wrong as we search for big, clear-cut causes to predict big, clear-cut effects.

Probabilities can't solve that problem because if you're calculating the risk of something, you're already aware of it. Who would think to check the past vacation history of American officials if the question you wanted to answer was "Where will the United States drop an atomic bomb on Japan?" Calculate all the probabilities you like, but to know that Kyoto would be spared, you would need just one crucial piece of information—whether the secretary of war had a soft spot for Kyoto and would intervene to protect it. It's a piece of information you'd never consider tracking down until *after* its importance became clear. Unknown unknowns are therefore directly related to what Nassim Nicholas Taleb calls Black Swans, in which we are surprised by rare, unexpected, and consequential events that can be neither anticipated nor quantified by equations. Black Swans are the inevitable outcome of complex adaptive systems, the by-product of a world too often in criticality. If you understand that seemingly insignificant flukes constantly sway an intertwined world, you'll recognize these limits of human understanding. By contrast, with the mindset that everything is controllable risk, you'll simply ignore these problems and rush headlong into catastrophe.

Hubris is particularly dangerous today because our world *is* changing, and it's changing in ways that would be alien to our animal ancestors, to early hominins, and to the ways of life that defined most of human history. Worse, the world is now changing so quickly that past regularities are becoming less predictive of the future than ever before. The shelf life of probability is getting shorter. This has created a strange paradox. The future is becoming more uncertain and often impossible to predict. At the same time, we are making increasingly precise predictions that often turn out to be wildly wrong. We put blind faith in probability at our peril.

If we take a step back, perhaps we don't always need to worry so much about some forms of uncertainty. Managed properly, a bit of uncertainty can sometimes be wonderful. Uncertainty is too often treated as a dragon to be slayed. Sometimes, that's quite reasonable, as being in the dark about the future can create crushing anxiety and agony when attached to, say, a cancer diagnosis with an unclear prognosis.

But contemplate a world that is fully certain. Imagine you're born knowing everything that will happen to you. Or, alternatively, you don't know with certainty, but you are given clear, stationary probabilities of key events. As a teenager, you're shown three potential life partners and told that there's a 64 percent chance you'll end up with partner A, a 22 percent chance of Partner B, and a 14 percent chance of Partner C. Few would choose that world, with the unexpected joys and disappointments of life becoming expected, etched into cold, fixed equations. If uncertainty is slain, so are surprises, serendipity, and flukes. The unanswerable mysteries of our lives, of our world, and of our universe spark curiosity, wonder, awe, and, yes, frustration and despair. But without them, we would not be ourselves. There can be upside to uncertainty.

Rather than embrace a healthy dose of uncertainty, we cling to false certainty. Much of our world now runs on complex models that few of us understand. The problem, however, is that the models have become so influential that we can forget that they are models—deliberate simplifications that are, by design, inaccurate representations of the thing itself, just as a map helps us navigate a territory. But the map is not the territory. There are trade-offs to using models. As the French poet Paul Valéry put it rather succinctly, "Everything simple is false. Everything which is complex is unusable." Nobody wants a map with a 1:1 scale.

We run into trouble when we conflate map and territory, mistaking representation for reality. It's obvious that Google Maps isn't the same as the complex beauty of the expansive natural world that it represents. But it's perhaps not so obvious to everyone that economic models that purport to explain human behavior are just like Google Maps, sometimes useful, but vastly different from the economy itself. When we begin to see the world through the prism of simplified models, we make mistakes from looking into our fun-house-mirror view of the world. We lose our way. The key is to remind ourselves that our methods of making sense of everything around us don't change, that beneath it all lies a far more chaotic, contingent world.

But we must still make choices. So, how *should* we decide?

The most common answer to that question lies with *decision theory*. The gist is, when facing a choice with uncertain outcomes, you should weigh up the various options, consider the payoffs of each outcome, and adjust according to your best guess as to the probability of each outcome. This allows you to factor in such things as catastrophic risk alongside marginal benefits. You'd probably not undertake a medical procedure if there was a 95 percent chance of getting marginally whiter teeth, but with a 5 percent risk of death.

Decision theory is used, often to great effect, to impose rigorous thinking on difficult problems. But there's a hitch. The assumptions for decision theory apply best to a simple social world that doesn't exist. What about how other people will respond to your decision? Crucially, the standard decision-making model assumes that you can make a decision in isolation *without affecting the system you live within*. That's a disastrously flawed assumption because, in an intertwined world, some of your decisions might inadvertently cause an outcome you're hoping to avoid. A bank run is a great example of this dynamic, in which it seems individually rational for you to withdraw your money from a risky financial institution. But in doing so, you make it more likely that the whole system will collapse, which is even worse for you. Decision theory often pretends, too, that your actions are isolated, not intertwined with everything else, and that just isn't true.

Decision theory also operates on short time scales, in which un-anticipated long-term effects aren't part of the probability calculations used to make a cost-benefit analysis. Henry Stimson didn't know that his vacation to Kyoto would matter in a future global war, nineteen years later. Similarly, we can't know which areas of our life that we discount in short-term cost/benefit analyses will turn out to be hugely consequential for us down the road, often in unexpected ways. Decision theory is therefore a flawed, sometimes useful, way of navigating the garden of forking paths before us. But everything goes disastrously wrong when we forget its serious limitations within our complex, chaotic world. When hubris combines with an overly neat map to navigate a messy world, we get into trouble. It's best to constantly remind ourselves that there will always be some uncertainty that can never be conquered.

The world works differently from how we imagine it. But so far, we've ignored a key question: Where do the flukes of life come from? In the next several chapters, we'll explore those dynamics in more detail, to examine four areas of human behavior that produce consequential shifts in our lives and our societies: *why* we act as we do; *where* we act; *who* acts; and *when* we act.

We start in Israel, where we will now meet a (mostly) red cow that could usher in the end of the world.

CHAPTER 7

THE STORYTELLING ANIMAL

*Narrative bias, belief, and the limits of rational
decision theory in a chaotic world*

Melody was born in August 1996, almost exactly three years before
the end of the millennium, in the Israeli village of Kfar Hasidim. She
was bright red from snout to tail, a moving canvas of vibrant color in a
paddock of black-and-white Holsteins. Melody was, by all accounts, a
normal, healthy cow. But that's not all she was. She was a ticking bovine
bomb. As the journalist Gershom Gorenberg put it in *The End of Days*,
she could have "set the entire Middle East ablaze." Melody was the most
dangerous cow on the planet.

For nearly two thousand years, Orthodox Jews have yearned for
the moment when they can rebuild the holy Temple upon its former
foundation, a site in Jerusalem known as Temple Mount. That rebuilding
will, depending on one's religious beliefs, either coincide with, or usher
in, the end of days and the coming of the Messiah.

But the Temple Mount isn't empty. It's also home to the Dome of
the Rock and the Al-Aqsa Mosque, the third holiest site in Islam. Some
interpretations of Orthodox Judaism have concluded that a Third Temple
can't be built—and the Messiah can't return—until these Muslim sites

are destroyed.* If that ever happened, it would almost certainly spark a global religious war.

There's another problem: before construction, anyone entering the Temple Mount must be purified. The Hebrew Bible, in the book of Numbers 19, provides peculiar instructions for purification. The Israelites were told to find a "red heifer without defect or blemish that has never been under a yoke." When that perfectly formed red heifer attains the age of three, the cow is to be slaughtered and burned, its remains used to create a mixture of ash and water, which can be used to purify the builders.

In the spring of 1997, excited whispers of a newborn fully red heifer began to spread. In the history of Judaism, only nine cows had ever been certified as bona fide red heifers. A suitable contender hadn't been identified for nearly two thousand years. Could Melody be the tenth? Rabbis descended on Melody's village armed with magnifying glasses. Was she properly red, or an unsuitable ocher hue? If more than one black or white hair could be found sprouting from even one follicle, Melody would be disqualified. Close, but no cigar.

After the inspection, a joyous verdict was pronounced: Melody was a fully red heifer. If she stayed red until she was three years old, it'd be time to lather construction workers with Melody's holy ash—and set the explosives. And when was her third birthday? It was a divine sign: it would happen just before the dawn of a new millennium.

A year and a half into Melody's life, a little splotch of white appeared on the tip of her tail. The book of Numbers didn't call for a *mostly* red cow. Melody's horns were removed. The dream was over. But what if Melody's tail had remained fully crimson instead of 99.8 percent red?

---

* Lest you think this is a far-fetched scenario: a sophisticated attempt to blow up the Dome of the Rock to build the Third Temple was foiled in the 1980s. One member of the extremist group had access to sufficient explosives before being arrested.

Someone would likely have tried to blow up the Islamic holy sites in preparation for building the Third Temple. It could have triggered a holy war. We may have avoided that tragic fate, quite literally, by a hair.

The saga isn't over. Melody's near miss galvanized a global effort of messianic Jews and millennialist Christians to start breeding red cows. In September 2022, the Temple Institute, an organization devoted to rebuilding the Third Temple, announced the arrival of five red heifers bred in Texas, "each one perfectly red, each one unblemished, each one just under a year old." A 2022 broadcast of Temple Talk Radio assured listeners that, while they wouldn't divulge details, preparations had been made for when the true red heifer was identified. Eventually, they will surely breed "the one." And when that happens, it's plausible that a holy war could be sparked by one cow.

To make matters even more contingent and arbitrary, the entire saga of the red heifer could possibly be chalked up to a mistranslation. Some religious scholars have suggested that an early interpretation of an ancient word got it wrong, and the zealots should be looking for either a yellow one, or a far more common brown heifer, instead.

—

In the storybook version of life, humans are rational utility maximizers who make choices according to a structured internal flowchart of risks and rewards, penalties and payoffs. In truth, humans act according to our beliefs—the "why" that drives us. Those beliefs are constantly swayed by the arbitrary, the accidental, and the seemingly random. But when we study ourselves—when we try to understand what makes society tick—we systematically ignore this obvious fact.

Rational choice theory and its intellectual offshoots have dominated social scientific thinking about human decision-making ever since Adam Smith advanced its core assumptions in the nineteenth century. It's a deeply flawed way of imagining the world, a map that is certainly not anything close to the territory. It suggests that we do everything with a clear purpose, based on rational assessments of objective data. We have a coherent strategy to achieve every aim. We make decisions with perfect information, always certain about the costs and benefits of each path, but also knowing precisely how many paths there are to choose from. The most dogmatic forms of rational choice theory present humans as bipedal calculators, evaluating comparative probability distributions among fixed preferences, progressing through life as optimizing agents, eager to squeeze the last ounce of efficiency out of every moment.

Even rational choice theorists don't behave as their purest models suggest. Gerd Gigerenzer, a German psychologist who studies decision-making, often tells the story of an (allegedly real) conversation between two decision theorists. One of them was considering whether to accept an offer for a job at Harvard, leaving behind his post at Columbia. "Why don't you write down the utilities of staying where you are versus taking the job, multiply them by their probabilities, and choose the higher of the two? After all, that's what you advise!" In reply, the other theorist snapped, "Come on, this is serious!"

In the past, rational choice theory was routinely used to suggest that humans try to maximize in financial terms. It sometimes works as a shorthand in crude economic modeling, but quickly falls apart upon even the lightest scrutiny in the real world. We're impulsive. We're emotional. We're swayed by irrationality, faith, and belief. We regularly act against our own rational self-interest.* In traveling through Madagascar, I've seen ornate marble tombs, the familial final resting places for the

---

* One of my favorite examples comes from the mid-fourth century, when a group of North African Christians, called the Circumcellions, actively tried to get killed so they could become martyrs. They would leap out and surprise well-armed travelers or feebly attack Roman soldiers with wooden clubs. They often succeeded—by getting killed.

Merina people of the island's highlands. In a country where the average person earns about $500 per year, each tomb costs about $7,000, the equivalent to fourteen *years* of individual earnings. For an American income, that would be the equivalent of spending $889,000 on a family gravesite. But within the logic of Madagascar's ritual belief system, in which they believe in a fleeting life on earth, but an eternal one in the marble tomb, their budgeting makes perfect sense.

Humans are many wonderful things, but objective, rational optimizers we are not. It's a good thing, too, as it would suck the richness and vibrancy out of life if every moment of our existence could be boiled down to a hard-nosed calculation of probability distributions and expected utility. What a bleak world that would be. If such people do exist, I wouldn't want to run into one of them at a party.

That's why, over time, a softer version of rational choice theory that doesn't assume such perfect information has become more prominent, called *bounded rational choice theory*. The *bounded* part refers to humans not being perfect in our decision-making. We make cognitive mistakes and lack crucial information. Rather than being optimizers, we're often guided by *satisfice*, a portmanteau of *satisfy* and *suffice*, in which we choose not what is optimal, but what is good enough. What's more, modern neuroscience research also makes clear that only a small sliver of our decisions are the product of conscious self-reflection. Much of our decision-making happens on autopilot. Some is even affected not just by the chemicals in our brains, but by the microbes that live within us, which have the power to alter our thinking.

Social scientists who used to be naive and apply rational choice or bounded rational choice theory uncritically are now more open about its limitations. Yet, its assumptions still form much of the core of the modeling we produce to understand and navigate the social world.

As a result, we have a serious blind spot. Many intellectuals systematically ignore thought that goes beyond empirical rationality and enters the realm of mysticism, even though mystical belief drives a significant amount of human behavior. In one analysis of the top journal in political science, for example, researchers counted how often a substantive article about religion is published. The answer? Once every four years. (The review took place a few years after September 11, when the discipline sheepishly began to acknowledge that, yes, perhaps religion *was* an important element of politics and international relations.) But things didn't get much better even after that wake-up call. Another review a decade after 9/11 found that just 97 publications out of 7,245 were primarily concerned with religion, a rate of about 1.3 percent.

The professional study of humanity is detached from how most people experience the world. Eighty-four percent of the world's population identifies with a religious group. In a survey conducted by Pew Research that spanned thirty-four countries, roughly two in three people agreed that "God plays an important role in my life." One 2022 study of ninety-five countries found that roughly 40 percent of the global population believes in witchcraft, defined as the "ability of certain people to intentionally cause harm via supernatural means." Trying to understand politics without a clear grasp of how such beliefs shape human action is like trying to drive a car without a steering wheel. It's a crucial component of humanity to ignore. But many rational choice models—and some of its offshoots, such as game theory—still mostly ignore it. In the real world, emotion, hunches, impulse, faith, and belief in the divine have profound effects on consequential decision-making, yet we pretend that the world is peopled with implicit probability calculators.

Even if decision-making models did a better job of capturing the messy and varied motivations within our heads, an insurmountable problem can still *never* be overcome. How can we ever truly understand why things happen in a world in which a single red cow could theoretically spark a world war? To maintain order in a system, rules need to be universally followed. If just 99 percent of planets followed the laws of physics, our cosmic calculations would quickly become meaningless. Our astronomical charts would become worthless. Theories of rational decision-making are perhaps the closest we've come to pretending natural laws apply to humans, too. But once you accept that those rules are not just occasionally bent but are instead routinely broken—daily by billions of us—then the entire pretense of an ordered, predictable society breaks down. Beliefs create unshakable, unfathomable contingency.

That's because humans, unlike molecules in a gas or comets in an orbit, are self-aware and self-reflective. Our thoughts are also influenced by sensory perceptions, experiences, and the thoughts of other thinking, self-reflective beings, all moderated by culture, norms, institutions, and religions. That level of complexity simply doesn't exist in a liter of gas. We can do our best to model religious groups and understand trends across time. We can use the most sophisticated algorithms and analyze billions of social media posts to determine whether new ideologies are taking root. But Melody the cow shows that even those attempts will always face limits because a small group of unusual believers can plausibly change the world for everyone else. And it's not just red cows. September 11 invalidated *every* geopolitical forecast for the next decade in minutes. Our beliefs aren't a sideshow. When it comes to understanding why things happen, they're often the main event. Yet, they're studied the least because we want to imagine the storybook reality exists, with our actions dictated by rationality, not narratives or beliefs.

—

Our beliefs are most easily swayed when ideas are put into a story. Generation after generation, from our earliest days, humans accumulated wisdom to make sense of the world. But how could that wisdom reverberate between generations? The neuroscientist Antonio Damasio provides the answer: "The problem of how to make all this wisdom understandable, transmittable, persuasive, enforceable—of how to make it stick—was faced and a solution found. Storytelling was the solution."

Our brains are so attuned to narrative that we will connect the dots into a story even when the dots aren't connected, which is called *narrative bias*. When we are given a snippet of incomplete information, the pattern-processing networks within our skulls fill in the gaps. Rukmini Bhaya Nair demonstrates this effect with a traditional Bengali story, told in six words.

A tiger.
A hunter.
A tiger.

Our minds turn six words into a plot. We can picture the scene, the narrative arc, the dramatic tension. The exact images we conjure up from those six words will differ from person to person, but the basic plot will be remarkably similar. Few assume the hunter ran away, or that a second tiger arrived on scene, but each is an equally plausible interpretation. Who's to say the six words are even related? They might be untethered from any narrative. We stitch them together instinctively. We can't help it. Our brains imbue clear-cut meaning into limited information. It's so automatic that writers can exploit it. In an (apocryphal) story Ernest Hemingway was said to have bet some doubters that he could cram a tale worthy of a novel into just six words. The onlookers took the bet, calling his bluff. He scribbled. They looked, then paid up.

For sale: baby shoes, never worn.

As the literary scholar Barbara Hardy argued, we "dream in narrative, daydream in narrative, remember, anticipate, hope, despair, believe, doubt, plan, revise, criticize, construct, gossip, learn, hate and live by narrative." In the last several decades, our innate desire to turn everything into stories has spawned a vast scientific literature, from literary studies to evolutionary biology and neuroscience. These studies have shown that information is retained much more easily when it's presented to us as a narrative. We are, to again borrow from Jonathan Gottschall, a storytelling animal. "The storytelling mind is allergic to uncertainty, randomness, and coincidence," he writes. "It is addicted to meaning."[*]

But here's the astonishing bit: narrative bias is causal. Stories drive us to act. And sometimes stories can be the difference between life and death.

On December 26, 2004, the earth beneath the sea shook, just off the west coast of Sumatra. Mammoth waves emanated from the underwater epicenter at five hundred miles per hour. There was no early-warning system, no blaring sirens. Even though the tsunami took hours to travel across the open ocean, hundreds of thousands only realized their fate when it was too late. An estimated 228,000 people died.

One group of people didn't die: the Moken. The Moken learn to swim before they walk. As ocean nomads, they spend much of their lives in wooden boats, deeply attuned to nature. That December morning, on the Andaman Islands off the coast of Thailand, the Moken heard an alarm that was only audible to those who were listening closely: silence. The clicking and buzzing of cicadas that normally filled the air abruptly stopped. Then, the sea began to recede. The Moken knew what to do.

For countless generations, the Moken have passed down a story that warns them of *laboon*, or the "wave that eats people." It's said to arise from the spirits within the ocean, and the story warns that the cicadas fall silent when the tsunami is unleashed. The Moken clambered to higher

---

[*] The discerning reader might object, "Wait a minute! You're telling us stories, too. *Fluke* has narrative! You're using our brains against us." To these charges, I plead guilty. I have a human brain and so do you, so it's the only way I know how to effectively convey meaning.

ground before the *laboon* arrived. Their settlements were battered into tiny pieces. But none of the Moken died.

This tale of survival illustrates the power of stories to shape events. Too often, we pretend that stories can be separated from the hard-nosed reality of causality and why things happen. It's remarkable how much we relegate narrative to the "unscientific" side of the ledger and mostly pretend it isn't a force for driving change. We pretend there is some objective reality, data driven and sterile, which determines how the world operates. The economy runs on numbers, not stories, we're told in school. But that just isn't true. Humans make up the economy—and humans navigate the world through narratives. Yet, from game theory to decision theory, the storytelling animal is transformed, in a modeling trick, into the rational animal. This compounds the problem because we automatically filter reality through our narrative-obsessed minds, and then the models we use to imagine ourselves are further distilled into a cookie-cutter version of rationality that doesn't exist. Nowhere in either process is there room for the accidental, the random, the contingent, or the chaotic.

Until recently, the notion that one could study, say, the boom-and-bust cycles of the economy by analyzing narratives and viral stories would've gotten you laughed out of an economist's office. Few are laughing now because the idea has been mainstreamed by several renowned experts, including one who previously won a Nobel Prize in Economics: Robert Shiller.

"If we do not understand the epidemics of popular narratives," Shiller wrote, "we do not fully understand changes in the economy and in economic behavior." This may seem so obvious as to be commonplace, but narrative economics was, until recently, a fringe niche within the field. Try going on CNBC or Bloomberg and talking not about falling price-earnings ratios, but about how viral narratives foreshadow a recession. Yet, they often do because they can act as self-fulfilling prophecies.

When ordinary people start hearing talk of a recession, they may curtail their spending, like squirrels preparing for winter. Businesses that were on the brink of investing might pull back, saving their capital to weather the economic cold, not because they already feel the chill, but because they hear winter is coming. The story of a possible future event can *cause* that event to take place. There's not a separate, objective, rational market economy that's detached from the storytelling animal because the market *is* the aggregation of billions of storytelling animals. If narratives drive us, then narratives drive everything we touch, and that includes politics, economics, our daily lives, you name it.

The problem is that measuring narratives creates them. When you stick a thermometer outside, the thermometer doesn't make the weather hotter or colder. But surveying consumers on their confidence in the economy and then reporting that number does affect consumer confidence. With humans, measuring and reporting changes what you are measuring and reporting.

It's not just economics that is swayed by stories, either. Shiller points to the 1852 publication of *Uncle Tom's Cabin*, depicting the barbarity of slavery through the embodiment of the vile Simon Legree. It played a role in the rise of Lincoln's antislavery Republican Party and certainly influenced events as the country lurched toward civil war less than a decade later. Our subjective beliefs drive change, which makes the world even more contingent.

What's perhaps most surprising, however, is that a science of storytelling is possible. Our narratives almost always conform to certain patterns, which raises the strange possibility that our mental processes have evolved for specific templates best suited to understanding change—a literal physical embodiment of storybook reality, encoded into our minds. Kurt Vonnegut, one of the greatest authors of all time, demonstrated that most human stories could be graphed, with the vertical axis related to whether good or bad things happen to the main character, and the horizontal axis representing time as the story unfolds. The idea came to him when he noticed significant similarities between the "shape" of the story of Cinderella and the New Testament of the Bible. In another story shape, what he called the "Man in the Hole," a person gets into trouble, then gets out of it to end the story on a happy note. *The Wizard of Oz* is this kind of story, as is virtually every sitcom episode ever written. If you're unlucky, you'll find yourself in a story arc that Vonnegut calls "From Bad to Worse," in which the character experiences one misfortune after another. (May you never find yourself in this kind of story, as in Kafka's *Metamorphosis*.)

Reality doesn't have a narrative arc. We cram it into that form nonetheless, as our storytelling minds distort our view of the world. Jonathan Gottschall, writing in *The Story Paradox*, notes that these conventions of narrative give us the false impression of a world never driven by accidents or chance. We have expectations of how stories end, and when stories violate those expectations, they flop. One study even found that higher Nielsen TV ratings are correlated with shows that produce narrative moral justice—in which the fictional universe is ordered such that the good characters triumph in the end, as the world should be rather than how it is. Every so often, we latch on to stories in which evil triumphs (*Game of Thrones* and *Breaking Bad* are notable exceptions). But what we almost never do is celebrate story endings that are brought about by randomness or chance. As Gottschall puts it, we know that "Harry Potter isn't going to defeat Voldemort . . . because the latter slips on a banana peel and breaks his head."

Conspiracy theories are driven by narrative bias on steroids. As Gottschall explains, conspiracy theories take a bewildering series of seemingly unconnected data points and put them into a coherent story. It's usually one hell of a good story, too—complete with cover-ups and shadowy cabals, orchestrated by cartoon villains who are hoping that you—the blindfolded chump—won't discover *the Truth*. Fact-checkers and debunkers have an impossible task. Their job is to tell you—the storytelling animal—that *there is no story*. It's a battle that's already lost. Evolution determined the winner. When forced to choose between a good story or none at all, we grab the popcorn, mesmerized by a hidden plot.

Each of us follows different narratives and incorporates new information into them moment by moment. That means 8 billion humans are making decisions based on 8 billion different sets of ideas. When we all interact, many strange, unpredictable effects are inevitable.

You have surely personally encountered the power of irrational belief, whether it's by trying to get through a holiday conversation with your crazy uncle, or dealing with someone who consistently behaves in ways that you consider self-destructive. You, too, are irrational. You're susceptible to the seduction of narratives. So am I. It's just the way we are.

That's a wonderful truth. We could live in a dystopian world in which uniform beliefs created regularity and patterns that some economists would no doubt enthusiastically fetishize for their mathematical beauty. Thankfully, we don't have to suffer that hellscape. While I seriously hope that the ashes of a successor to Melody—the (almost) red heifer—are never used to spark a major religious conflict, I'm glad to live in a wondrous, maddening universe where societies can shift and history can be reshaped by the stories our ancestors tell us, by our being storytelling animals, and even, God forbid, by one crimson cow.

CHAPTER 8

THE LOTTERY OF EARTH

How geology shapes our destinies and
geography diverts our trajectories

Now, we move from *why* to *where*.

When we hear the phrase *space-time*, many of us have a vague association with Einstein and the impenetrable mysteries of physics. But it's a more useful word than it first appears for thinking about our daily existence and social change. It is, just as it seems, a smooshing together of the three dimensions of space with the fourth dimension of time, to describe a profound idea: that where and when something happens matters as much as what is happening. Unlike coin flips, which behave the same way across time and space, many aspects of our social world can shift based on location and timing. Before we move to timing, though, we need to grapple with a dumbfounding truth: the trajectories of our lives and our societies are often shaken by the hidden movements of the earth's tectonic plates.

Consider the intertwined histories of Britain and its former colony the United States. Britain was cut off from the European mainland eight thousand years ago, when an enormous landslide in Norway triggered a world-changing tsunami, creating an island from seas that had been steadily rising since the end of the last great ice age. Becoming an island was arguably the most consequential event in the history of Britain, but you won't find it in most British history books. Nonetheless, every subsequent event was determined, at least in part, by the absence of a land bridge between Britain and Europe. Perhaps nowhere was that effect more obvious than with the development of an empire built with its fearsome navy.

Navies require ships, and ships require timber. By the end of the eighteenth century, the Royal Navy had three hundred ships in active service, built with wood from 1.2 million trees. The Royal Navy's voracious appetite for wood, which thinned forests and felled soaring trees, forever altered Britain's landscape. As demand for solid, soaring timbers grew, supply dwindled. Good trees became precious. "Statesmen plotted to obtain them, ships of the line fought to procure them."

America was to be the saving grace of the Royal Navy, a vast conti-nent of untouched forests. In Connecticut, the governor boasted of the "cloud-kissing" pines. Early American settlers harvested that pine, turning trees into houses.* But across the Atlantic, the king wanted the trees for the Royal Navy. To ensure that none of the finest specimens of pine were harvested, government officials went around forests and farms marking tall trees with the King's mark, a "broad arrow" shape imprinted into the bark with three blows from a hatchet. Soon, an illicit trade emerged, violating the king's laws.

In the winter of 1772, a royal surveyor discovered six sawmills near Weare, New Hampshire, that were processing wood with the telltale broad-arrow mark upon the bark. The owners were arrested, which the townspeople saw as an egregious injustice. In the early hours of April 14, 1772, a mob descended on the Pine Tree Tavern, where the king's

---

* Trees that were more than twenty-four inches in diameter typically belonged to the Crown. In truly old New England houses, a suspiciously large number of floorboards are just below that threshold, suggesting that the king's trees were cut to appear below the legal limit.

enforcer lay asleep. The mob whipped him with switches made from the branches of nearby trees, one lash for every tree he had reclaimed for the Crown.

The Pine Tree Riot, as it came to be known, was an indirect trigger for revolution. The king feared that harsh punishments would spark an uprising, so the mob got off lightly. That slap on the wrist emboldened America's colonial subjects, who were growing increasingly frustrated with royal rule. Historians view the Pine Tree Riot as a major catalyst for the Boston Tea Party, and by extension, the Revolutionary War and American independence. Tall trees were a key, but often forgotten, factor in America's founding. In the war that soon followed, the new American navy sailed under a flag of arboreal resistance: a single tall pine tree set against a white background.

Geography, it is sometimes said, is destiny. That's hyperbole, a statement that erases humans as authors of their own histories. But geography does provide the folio within which we write, as our lives are shaped and diverted by the physical environment. We mostly focus on the human characters, fixating our attention only on the ink we spill. The leaves of the pages—the natural world that history happens within—seems like a mere backdrop. But the natural world drives enormous change. We too often imagine ourselves as aloof and separate from the forces of geography and the endless expanse of geology. We construct houses that try to keep "the elements" out, giving us comfort that we can separate ourselves from disease, animals, and dirt. We speak of going *into* nature, as on a hike or a camping trip. But we are part of the earth, it is a part of us, and we are often the beneficiaries or the victims of our contingent landscape.

From the beginning, our bodies were shaped, quite literally, by our physical environment. Until about 2 million years ago, our primate ancestors slept in trees, curled up in nests they crafted for comfort. Our fingerprints may be leftover relics from this period in our history.

Fingerprints worsen grip on smooth objects, as the ridges reduce the amount of surface contact, but they improve our grip in wet conditions, particularly against rough surfaces "such as branches, since the ridges interlock with ones in the bark." It provides one possible explanation for those unique whorls on our fingertips—a lingering reminder of our time in the trees. Roland Ennos, author of *The Wood Age*, also argues that our earlier arboreal existence provides a possible origin story for our fingernails. With soft finger pads that gave prehuman primates the ability to navigate branches and twigs with ease, "they no longer had any need for claws; instead these were flattened into self-trimming nails, which act as a hard backing to the pads, just as the rims of wheels act as a backing to car tires."

We descended from apes, but which kind of ape was determined by plate tectonics. Twenty million years ago, two enormous plates crashed together, creating the Tibetan Plateau. This siphoned moisture away from East Africa, drying the region out, shifting the environment "from the set of *Tarzan* to that of *The Lion King*," in the words of the scientist Lewis Dartnell. Ape populations were separated by climate and divided into two branches: the African apes and the Asian ones. The African apes eventually became us.

The earth also likely shaped the development of our advanced intellects. Our ape ancestors lived in the Rift Valley in East Africa, where the climate was volatile, the landscape varied. Because of tectonic forces, the Rift Valley had rugged terrain. To survive, our ancestors needed to adapt to and conquer multiple environments. The time had come for a generalist with a nimble intellect. This evolutionary pressure to get smarter also likely became more intense due to drastic, unexpected shifts in the climate. Basins in the Rift Valley would sometimes fill with water, creating "amplifier lakes," which were sensitive to even tiny changes in climate patterns. The lakes could be filled to the brim only to become bone-dry in a comparative blink. Such wild swings created intense pressure on life in the region. Astonishingly, recent research on the fossilized remains of hominins living in the Rift Valley shows that periods of abrupt climate changes overlap with the expansions of brain size observed in the fossil record. Studies also suggest that humans invented more advanced kinds of tools during three different periods of extreme climate volatility. These correlations have led some scientists to conclude that our intelligence evolved to cope with these sudden, sharp environmental shifts, as intelligence and the social cooperation it made possible were useful for survival. A chaotic climate in a geological hot spot may be the reason why we're smart.

Later, when *Homo sapiens* emerged from Africa—likely triggered by another climate shift—early humans fanned out across Eurasia and found new places to call home. But, as Dartnell points out, if you look at a map of the major ancient civilizations and superimpose it on top of the earth's tectonic plates, there's a striking relationship. Persia and Assyria hug the dividing line between the Arabian and Eurasian plate. The ancient Greeks built their city-states near tectonic boundaries. Ancient empires, it seems, did not sprout randomly, but were instead guided by hidden fault lines below the surface of the earth.

Once settled, our environments shaped early cultures. Why did the Greeks develop their famously diverse city-states rather than a unified empire? Again, the answer may lie partly with geography. Around one thousand early Greek city-states emerged, mostly on distinct islands separated by stretches of the Aegean, Ionian, and Mediterranean Seas. With rugged, mountainous terrain and stretches of the wine-dark sea between them, the landscape was difficult to unify by conquest. Instead, countless independent city-states developed. Each experimented, testing out new ways to organize society. Political diversity triggered intense philosophical disagreement, which is so often the catalyst for innovation in human thought. This leads to a tantalizing question: Would the modern West have been so influenced by ancient Greece if Athens had existed on an easily conquered steppe instead?

—

Modern explanations of social change rarely include geographical or geological factors. The fields of economics and political science, for example, routinely produce models that ignore geography completely. In those equations, it is as though we live in a uniform world, flat and featureless. We think so much about how we shape history that we rarely stop and think how the earth shapes us.

To more precisely understand the role of geology and geography, we need a few concepts. The first can be thought of as *the lottery of earth*. This refers to the arbitrary characteristics of the physical environment we inhabit, which are mostly unchanging (at least on the time scales we use to measure history). For example, it's crucial that Britain is an island, or that the United States has no inland sea, but those are static facts on the time scales that matter to us. Nonetheless, arbitrary landscapes shape human choices.

When humans make decisions, however, one crucial choice can create a fixed trajectory for quite a long time. This is the concept of *path dependency*. Past decisions constrain future ones. To use the Borges analogy of the Garden of Forking Paths, walking down one path may close off the possibility of going down another in the future, while opening fresh pathways to explore. But some of those paths are not easily reversible—you can get stuck on a given trajectory. How past humans interacted with their environment can alter our present societies—and even dictate how we live our individual lives.

That becomes clearer when you live somewhere that's been populated by human civilizations for millennia. I now live in Winchester, England, where it's impossible to ignore how the natural landscape diverts human trajectories past and present. I sometimes walk my dog up a hill near the city. Thousands of years ago, a small group of Iron Age settlers saw that hill as a useful natural defense. They established a fort on its summit, anchoring what we now call Winchester to the spot. The Romans decided to set up shop in the ruins, then the Anglo-Saxons followed, then the Normans, on and on to the present. It's a charming thought—and an accurate one—that where I live, my social life, even my dog walks, were partly determined thousands of years ago by an Iron Age settler scouting out defensible hills. That's geographical path dependency.

Path dependency can make it harder to change course. For example, most railways use a standard gauge width. Once you start building a rail network and have trains that fit on it, any changes to the track would be exorbitantly expensive because you'd have to replace the entire network and change the trains. With that example, it's also clear that path dependency can come from outside a system, as some countries have rail gauges dictated by historical decisions made in other countries, to ensure that their trains can keep running even across borders. A single human choice, or a small set of human choices, about how to interact with the physical environment in a specific historical moment can create a trajectory that is then followed by future generations. But here's the maddening bit: it's often impossible to tell when a decision will create path dependency. Most Iron Age settlers had no obvious, discernible impact on modernity. Every so often, in hindsight we can tell that a long-dead human diverted historical trajectories in ways that still affect us.

Finally, there's the most interesting type of geography and geology rerouting history. I call this *human space-time contingency*. Geographical or geological facts matter to us more, or less, over time, only becoming drivers of change when they interact, in contingent ways, with human civilization. For example, oil has been lying beneath what's now Saudi Arabia for roughly 160 million years, but that only mattered to human society after the invention of the internal combustion engine in the nineteenth century. Saudi oil was discovered in 1938. That year, the wheel was little used in the Arabian Peninsula, as most transport was still done by camel. Saudi Arabia was one of the poorest countries on the planet. Today, it's one of the richest. That abrupt change can be explained neither by geological nor human factors alone; the interaction between them in a specific space and time allowed the Kingdom of Saud to cash in on its black gold.

Once you start thinking this way, it becomes obvious that our interactions with our physical environment are a major catalyst for flukes, upending the neater reality we pretend exists. The idea that geography shapes human history—and our individual lives—isn't new. Yet, it has fallen out of favor as an explanation of change. This poses a puzzle: If it's so obvious that we're shaped by our environment, then why is it so controversial to say so? Why has the physical world largely been deleted from social explanations for change? The answer, like so many, comes from an unfortunate contingent moment of history. In the past, influential thinkers misused geographical explanations for insidious purposes, rendering even somewhat adjacent ideas toxic, which persists to the present day.

These days, saying that an argument relies on "geographic determinism" or "environmental determinism" is a grave insult in history and social science, a way to instantly dismiss a scholarly claim. That's understandable because the idea that geography shapes outcomes has been used to justify racism for thousands of years. In ancient China, a chancellor named Guan Zhong argued that those who lived near fast-flowing, meandering rivers were inevitably "greedy, uncouth, and warlike." In ancient Greece, Hippocrates, the father of medicine, claimed the Scythians inhabited a barren landscape, so he deduced their men must be impotent, too. Ibn Khaldun, the fourteenth-century Arabic scholar and father of social sciences, argued that darker skin was produced by hotter climates, and that the environment also determined whether peoples would be nomadic or sedentary. Centuries later, these theories influenced the French historian and political philosopher Montesquieu, who returned to climate-based theories that placed Europeans on the top rung of a racial hierarchy. In turn, geographical racism became enshrined in the intellectually bankrupt pantheon of concepts that white oppressors used to justify colonialism. There is therefore good reason to be deeply suspicious of any line of thinking with such a despicable racist past, used to justify bigotry, violence, even enslavement.

Nonetheless, our environment *is* a key factor that partially determines human history, even though past thinkers have perverted geographical explanations as a stalking horse for racism. There's a crucial difference between theories that claim that the physical environment makes certain people inferior (which is racist and absurd), and those that demonstrate that environmental factors constrain choices and create historical paths that societies in certain geographies are more likely to follow. The intersection of human action with environmental factors often produces unexpected results. Britain could build ships because it had wood, and it wanted to build ships because it was an island. Had modern humans emerged at a different time in geological history, Britain might have been a landlocked wasteland. There would be no Royal Navy, and, likely, no British Empire. Geographic factors alter the choices that people make. That changes history.

In the mid-to-late twentieth century, however, long-standing intellectual dogma had a long overdue reckoning. Environmental or geographical determinism was largely culled from social theories. It became a scholarly sin to even consider whether some aspects of human history—including gross injustices and inequalities—were determined not exclusively by choice, but partly by geological chance.

In the late 1990s, the geographer and ornithologist Jared Diamond brought geographic determinism back into vogue. His book *Guns, Germs, and Steel* was a surprise international bestseller, reviving ideas that had long ago been relegated to the intellectual fringe. Diamond argued that modern inequalities are derived not from innate intellectual capacity or cultural strength, but from geographical endowments that made it harder for some societies to thrive, while others got lucky, with the ideal conditions to build advanced civilizations. The earth doesn't fairly distribute resources, predators, or diseases across space, and those unfair geological and geographical variations have manifested in a profoundly unequal modern world.

In *Guns, Germs, and Steel*, Diamond observes that human history was also diverted by the shape and orientation of the continents—an idea known as the continental axis theory. Climate, habitat, vegetation, soil, and wildlife are mostly dictated by latitude, not longitude. Move north or south, and the climate changes drastically, which means you need different strategies to survive. But if you move east or west, particularly across the vast horizontal stretch of Eurasia, you can travel thousands of miles and still be in broadly the same kind of biome (a large area with similar climate, vegetation, wildlife, and soil). As a result, people, ideas, trade, technological exchange, and even empires had an easier time spreading east to west rather than north to south. This, Diamond argues, conferred advantages on Eurasia that didn't accrue within, say, Africa. (It didn't help that the north/south pathway from Europe to North Africa to sub-Saharan Africa had a rather large desert within it.) Sure enough, when historians tested the spread of mega-empires throughout the long stretch of history, they found that they do tend to follow an east/west pattern.[*] That makes sense, as armies tended to be most effective

---

[*] These are not ironclad "laws of history," but rather patterns that have generally held. There are exceptions, such as Nile empires and Andean empires, which makes sense within the theory because you can travel up or down the Andes or up and down the banks of the Nile and still be in broadly the same kind of environment.

within their own biome. Warm-weather armies don't tend to do well in cold-weather warfare, and mountain armies don't tend to do well in deserts. Through these mechanisms, the arbitrary nature of climate, geographical terrain, and the geology of soils has shaped who we are and how our history has unfolded. The debate just lies over how much is driven by human action—and how much is due to the lottery of earth.

Critics have nonetheless accused *Guns, Germs, and Steel* of resurrecting the racism embedded in previous geographic explanations for global inequality. Diamond emphatically disavows racism. But academic vultures circled. Some pointed to factual errors or debatable evidence in some parts of the text, which were worthy of serious critique. But others went much further, dismissing the basic premise of his argument altogether, unfairly lumping Diamond in with odious thinkers from eras past simply because he advanced the obviously true position that we are creatures affected by the geographical accidents of our landscapes, our crops, our diseases, and our resources. One even wrote an article in a scholarly journal called—I'm not making this up—"F**k Jared Diamond."

Diamond has faced so much criticism that he has now posted a catchall response on his website: "Whenever I hear the words 'geographic determinism,' I know that I am about to hear a reflex dismissal of geographic considerations, an opinion not worth listening to or reading, and an excuse for intellectual laziness."

What's at stake here is a schism between extreme left-wing and extreme right-wing explanations for history's inequalities. As the social scientist Clint Ballinger has pointed out, some dogmatic right-wing thinkers look at inequality and place blame on those who are poor, often with racist overtones. These thinkers say that the culture in poor countries is deficient in some way, or that those who live in poor countries haven't worked hard enough to build functioning governments, or that their religion doesn't foster a sufficiently "Protestant work ethic." This is the "it's their fault" view. That view is naive, simplistic, and not backed up by the evidence.

On the left wing, some thinkers chalk the wide gulf of inequality between societies purely up to oppression, such as colonialism, with a "they were victims" view. The colonized *were* victims—and the scars of colonialism continue to rip apart societies and undermine prosperity. A large proportion of the explanation *does* come from colonialism and the atrocities of history. On the left, then, Diamond's argument was seen by some to let colonialism off the hook, as though making some room for geographical explanations whitewashes the stain of colonialism.

But there's a crucial problem with this objection: Explanations that begin and end with victimhood only kick the can down the explanatory road. Colonialism was an abomination and it severely worsened inequality. But even if we accepted that modern inequalities were *exclusively* caused by powerful European states oppressing weaker non-European ones, why were powerful European nations able to victimize comparatively less developed societies in the first place? We still must explain why Europe was able to colonize Africa, rather than Africa colonizing Europe. Something must account for the disparities *before* colonialism. We're back to square one.

The critics have it backward. The core idea that some inequalities are made more likely by geographical and environmental factors is not racist, but anti-racist. Dismissing this obvious truth disarms anti-racists of a powerful evidential weapon, for if geography is meaningless to our trajectories, then some thinkers will be more tempted by pernicious explanations that peddle myths of racial essentialism—that some people are innately better than others. The vast ills of colonialism are indeed a major factor in explaining modern inequalities between societies. But there are other nonhuman factors, too. Geography isn't destiny, but it matters.*

---

* The Oxford historian Peter Frankopan's recent book, *The Earth Transformed*, provides the definitive account of how climate shaped human history, one of many examples of environmental factors intersecting with us.

The world plainly varies wildly in geographic features that directly affect human prosperity. Fresh water is required not just for survival, but for irrigation. Some places have it, others don't. The growing season is affected by latitude, soil type, minerals, rainfall patterns, the climate, even the angle of the sunlight. Some regions are blessed with fertility, others cursed with barrenness. Some regions face voracious predators and crippling diseases, others are free from both. The earth produces a geographic lottery. Some societies won, others lost.

This becomes obvious if you consider the following thought experiment. Imagine an earth without humans. Then, by some magic, three groups of humans are placed somewhere on the earth's landmass to start their new civilization, but the locations are completely randomized. One group ends up in France's Loire Valley, with plenty of fresh water, fertile soils, and a lovely, temperate climate. Another group ends up in the Australian outback. The third group has the misfortune to be placed, for their brief lives, in Antarctica. Obviously, geography, geology, and climate will partly determine the groups' fates. The notion that geography influences human trajectories—and inequality—doesn't in any way negate the atrocities committed throughout history or the importance of human decisions, cultures, and other aspects of more traditional historical narratives.

Our world and the long historical trajectories of our species have been shaped by flukes and calamities produced by the movements of magma and the crust that surfs upon it. If we lived in a uniform world, where every location was identical to every other one, there would be little trade and little reason to migrate. Cultures would converge, killing off one of the richest gifts of the human experience. Thankfully, tectonic plates crashing together, ripping apart, and sliding past one another have created a fascinating place to live. We should be grateful for that, while also working to right the grotesque inequalities that have been inflicted by the combination of deep historical injustices produced by racist abuse, along with the contingent movements of the earth's crust.

—

What do the lottery of earth and human space-time contingency look like in practice? Well, you can find causal links in the most unexpected places. The way Donald Trump lost the 2020 presidential election can be partly traced back to ancient geology.

During the Cretaceous period, when velociraptors roamed the earth, an enormous inland sea covered the land that now forms America's Great Plains and most of the Deep South. In that shallow sea and along its coastline, trillions of microscopic plantlike organisms known as phytoplankton thrived. When they died, they sank to the sea bottom and, over vast stretches of time, turned into a nutrient-rich chalk layer of rock. Eventually, the sea receded, revealing the land of modern-day Mississippi, Alabama, and Georgia out from under the water. The nutrient-rich chalk remained, however, and later became a rich dark soil. Millions of years later, the crescent-shaped coastline of that ancient inland sea would create some of the most fertile land anywhere in the future United States.

A few hundred years ago, in Britain, the Industrial Revolution began, as new tools were invented to spin cotton. The best place to grow cotton was in the American South, on plantations in an area known as the Black Belt, named for its rich dark soils—soils created by the coastline of the inland sea during the time of the dinosaurs. When Europeans enslaved Africans and brought them to North America, they forced them to live and toil where cotton thrived.* The location of the slave

---

* In another grotesque interaction between human atrocities and the natural world, enslaved Africans abducted from areas in West Africa that were prone to malaria sold for a higher price because they tended to have immunity from

plantations on the eve of the American Civil War is shown below, and the crescent-shaped swoop of cotton production corresponds almost perfectly to the crescent-shaped swoop of where the coastline of that inland sea once was, where the microscopic corpses of trillions of phytoplankton created fertile soils.

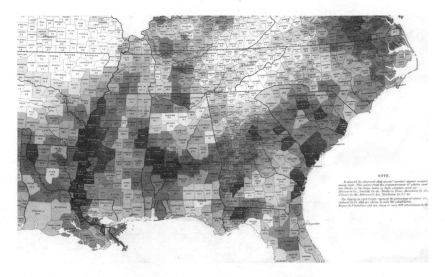

But the rich dark soils from that ancient inland sea weren't done diverting human trajectories. In the 2020 U.S. presidential election, Donald Trump's defeat depended, in part, on a narrow loss in the state of Georgia. Moreover, control of the U.S. Senate—and the entirety of Joe Biden's political agenda after his 2020 victory—hinged on nail-biting Democratic victories in Georgia. The margins for that victory were racked up, believe it or not, on that Cretaceous coastline. If you look at county-level election results, you can still clearly see the coastline, not in rock or soil, but in voting patterns. Many African American descendants

a disease that, at the time, also plagued the American South. It was another contingent interaction, between racism, the prevalence of parasites based on climate, the emergence of industrial cotton production, and the distribution of cotton-friendly soils.

of formerly enslaved ancestors still live near former cotton plantations. In most U.S. elections, roughly nine out of ten African Americans support Democratic candidates. Donald Trump's defeat and Democratic control of the U.S. Senate was partly caused by the historically contingent demographic impact of phytoplankton in an ancient sea.

It's contingency all the way down. Our lives are shaped by the decisions of humans, alive and long dead, but also by the lottery of earth. As we'll now see, that also means that every individual—including yourself—will, quite literally, change the world.

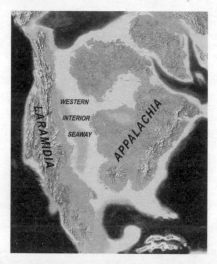

CHAPTER 9

EVERYONE'S A BUTTERFLY

How every person—including you—is
constantly changing our world

Motivational posters tell you that if you set your mind to it, you can change the world. I've got some good news for you: you already have. Congratulations! You're changing it right now because your brain is adjusting slightly just by reading the words I've written for you. If you hadn't read this sentence, the world would be different. I mean that literally. Your neural networks have now been altered, and it will—in the most imperceptible, minute way—adjust your behavior slightly over the remainder of your lifetime. Who knows what the ripple effects will be. But in an intertwined system, nothing is meaningless. Everything matters.

You may think this all sounds a bit trivial or abstract, but consider this: You might decide, or you have already decided, to bring some new humans into the world. Without getting into graphic detail, the precise moment that a baby is conceived is one of the most contingent aspects of our existence. On the day it happens, change any detail—no matter how seemingly insignificant—and you end up with a different child.*

---

* The philosopher Derek Parfit has developed this astonishing truth into a realm of thought known as the non-identity problem, in which he explores the moral and ethical implications of the contingency of *who* gets born, based

Suddenly, you have a daughter instead of a son, or vice versa—or just a different son or daughter. Siblings often diverge in unexpected ways, so any change in *who* is born will radically change your life—and the lives of countless others. But it's not just the one day that a child is conceived that matters. Instead, amplify that contingency by *every* moment of your life. Each detail in the entire chain-link architecture of your lifetime had to be exactly as it was for the exact child who was born to be born. That's true for you, for me, for everyone.

Yet again, the motivational posters have sold you short. "You're one in a million!" they shout at you with uplifting glee. Try one in a *hundred* million, because that's how many competitors, on average, your single-celled predecessor outswam to successfully become half of yourself.

You matter. That's not self-help advice. It's scientific truth. If someone else had been born instead of you—the unborn ghost whom you outcompeted in the existence sweepstakes—countless other people's lives would be profoundly different, so our world would be different, too. The ripples of every life spread out, in unexpected ways, for eternity.

These are awe-inspiring truths. Yet, in modern life, many of us feel like easily replaced cogs in a vast, cold machine. As global corporations sprawl and we seek help from call centers rather than corner stores, many modern systems make us feel interchangeable. Workers robotically follow protocols, checklists, and scripts, engines of efficiency that strip us of our individuality. Humans begin to feel like robots who eat. It dehumanizes us. It doesn't matter who turns the crank, so long as it gets turned.

But what if that dystopian viewpoint is completely wrong?

Let's consider two opposite conceptions of how history works. In one vision of historical change, there's the storybook reality: Change is

---

on even the smallest tweaks in our behavior. The philosophical implications are mind-bending.

ordered and structured. The convergent trajectory of events means that individuals come and go, but trends dominate. Where do the trends come from? We're never explicitly told, only that the aggregation of humans has produced a path toward an inevitable outcome and we'd better prepare ourselves. The trend is destiny. History is written by unseen social forces, and the main characters are powerless to alter the plot.

On the opposite extreme, individuals reign supreme because the idiosyncratic behavior of a single person can reroute us all onto a different path. The logical extension of that viewpoint—rooted in chaos theory— means that every individual isn't just capable of changing history. Rather, we *are* each changing history constantly, with every action—even every thought. Who is doing something can matter as much as what they're doing. If that's true, it would yield an empowering fact: it's not just that everything you do matters, but also that it's *you*, and not someone else, who's doing it. Perhaps every one of us creates our own butterfly effect because each of us flaps our wings a little bit differently.

These two conceptions of change are fundamentally different. So, are we just along for the ride, or does each of us determine the destination?

In late 2015, the *New York Times Magazine* polled its readers with a hypothetical question: If you could travel back in time and kill Hitler when he was still a baby, would you do it? If you shove aside all the glaring problems with the logic of time travel and accept the premise of the question, it seems at first glance to be a straightforward moral dilemma. For a utilitarian, it should be an easy calculation: yes, you should kill one baby to save the lives of millions of innocent future victims. Others who take a more puritan, Kantian approach to morality see it differently. Baby Hitler may grow up to be adult Hitler, but one may never justify killing an innocent infant. Forty-two percent of readers said they'd kill baby Hitler, 30 percent said they wouldn't, and 28 percent said they weren't sure.

But the baby Hitler question is more profound than a thorny moral dilemma. The right answer pivots on our view of how history works and why change happens. Chaos theory proves that small changes can produce enormous impacts, so any manipulation of the past would risk drastic change, making the thought experiment even more uncertain.

Implicit in the baby Hitler thought experiment is the idea that without Hitler the Nazis wouldn't rise to power in Germany, World War II wouldn't happen, and the Holocaust would be avoided. It therefore assumes that Hitler was the sole, or at least the crucial, cause of those events. Many historians would take issue with that viewpoint, arguing that those cataclysms were all but inevitable. Hitler might have affected some outcomes, they'd say, but not the overall trajectory of events. The Nazis, the war, and the genocide were due to larger factors than just one man.

Even if you're willing to accept that killing Hitler would reshape history, the baby Hitler hypothetical also (understandably) assumes that a world without Hitler would turn out much better. While it's hard to imagine, some have suggested that a world without Hitler could have been even worse. The British writer and actor Stephen Fry wrote a novel in which a graduate student travels back in time and makes Hitler's father infertile. Nazism still emerges, but the leader who rises to power is more rational and less impulsive than Hitler was, which leads to Germany acquiring nuclear weapons, winning the war, and killing millions more Jews. Would that have happened? It's impossible to say. But what's certain is that changing a complex past would create unpredictable futures. In that way, the baby Hitler question hinges not just on morality, but on views about historical causality—and whether and how deleting one individual from the past would change the story of our species. We can never know.

Some historians, such as the renowned British scholar E. H. Carr, have argued that engaging in such counterfactual history is a preposterous waste of time, a fantasyland parlor game with no bearing on the real world. Another British historian, E. P. Thompson, called counterfactuals *Geschichtenscheissenschlopff*, which can be translated as the charming phrase "unhistorical shit." That's a curious view for a historian to take because even if the past can't be changed, considering alternative pathways is a useful tool in trying to understand why any given event took place. Speculating on what might have been can reveal insights about what really was. This is important to get right because, as we've already seen, the narratives we believe shape our behavior—and history is all about narratives. "History is not what happened, but it is what we agree happened," observes David Byrne.

For centuries, it was broadly accepted that key individuals determine history. Long-dead early historians wrote glowing biographies of emperors and kings. In China, the "mandate of heaven" bestowed legitimacy on rulers because they were seen to be driving history forward by advancing the divine will on earth, a concept referred to as the divine right of kings in medieval Europe. In the nineteenth century, the Scottish philosopher Thomas Carlyle turned this mindset into an explicit philosophy of history known as the Great Man Theory. Carlyle argued that leaders of nations and titans of industry had been sent by God to transform the world according to His wishes. "The history of the world," Carlyle claimed, "is but the biography of great men." Paradoxically, though, in Carlyle's version of history, it doesn't matter *who* is the Great Man. Because the Great Men were simply implementing a preordained divine plan, you could swap anyone out with no consequences. If it hadn't been Napoléon, somebody else would have stepped in to do the Lord's bidding. For Christian Great Man theorists, it was divine prophecy, not personality, that mattered.

Over time, the Great Man Theory morphed into something broader, an approach to history that looked to powerful figures to understand why change happened. To understand the War on Terror, study George W. Bush and Osama bin Laden, not underlying trends or social dynamics.

This new reading of Great Man history put its faith in counterfactual contingency that pivots on specific mortals, not divine will. Leaders shape outcomes—and their personalities, their quirks, even their moods, can sway events. Steve Jobs didn't just carry the baton of technology forward, he created a new baton altogether. If someone else had replaced Jobs, or if Jobs's father hadn't emigrated to the United States from Syria, our world would be different.* In this view of history, individuals are not interchangeable. Key people, in key moments, matter.

Then, in the late nineteenth and early twentieth centuries, historians, philosophers, and economists pushed back hard against the Great Man view. In *War and Peace*, Leo Tolstoy painted Napoléon as merely a man of his time. Imperial conquest was in the air, so any French leader would have invaded Russia if faced with the same historical and political context. History shaped the leader, the leader didn't shape history. Similarly, Hegel, and later Marx, presented history as a predictable march toward an end goal. For Marx, every event was part of a relentless quest through a series of stages, culminating in a world dominated by the proletariat. Some could speed up the process, but nobody, no matter how powerful, could stop the inevitable outcome. On the other end of economic ideology, the economist Adam Smith spoke of an invisible hand that guides human behavior. Though Smith and Marx disagreed on almost everything, they shared the view that the end goal of history is determined, though individual characters may come and go.

In the 1920s and 1930s, the *Annales* school of history emerged in France, founded by a group of scholars who looked to understand social change by analyzing long-term, societywide trends rather than specific individuals or key events. It became hugely influential. One of its founding members, Marc Bloch, was a Jewish historian who later became a

---

* Today, historians have thankfully recognized that Great Man terminology neglects the role of influential women, so some now refer to it as the Big Beasts view of history (not the most flattering replacement term).

member of the French Resistance during World War II. In mid-1944, he was arrested, tortured, and executed by the Gestapo. His philosophy of history would point to long-term social dynamics, rather than tracing events back to baby Hitler, to explain his own death.

The *Annales* school changed what it means to "do history." Rather than fixating on key movers and shakers, many historians subsequently adopted what is sometimes referred to as "history from below," examining how long-term shifts in the lives of ordinary people create social change. Modern historians often look down their spectacles with disdain at those who cling to the Great Man / Big Beast mindset, as though they're ignoring "real" history for the sexier Hollywood biopic version.

Political scientists and economists tend to treat individuals as interchangeable, too, dismissing explanations that lie with specific people. Game theory, economic equations, and rational choice models don't usually rely on understanding varied personalities, but rather on modeling the incentives *anyone* would face, completely collapsing individual differences into an imagined "generic" or "standard" human.

David Ruelle, a Belgian mathematical physicist, offers a useful thought experiment to show the limits of this kind of thinking. Imagine placing a single flea in the middle of a checkerboard. Probability theory could effectively predict, on average, how often that flea will leap to any specific square on the board. So far, so good.

Now, consider adding sixty-three additional fleas to a sixty-four-square checkerboard, and affixing a name tag to each one: there's Rick the flea, Ellie, Joe, Ann, Caspian, Anthony, and so on. Trying to accurately predict where Rick or Ellie will be at any given time is likely to be impossible. There are too many potential combinations with sixty-four fleas on sixty-four squares. However, social science models will be exceptionally good at predicting, based on behavior over time, how the fleas will generally arrange themselves on the checkerboard—the space between them, their rate of movement, the average height of their leaps, and so forth. These kinds of problems—such as predicting traffic flows, where it doesn't matter as much which specific driver is on the road—are perfectly suited for our research tools.

Now, what if just one flea—let's call him Nigel—is a cannibal? Suddenly, any attempt to predict or understand the dynamics of that checkerboard based on averages or equilibriums are no longer useful because the individuals are no longer interchangeable. The fleas will flee from Nigel. Next, imagine if *every* flea is a bit idiosyncratic. One flea, Barbara, will leap off the board completely if she ends up within two squares of Nigel. Two others, Paul and James, refuse to move, no matter what. One flea, Kelsey, prefers the corners of the board, so she'll stay put if she ends up in a corner square. To make matters more complex, these behaviors change over time, as the fleas learn, adapt, and develop new preferences based on their experiences. Suddenly, the initial conditions of the flea's positions matter enormously. Every time you rerun the experiment, something completely different happens.

Yet, the study of humans, which are vastly more complex than fleas, too often pretends that the specific people don't matter much. For example, many political scientists who study American politics have long tut-tutted those who analyze the traits of U.S. presidents rather than studying the American presidency. A biography of Abraham Lincoln should be left for the cable TV hosts to write, not the serious academic. The mathematized, scientific turn in social science has meant that those who try to understand individuals are often seen as unsophisticated, or not rigorous enough. Palace intrigue and personality profiles are viewed much as E. P. Thompson viewed counterfactuals: as unscientific shit. Western knowledge production systematically prioritizes general rules—even if they're misleading or wrong—over specific and idiosyncratic understanding of individuals. Let the armchair psychologists, or the amateur historians, deal with such trifling questions. The pistons of social change move within the institution, not the person.

I've studied power and those who hold it for more than a decade, and I've always found this view of history bizarre. The presidency matters, but so does the president. The Cuban Missile Crisis might have unfolded differently not only if JFK or Khrushchev had been different leaders, but also if one of them had had a mood swing at a crucial moment. That viewpoint was rare among those who research the American presidency—the more sophisticated "institutionalists." Then, Donald Trump rose to power. It became impossible to ignore that American political history was radically transformed by one man. Does anybody really believe that America would be the same place today if Jeb Bush or Hillary Clinton had won in 2016 instead?

Even the people around power can matter enormously. Ask a historian why the North won the American Civil War, and you'll get plenty of answers. All will have a clear logic. The North had superior supply lines and manufacturing. The North had a larger navy, making blockades possible. The North had more men. All true. But the war could have turned out differently with a few small changes, particularly in the early stages, when the Confederate Army had several decisive victories over an overly timid, mismanaged Union Army. By the autumn of 1862, an additional crushing blow to the Union could have kicked off a chain reaction. Britain was contemplating official recognition of the Confederacy. The United States might have permanently split in half. One partial explanation for why that didn't happen lies not with a brilliant general, nor with a robust supply line, but with three discarded cigars—and the right man to find them.

Around 9:00 a.m. on Saturday, September 13, 1862, Corporal Barton W. Mitchell of the Twenty-Seventh Indiana Regiment in the Union Army was taking a break from marching. Scrambling to escape the autumn sun, he settled into the shade of a nearby tree next to a fencerow. As he stretched himself out to rest, something caught his eye, hidden in weeds next to the tree's roots. A sheet of paper was wrapped around three cigars. The heading on the paper read, "(Confidential). Hd Qrs Army of Northern Va. Sept 9th, 1862. Special Orders 191." Barton had accidentally discovered the marching orders for the Confederate Army. The army was mounting a surprise attack. Barton had stumbled across priceless intelligence that had fallen out of a courier's satchel. It could turn the tide of the war. But was it genuine?

The document was signed "R.H. Chilton," by command of "Gen R.E. Lee." It seemed plausible enough, but falling for a phony document could be catastrophic. The letter was brought to a division commander of the Union Army, General Alpheus S. Williams. Outside his tent, the document was first handed to his adjutant general, Colonel Samuel Pittman. Unrolling the paper, Pittman read it, grasped its significance, then paused as he saw the signature at the bottom. Immediately, he knew the orders were genuine.

Armed with this secret intelligence, the Union Army marched to meet the Confederate troops. The bloodiest day in American history, the Battle of Antietam, ensued four days later. The Union suffered severe casualties—but they had been prepared for the assault. Antietam forced the Confederates to retreat, reversing the momentum of the war. Historians suggest that the battle's outcome also gave President Lincoln the confidence to issue the Emancipation Proclamation five days after the battle ended, ordering enslaved people in Confederate territory to be free. Such pivotal events could be traced back, in part, to three discarded cigars.

But how had Samuel Pittman known the orders were genuine? They had been signed by R. H. Chilton. Before the war, Pittman had been a bank teller in Detroit, where Chilton was the paymaster for the U.S. Army. Chilton had had to sign checks to make payments. Pittman had seen Chilton's signature thousands of times. When he saw the signed paper unrolled from the cigars, he instantly knew it was authentic. It's a strange, but plausible, possibility that modern history pivoted on three lost cigars, a soldier resting in just the right patch of shade, and enemy orders arriving, by happenstance, into the hands of the only man in the Union Army who could have been sure they were genuine. We often write such events out of history, searching instead for more definite, sensible "reasons" for why things happen. Nevertheless, in our arbitrary, accidental world, sometimes the right place to look, as Corporal Mitchell discovered, is in the weeds.

—

We cling to the idea that *what* matters more than *who*—and by extension that the message matters more than the messenger. But for most of history, it's been clear that often isn't true.

In Greek mythology, Cassandra of Troy caught the eye of the god Apollo, for her beauty and intelligence. Apollo gave her a divine gift: the ability to accurately see the future. But Cassandra later scorned Apollo. Unable to revoke the gift of foresight he had bestowed upon Cassandra, Apollo did the next best thing by cursing her with the punishment of disbelief. No matter how accurate her prophecies, nobody would believe her. Cassandra could warn men of their impending deaths or alert kings of disastrous wars, but she would always be howling into the wind, her sagacity ignored.

The myth of Cassandra is one of the earliest indications that humans have long understood that if there is a fixed truth, our interpretation of it is often subjectively tied to who promotes that truth. We are a species that takes intellectual shortcuts, sometimes through a concept known as signaling and other times through schemas.

Signaling involves deliberate attempts to convey information using socially accepted clues. Experts, for good reason, rarely appear on television wearing a Hawaiian shirt with flip-flops. We humans are adept at picking up on these clues, asking probing questions of the people we meet about their education, their job, or which neighborhood they call home, to quickly size people up so we can determine how much stock to place in what they say. One of the first questions most people ask in a first encounter with someone new is "What do you do?" The answer instantly rejiggers our interpretation of the person. This produces bias. The right information with the wrong signal gets ignored, producing yet another challenge to the structured, systematic view of change.

Schemas are psychological tools we use to distill vast amounts of information into easily maintained categories. Neuroscience and psychology research repeatedly finds that these mental labels provide the filters through which we process fresh revelations about the world, and about the people we meet within it. You may not know who someone is, but if the person is labeled a Democrat or a Republican, a Tory or a Labour supporter, the person becomes connected in your brain to ideas that you hold about those categories. We're again trapped by the contingencies of language, as you're likely to radically change your assessment of someone you meet if the person is introduced as an "entrepreneur" as opposed to an "influencer," even if it's the same individual. Yet, those meanings—and the credibility we attach to them—change over time. What would someone in the 1990s make of a person called an "influencer"? Who knows? But it would certainly be different from the connotations glued to that word today. Our mental maps and schemas are not fixed, but constantly shifting. That means that the very words we use to describe people, or to categorize them in our minds, can affect whether the information we receive from them is trusted or discarded, which produces more unpredictable outcomes.

Our brains are therefore designed to allow us to quickly categorize people and assess, even subconsciously, whether we should listen to them. We often get it wrong. Plenty of serious-seeming people in slick suits with eminent degrees and an abundance of charming confidence have repeatedly crashed the economy, dragged us into wars, and inflicted tremendous global suffering. So, it's not just who says something, but how we perceive the person saying it. Contingency upon contingency upon contingency. We may refer to the messenger mattering as much as the message as the Cassandra problem, yet another cognitive bias that can change history in irrational, arbitrary ways.

If we're prone to these biases, then so, too, were other humans throughout history. For example, in April 1865, Charles Colchester warned Abraham Lincoln that his life was in danger just days before Lincoln was killed at Ford's Theatre. Colchester, a "red-faced, blue-eyed Englishman with a large mustache," had the trust of Lincoln's wife, Mary Todd. But Lincoln ignored Colchester's warning. Why? Because Colchester had become a fixture in the White House not as a political adviser but as a clairvoyant, a soothsayer who claimed that he could put Mary Todd back in touch with her dead son Willie, who passed away in 1862. Lincoln never believed in Colchester's spiritualism, though Lincoln dutifully attended the séances to comfort his wife. But when Colchester warned Lincoln that his life was in danger, he dismissed it as just another fabricated prophecy, the easily ignored drivel of a con man.

Lincoln would have been better off if he'd believed Colchester. Not because Colchester was a genuine clairvoyant—he clearly was a charlatan. Instead, Colchester had access to inside information. One of Colchester's close associates was a man who also attended séances and believed in spiritualism: John Wilkes Booth. Colchester's warnings to Lincoln probably weren't mere conjecture but were instead the Cassandra-like warnings of a man who knew what was to come. Lincoln ignored Colchester's counsel, went to Ford's Theatre, and was murdered by Booth.

Now, you may object that anyone can point to historical curiosities, but that some realms of knowledge are immune from these individual variations. After all, good ideas that work float; bad ideas that don't, sink. Humans often come up with similar ideas across time and space, a phenomenon known as multiple discovery. The crossbow, for example, was independently invented in China, Greece, Africa, Canada, and the Baltics. Oxygen was discovered by at least three people, on three separate occasions, all around the same time. Two men filed patents for the telephone on the same day.

Perhaps the genius matters less than the idea that forms a stroke of genius. Maybe our world wouldn't be that different if Einstein had been ignored, his ideas dismissed as the fantasies of a delusional patent clerk. Somebody else would have made his discoveries and it would've been a wash because it's the equations that matter, not who writes them. But is that true? This is an important question because if even scientific ideas are at least partly contingent on which individual comes up with them, then it's hard to dispute that just about *everything* is contingent and prone to flukes created by individuals.

In the twentieth century, two titans of the philosophy of science, Karl Popper and Thomas Kuhn, sparred over how modern science works. Popper emphasized how disproving bad ideas drives change in a more objective process; Kuhn emphasized the subjective role of individuals. To Popper, scientists try to tear down bad ideas to expose the truth, jettisoning flawed theories through falsification. They continually try to disprove every proposed hypothesis, and when they do, that idea goes to the junk heap of scientific history. When done properly, scientific discovery moves forward by relentless testing, unfeeling and unswayed by personalities or politics. Ideas go through gladiator-style combat in the scientific arena, and only those that survive unscathed live to be tested again.

By contrast, Thomas Kuhn, who wrote *The Structure of Scientific Revolutions* in 1962, argued that scientists, like all of us, have prejudices and biases. Individual scientists have an established set of beliefs, they believe in certain theories, and they devote their professional lives to proving those views right. But when scientific theories are wrong, the cracks eventually get exposed despite the best efforts of researchers who want to protect their pet hypotheses. When the cracks get big enough, the entire edifice of science can collapse, decades of accepted truth destroyed in a bewildering crash. Kuhn refers to these moments as revolutions in science, where previously dominant paradigms are replaced by fresh ones, and the process repeats. (If you've ever spoken of a "paradigm shift," you've been using terminology coined by Kuhn.)

To Kuhn, scientists themselves matter—and they matter a lot. Individual researchers can sway which questions science asks, which hypotheses are taken seriously, and who gets funding. This doesn't mean that scientific truths are subjective, but rather that making science is a human endeavor, which makes it vulnerable to the contingencies and arbitrariness that accompany any action undertaken by human beings.

In 1906, a German meteorologist named Alfred Wegener set the record for the longest continuous balloon flight ever made, drifting high above the earth for fifty-two hours. Six years later, he proposed that continents, like balloons, could drift, moving apart over long periods of time.* When Wegener proposed his theory in 1912, the backlash was swift and harsh. Who was this meteorologist and champion balloonist to tell geologists that the earth's crust moves?

In Britain, which was on the brink of war with Germany when Wegener's theory was published, few scientists even took notice of his theory until the early 1920s. In 1943, the American paleontologist George Gaylord Simpson wrote a strong rebuke to the idea that the earth's land moved. With America at war with Germany at the time, American sci-

---

* Wegener wasn't the first to propose this intellectual heresy. In the late 1500s, a cartographer named Abraham Ortelius proposed that the continents had once been joined together before separating toward their present locations. Several others proposed a similar idea. Each time, it was considered preposterous, despite how strikingly South America and West Africa seemed to fit together nearly perfectly, like two pieces of a jigsaw puzzle.

entists sided with Simpson. Despite compelling evidence, only by 1967 did plate tectonics and continental drift become accepted, sparking a revolution in earth sciences. For nearly fifty years, people misunderstood the world because of the nationality and professional background of *who* proposed an idea, rather than what was being proposed. A German meteorologist most known for his ballooning prowess wasn't the right messenger for the moment.

I'm certainly not the first to raise the notion that individuals can radically alter the history of science. But the standard rebuttal to this argument almost always points to the same man: Charles Darwin. Does it matter that it was Charles Darwin, specifically, who proposed evolutionary theory? Wouldn't someone else have come up with the same theory if he hadn't, the same way that Gottfried Wilhelm Leibniz invented calculus around the same time as Isaac Newton?

The objection is apt because someone else *did* propose a theory of evolution at roughly the same time as Charles Darwin, an English naturalist named Alfred Russel Wallace. The tale of these two men is frequently used to support an anti-Kuhnian, dispassionate, convergent view of science. Great discoveries are "in the air" when they're made, part of a scientific trend. It wouldn't particularly affect the trajectory of progress whether it was Darwin or Wallace who pioneered evolutionary theory. To find out how the history of ideas works, let's take a closer look.

—

The most important book of the nineteenth century almost didn't get written.

On its first voyage, the HMS *Beagle* was captained by a man with the memorable name of Pringle Stokes. In 1828, while the ship was anchored at the southern tip of South America, Stokes fell into a deep depression.

The dreary weather was so bleak, he wrote in his diary, that "the soul of man dies in him." Stokes locked himself in his cabin, shot himself, and died several days later. Had he stayed alive, Charles Darwin would never have set foot on the *Beagle*.

Instead, the captaincy of the *Beagle* soon passed to Robert FitzRoy, an aristocratic officer in the Royal Navy. As FitzRoy prepared to launch the second voyage of the *Beagle*, he was aware of the lonely isolation of command, as it would be unbecoming of an aristocrat such as himself to converse with the lowly members of the crew. Hoping to avoid the fate of Pringle Stokes, FitzRoy began an informal search for an onboard companion for the upcoming years at sea. His first choice was a clergyman, who rejected the offer because he didn't want to neglect his religious duties. The second choice was a professor, who refused because he didn't want to upset his wife. But the professor recommended a former student who might be a suitable contender: Charles Darwin.

FitzRoy believed in physiognomy, the notion that physical traits reflect a person's underlying disposition. When FitzRoy set eyes on Darwin, the captain was alarmed by the sight of Darwin's nose. FitzRoy "was convinced that he could judge a man's character by the outline of his features," Darwin later wrote, "and he doubted wheather [sic] anyone with my nose could possess sufficient energy and determination for the voyage. But I think he was afterwards well-satisfied that my nose had spoken falsely." In one of the more striking contingencies of the nineteenth century, Darwin was nearly kept off the fateful voyage that would change science forever because of the shape of his nose.*

Darwin returned from the second voyage of the *Beagle* in 1836, his brain teeming with fresh insights that could revolutionize biology. Darwin sent drafts of his ideas to friends and fellow scientists. But he

---

* This was a quite literal affirmation of the "Cleopatra's nose" view of history, made more prominent by J. B. Bury, which argues that the pleasing shape of Cleopatra's nose set off a chain reaction that forever altered history.

delayed publishing his core insights for various reasons, ranging from personal illness to the potential social stigma for publishing a set of ideas so at odds with prevailing religious dogma. He stuck his early drafts in a drawer and went about his life without any urgency to publish them in a book.

Then, in 1858, Darwin received a parcel that would change his life—and science—forever. It was a letter from the British naturalist Alfred Russel Wallace. As Darwin read what Wallace had written, Darwin was shocked to see a remarkably similar idea to his own concept of natural selection. "I never saw a more striking coincidence," Darwin later remembered. Fearing that Wallace would get the credit for an idea that Darwin had come up with decades earlier, Darwin quickly produced the manuscript for *On the Origin of Species* and sent it to a publisher, John Murray, for review. The review was completed by Whitwell Elwin, a clergyman. In Elwin's letter to the publisher, he tried to dissuade publication of the manuscript as written, arguing that it would be better if Darwin wrote a book about pigeons instead, noting that he had been assured that Darwin's thoughts on pigeons were "curious, ingenious, and valuable in the highest degree." The book would sell better, too, Elwin insisted, noting, "Every body is interested in pigeons." Thankfully, Darwin ignored the advice. *On the Origin of Species* was published a few months later. It has never been out of print since.*

This story is often used by advocates of dispassionate, convergent science to argue the "in the air" thesis, the notion that scientific progress makes profound discoveries all but inevitable once the right intellectual ethers are floating around. Although it makes a good story to say that science would have been radically changed if the shape of Darwin's

---

* John Murray is the UK publisher of this book. They finally published a book about pigeons in 2019, 160 years after releasing Darwin's masterpiece. It has not (yet) enjoyed the same level of success as *On the Origin of Species*.

nose had bothered Captain FitzRoy just a little bit more, plenty have argued that, without Darwin, evolutionary theory would just have been proposed by Wallace instead. Wallace would have written up the same theory, gotten the credit, and he, not Darwin, would be a household name. Flukes tied to individual scientists don't change scientific history, they just determine *which* scientist gets the credit, fame, and glory.

Is that true?

Wallace was an outsider, which meant that established scientists would have been skeptical of someone from his background producing such a sweeping theory that upended all scientific knowledge, such as evolution by natural selection. But it wasn't just Wallace's outsider status that would have changed how the theory of evolution was received had he been the messenger. As a young man, Wallace had consulted a phrenologist and had been struck by how skull reading could reveal deep truths about one's nature. He continued to swear by phrenology his entire life. Wallace once published an account of a séance he attended in which he insisted that the medium had conjured flowers out of thin air, thirty-seven stalks appearing "all fresh, cold, and damp with dew, as if they had that moment been brought out of the night air." Wallace also swore by hypnotism. In one publication, Wallace wrote that "thought-transference, automatic writing, trance-speaking, and clairvoyance and phantoms" were all real phenomena, as verifiable as gravity. In prominent scientific publications, Wallace became a subject of ridicule.

Today, Darwin's core ideas are almost universally accepted by scientists. But at the time, Darwin's theory was, to put it mildly, controversial. Even today, despite mountains of evidence backing evolutionary theory, just 54 percent of Americans agree that "human beings, as we know them today, developed from earlier species of animals." If that skepticism remains stubborn now, how would evolutionary theory have fared in the nineteenth century if its chief proponent was equally insistent that phantoms were real and flowers could be conjured from the night air by a skilled medium?

Evolutionary theory would've eventually carried the day because it's correct—and correct ideas do tend to win out in scientific inquiry. But it likely wouldn't have gained widespread acceptance so quickly, delaying a key branch of science for decades. Unexpected ripple effects might have occurred, too, since everything is intertwined. Darwin's cousin was Francis Galton, a polymath who warped Darwin's ideas to establish the fledging field of eugenics, later inspiring mass sterilization campaigns and hateful ideologies that inspired the Nazis. Would Galton have established eugenics if a séance-obsessed stranger, rather than his cousin, had been behind the apparently outlandish theory? Would somebody else have developed eugenics in place of Galton?

We can't say. But in our interlaced world, the same idea proposed by someone else can produce radically different effects. Yet, who discovers something is, as it was with Darwin, sometimes determined by something as arbitrary as the shape of one's nose. No corner of our world, no matter how seemingly rational, can escape from the grip of contingency. What you do matters. But it also matters that it's you, and not somebody else, who's doing it.

For a fitting conclusion to this saga, we shall briefly return to Robert FitzRoy, the captain who sought to stave off depression and loneliness by taking a chance on a naturalist with an unseemly nose. FitzRoy went on to develop the field of meteorology, founding the precursor to Britain's modern weather service, the Meteorological Office, and producing the foundational work that inspired Lorenz, the meteorologist who discovered chaos theory a century later. In his work, FitzRoy coined the word *forecast*, a term central to prediction.

FitzRoy's story, alas, doesn't have a happy ending. Despite his efforts to stave off depression and avoid the fate of his predecessor, Pringle Stokes, FitzRoy fell into despair. His malaise was partly due to his weather forecasts being mocked for their laughable inaccuracies, and partly because he felt guilty about enabling Darwin's heresy. FitzRoy committed suicide on April 30, 1865—two weeks after Abraham Lincoln had been shot after failing to heed the warning of a particularly well-informed clairvoyant.

And now, we turn to another source of flukes: the power of when.

CHAPTER 10

OF CLOCKS AND CALENDARS

How timing, down to the split second,
produces world-changing impacts

Joseph Lott is alive because he chose the right day to wear a green shirt. Elaine Greenberg, the woman who saved Lott's life, is dead because she took her vacation one week too early. If necessity is the mother of invention, then timing is the mother of contingency. Flies buzz around roads constantly and, usually, harmlessly. But, every so often, a fly zips into a motorcyclist's eye, causing a crash. Two unrelated trajectories are brought together in arbitrary, seemingly random ways by the unshakable mysteries of time. Such "Cournot contingency," of two unrelated paths converging in a specific place, at a specific time, can produce death by millisecond. We are at time's mercy.

In the autumn of 2001, Elaine Greenberg took a vacation to Tanglewood, Massachusetts. While there, she spotted a necktie she knew her coworker would love—featuring Monet's *Sunset at Lavacourt*. Her colleague, Joe Lott, was known for wearing ties with paintings on them, and Greenberg knew impressionist paintings were his favorite. She bought the tie, figuring it would be a nice gesture for Lott, who was due to fly to New York City the following week for a work conference.

On the Monday before the conference, Lott got on the plane, but with storms across the country that evening, the flight, which should have taken a few hours, took fourteen instead. Lott arrived in lower Manhattan well past midnight, with the long journey leaving him looking a bit worse for wear. He had been due to have dinner with Greenberg so they could go over their presentation together before the conference, but was forced to reschedule. They agreed to have an early breakfast instead. Before Lott collapsed exhausted onto his hotel bed, he set out his clothes for the next day. As he did so, he realized his crisp white dress shirt that he had been planning to wear for the conference was crumpled and wrinkled.

The next morning, Lott woke up, took one look at his crumpled white shirt, and felt glad he had brought a spare, a pastel-green one that would do the trick. At 7:20 a.m., he arrived at the hotel breakfast room, where Greenberg helped him go over the presentation. At the end of breakfast, around 8:15 a.m., she handed Lott her gift, the Monet tie, with the shimmering blues of the Seine set against a fiery red-orange sky at sunset. Lott was touched. He thanked her and, to show he meant it, said, "Elaine, I'm going to put this tie on and wear it today for good luck." She shot back, "Not with *that* shirt, you're not." Lott laughed, but agreed. Even he knew that the tie would clash horrendously with pastel green. He decided to return to his hotel room to swap shirts—even if it meant being a few minutes late. "See you shortly," Lott said. Greenberg waved goodbye, then went up to the conference venue, on the 106th floor of Tower 1 of the World Trade Center.

Lott returned to his hotel room and began to iron his wrinkled white shirt. It took him about fifteen minutes, long enough that he was still getting ready when the first plane hit the tower at 8:46 a.m.

Lott survived. Greenberg died. Lott now exclusively wears art ties, a subtle tribute to his lost friend and that little piece of fabric, a thoughtful gift timed perfectly to save his life.

All of us have read stories that make us marvel at someone's astonishing luck or horrifying misfortune. These stories seem so improbable, so incredible, that they stand out. But here's the secret: they're *not* outliers for how change happens. The contingency of timing is determining and diverting our lives constantly, though some diversions have larger immediate consequences than others. The immediate cause of Lott's fortune and Greenberg's misfortune may have been a rainstorm, a delayed flight, and a gift given at the right moment—each produced by timing. But we live within an endless chain mail of interlocking causes, stretching far into the past, each link forged by the vagaries of time.

When Lott retired from the Marines, he began traveling the world more for work and once passed an art museum. He had time to kill, so he ventured in. Had Lott been in a hurry that day, he might not have done so, might not have discovered his love for impressionist painting, might never have worn an artistic tie, and Greenberg would never have bought the *Sunset at Lavacourt*. When you consider what had to happen for that breakfast to unfold just as it did, there are a near-infinite number of contingencies. If even trivial moments had been sped up or delayed by seconds, even in the distant past, that breakfast wouldn't have happened as it did. *Everything* up until that moment had to be exactly as it was for Joe Lott to receive that tie precisely when, and how, he did on September 11. Although incredible stories such as Lott's survival pull back the curtain and allow us to see the incredible fragility of our life trajectories, such contingencies of timing constantly shape us. We're not aware of them until, like Lott, it becomes impossible to ignore them in a consequential moment when we pause to think about what could have been. Could we have taken a different path?

In the first chapter, I briefly mentioned a short story by the Argentine writer Jorge Luis Borges called "The Garden of Forking Paths." It's an illuminating metaphor for our experience of time. Each moment of our lives is a fork of near-infinite possible paths. What we do in each moment affects the path we're on, as well as which forks we'll face next.

Rather than a "fork in the road" being a metaphor for life's big decisions, the Garden of Forking Paths is a metaphor for the unbroken journey of our lives. It's constant, relentless, branching infinitely. Right now, by reading this sentence rather than doing something else, your path is forking. Put the book down, and your path forks again. But here's the astonishing bit: some paths that appear available to you now are about to be cut off, not by your actions, but by other people you'll never meet wandering through their own gardens. As you move forward on your path, you change the paths of others, too, ad infinitum.

It's not just humans that divert your path with timing. By September 11, the storms that delayed Lott's flight had cleared away, leaving blindingly blue skies. None of the hijacked planes took off late or had trouble finding their targets due to cloud cover; there was to be no Kokura's luck that day in Manhattan or Washington. The Garden of Forking Paths is affected by everything, everywhere, constantly.

The Garden of Forking Paths is also a useful metaphor to explain change in the natural world. When mutations happen in organisms, some pathways become possible that weren't before, while others are closed off. Yet again, timing matters. In the last several decades, it has become clear that "mutational order" matters tremendously, even playing an important role in why and how cancers develop. It doesn't just matter what the random mutations are, but *when* they happen, and in which order they occur relative to one another. Each path we take, moment by moment, makes some worlds possible, others impossible.

Time is life's invisible variable. It's impossible to imagine a world free of time because we can't experience any moment but the present. But when you peer closer at the nature of time, the world of apparent human control that is embedded in clocks, timetables, and calendars starts to fall apart, being yet another seeming bastion of stability that is teetering on the precipice of contingency. Time, it turns out, is an incredibly strange thing.

—

"Let's begin with a simple fact," writes Carlo Rovelli, the theoretical phys-icist. "Time passes faster in the mountains than it does at sea level." This isn't a poetic statement about how we perceive ourselves in the pristine setting of nature, but an objective, verified truth. The gravity of a mass, such as the earth, warps time, making time move slower closer to the mass, an illustration of a phenomenon known as *time dilation*. Using precise atomic clocks, scientists have now been able to experimentally verify this effect, which was originally proposed by Albert Einstein. Even minuscule variations matter.

In 2010, extremely precise clocks were placed at different heights, with one clock just over a foot above the other. Astonishingly, time passed a tiny bit faster for the higher clock. Technically speaking, your head is older than your feet. The differences are infinitesimal. Over a human lifetime, if two people were born in the same moment, but one lived atop Mount Everest and the other lived at sea level, the mountain twin would be just a few thousandths of a second older after one hun-dred years. For the pragmatic purposes of our lives, it's a curiosity, not a driver of change. But even though the differences from time dilation are tiny, invisible, and irrelevant to our daily lives, the implication is profound. *There is no such thing as objective time.* Time exists relationally, yet another instance of reality being intertwined, not separable. Time, itself, remains a mystery.

Our experience of time can also be warped and altered by human decisions. Our lives unfold according to patterns and rhythms made not only by the laws of the universe but by us. Our ancestors chose to parcel time into discrete chunks that we still use to organize our lives today, another contingent fluke of the past. So it's not just that every bit of timing matters, but also that our division of time is, itself, arbitrary. When you consider the ways that your life interacts with time, you'll be astounded to realize how much of your day-to-day schedule has been determined by people who are long dead.

We look at calendars to gaze into our future and see what comes next. But at a more fundamental level, our calendars are the result of a few key decisions made by small groups of people thousands of years ago, shaping the rhythms of our lives and the patterns of modern society. Months, named after the moon, were originally tied to lunar cycles. In the earliest days of Rome, people followed a ten-month calendar, adding up to 304 days, with the remainder of the days of a year being lumped together into a winter period of varying length.* Later reforms added two months, January and February, but the original numbering system remains. That's why the names September, October, November, and December refer, linguistically, to the numbers seven, eight, nine, and ten, even though they are now—with the addition of January and February—the ninth, tenth, eleventh, and twelfth months. Even our naming systems are the living ghosts of past decisions. Nonetheless, many of our household budgets rise and fall as we are paid in intervals determined, originally, by the phases of the moon.

Next, consider the days of the week. In English, unlike most romance languages, the names are not Latin, but are instead derived from Norse/ Anglo-Saxon deities. Tiw, the Norse god of war, survived as Tuesday. Woden's day follows, from the god who oversees Valhalla. Thor's day comes next, followed by Frige's day, in honor of the goddess of love, who was married to Woden. We speak their names constantly without pausing to reflect on their origins, an unfamiliar snapshot from a for-

---

* If you ever want to win a bet, challenge someone to find any historical event, anywhere in the world, that took place between October 5 and October 14 in the year 1582. At that time, the old calendar system was out of sync with the sun and the moon, so Pope Gregory XIII introduced a more accurate calendar. But to make it work, ten days had to be eliminated. Those ten days simply don't exist in history.

gotten history. But why do we set the rhythms of our lives to weeks in the first place? Who decreed that everything in our lives should follow a cycle of seven?

Unlike many measures of time, the week is unrelated to cycles in the natural world. Instead, the first documented instance of time being broken up into seven-day chunks comes from a decree around 2300 BC, made by King Sargon I of Akkad, who saw the number seven as sacred. A seven-day week later appeared in the Hebrew Bible. However, the Hebrew Bible never suggests using the week as a method of timekeeping, and its own referencing system for dates ignores days of the week completely, cataloging dates using a numerical system within months.

In the first century BC, the planetary week—also seven days long—first appeared in Rome. It had nothing to do with rest or work, but instead referred to a belief that certain planets ruled human fates at specific times, an early form of astrology. Why are there seven days in the planetary calendar? Because five planets were visible to the naked eye (Saturn, Mars, Mercury, Jupiter, and Venus), and with the sun and the moon, that makes seven. Romance languages still enshrine these visible celestial bodies in their day names. In French, for example, *mardi* for Mars is Tuesday, *mercredi* for Mercury is Wednesday, *jeudi* for Jupiter is Thursday, and *vendredi* for Venus is Friday. The French word for moon is *la lune*, so Monday is *lundi*. If the Romans had had telescopes and could see other celestial bodies (such as Uranus and Neptune), perhaps humans would now subdivide our lives by nine instead of seven. (Early Welsh texts speak of a nine-day week.) Or, if the Romans stuck to the planets rather than adding in the sun and the moon, perhaps we'd have five-day weeks. There were always other options. The ancient Chinese and ancient Egyptians structured their lives in weeks of ten days. How different our lives would be. And it's all derived from a contingent mixture of history, vision, technology, and astronomy within a small group of humans who existed during a little sliver of time long, long ago. We synchronize our lives with rhythms produced by accidents of history. Time, divided in arbitrary ways, lurks in the background of every major event in modern human history and in our own lives. We mostly ignore it.

We're also shaped by how our biological clock interacts with these arbitrary divisions of time. Researchers have found a consistent diurnal pattern in mood, such that more people express feelings of optimism or positive thoughts during the morning, followed by an afternoon slump, with a rebounding mood in the evening. This is also reflected in music streaming preferences, as humans, on aggregate, listen to more relaxing music at night and more energetic tunes during work hours. Most people, as you might expect, are also happier on the weekends, but the timing of that mood peak is two hours later than on weekdays (which makes sense given how many people relish sleeping in on Saturdays and Sundays). This all may seem somewhat obvious, but across populations, it can have a large effect. Given how variable humans are depending on their mood, serious consequences can reverberate due to timing.

When publicly traded companies announce their quarterly earnings, for example, they are legally bound to accurately represent the economic profile based on the numbers. Mood should be meaningless, as businesses report sterile numbers. Yet, researchers Jing Chen and Elizabeth Demers found that the morning calls were systematically more upbeat and positive than calls about similar data that were announced in the afternoon. These differences were so stark that stocks would become temporarily mispriced based on the tone of the calls relative to the actual numbers. There's no such thing as neutral timing.

———

How we understand our world is shaped, to a remarkable degree, by people who produce research that tells us how the world works. Yet, social science mostly ignores specific timing. This may be news to you. But most economists, political scientists, and sociologists use quantitative tools that are unable to effectively model exact timing. Few datasets account for the precise sequence of events. In most quantitative methodologies used by social researchers, such as economists and political scientists, it would be exceedingly difficult to model something like a coup pivoting on a split second, or the notion that sometimes an outcome depends on the precise order of seemingly random events. Instead, crude measures are used, such as interaction effects—the presence of two variables together, but usually without regard to specific timing. Variables are often just lumped together, like a cooking recipe where the order in which the ingredients are added doesn't matter. But most recipes don't work like that, and you'll get unfortunate results if you add flour to a cake after you've baked it, just as you'll get the wrong answers in social research if you pay little attention to aspects of timing and sequence.

Moreover, when we study ourselves, we forget that we are quite unlike a cake. A recipe works in different times and places. But we frequently rely on the deeply flawed assumption that the same is true in human society: that the same factors, once mixed together, will produce the same outcome at time A as they will at time B. That's plainly wrong. The term for this flawed assumption, which is so ubiquitous that it's often implied rather than explicitly written, is *ceteris paribus*, or "all else being equal." In a constantly changing world, all else is never equal, and it's rarely a safe assumption to make, unless a given cause and effect is stationary and stable, such as a coin flip. In messy reality, a pattern in one place won't necessarily hold true in another, as we saw with the lottery of earth. Outcomes vary not just across space, but also across time. After all, it's not as though giving a Monet tie to Joe Lott will always produce a life-and-death moment. Many social scientists readily acknowledge these flawed assumptions, but nonetheless choose to use the "snapshot" view of time as a crude, but sometimes useful, simplification of reality.

Consider this apparently straightforward question: "Do pandemics reduce productivity?" Answering it relies on the implicit assumption that pandemics, across time and space, generally are the same, and you can apply the lessons from one to the other. During the COVID-19 pandemic, a surprising amount could be accomplished by office workers Zooming in their pajamas. Could you then infer, based on the coronavirus pandemic, how pandemics generally affect productivity?

The answer becomes plain if you consider what might have happened if a novel coronavirus had spread in 1990 instead of 2020. Without personal computers, video conferencing, or the internet in most households, widespread working from home would've been impossible. If the same virus had emerged in Wuhan in 1950, it would have taken quite a while to move from China to the rest of the world. The effects of the exact same virus would diverge enormously based exclusively on timing. We too often wave away these truths with two magic words: *ceteris paribus*. Such assumptions can lead to catastrophic miscalculations.

Even when we tease out seemingly stable patterns and regularities, it's always possible that the exact same causes may bring down a government or crash an economy one day, but have no effect, or a different effect, the next day. The passengers on United Airlines Flight 93 took down their hijacked airplane on September 11 before it could reach its intended target, but it's perfectly plausible that a different set of passengers on September 10 or September 12 might have acted differently—and the White House or U.S. Capitol might've been destroyed. Contingency, upon contingency, upon contingency, all stacked atop the precarious quirks of clocks and calendars.

However, time is no free-for-all. Just as systems can stay stable for a long period before breaking apart or radically changing, some changes are fleeting, while others get locked in and last, such as the seven-day week. This adds to the uncertain effects of timing because lock-in is, itself, arbitrary. For example, the words you're reading right now have a specific spelling that's been produced by contingent historical developments combined with a lock-in event caused by new technology.

"English spelling is ridiculous," writes Arika Orent, a linguist and neuroscientist who studies how language changes over time. "*Sew* and *new* don't rhyme. *Kernel* and *colonel* do." Why is that? Our language has been swayed by contingent events of history that occurred at specific moments of linguistic change. The Anglo-Saxons in England spoke Old English. Viking invasions injected Old Norse. In the eleventh century, the Normans effectively obliterated written English, replacing it with French. But when written English returned in the 1300s, the language was in flux, with word spellings depending on the preferences of individual monks and scribes. "*People*, taken from French *peuple*, might be spelled *peple*, *pepill*, *poeple* or *poepul*," Okrent notes.

Then, the printing press was invented. Standardization became essential, and words had to be shortened for efficiency. *Hadde* became *had*, *thankefull* became *thankful*. As spellings became recognizable, it became harder to experiment. But because the language was rapidly evolving, if the printing press had arrived a few decades earlier or later, this book and everything else you've ever read would be written differently. Lock-in, therefore, means that some timings are more important than others. Some flukes have staying power.

W. Brian Arthur, an economist who became one of the founding fathers of complex systems theory, demonstrated this effect with technology, coining a new term called *increasing returns*. In the 1970s battle between video being displayed using VHS or Betamax, it wasn't clear which technology would win. But once VHS started winning more market share, more people bought VHS players, locking them into the technology for several years because it would be expensive to switch. Soon, Betamax died out. This arbitrary lock-in effect was largely dependent on timing. Musical instruments are another example of increasing returns and lock-in, in which there are almost infinite ways in which sound can be produced, but most people learn how to play a tiny, arbitrary subset of all possible instruments. Ever heard of less common instruments such as a gue, lituus, sambuca, or peri yazh? For contingent reasons, partly based on timing, some instruments dominated while others died out. Once a set of characteristics are locked in for what it means to be classified as a "guitar," design experimentation plummets. Standardization reigns supreme.

The same is true for modern dogs, which are also contingent accidents of timing. Dogs were domesticated in the mists of prehistoric human history, but modern dog breeds as we know them arose in a tiny sliver of time within Victorian-era Britain. Up until the late 1800s, variation between dog types was limited, and all were classified by their function. Then, a small number of people in the upper classes of English society—who were both rich and bored—decided to develop dog shows. The aristocrats associated with these shows, known as doggy people, gained prestige by breeding new types and classifying them. They established idealized breed characteristics, which drove specialization and standardization. There were two kinds of terriers in 1840. Now, thanks to that Victorian experimentation, there are twenty-seven. Jack Russell terriers are named after Jack Russell, a Victorian parson who created them to help him with fox hunting.* If you, like me, have a border collie for a best friend, its standardized features were locked in after a Scottish court case called the Great Collie Ear Trial, to determine whether a collie's ears should be pricked, tipped, or floppy. The dogs we see today would be completely different if new breeds were produced and standardized in America in the 1930s, or France in the 1770s. Our canine companions are yet another happy accident of timing and lock-in.

---

* If you own a Jack Russell terrier, you will either be pleased or dismayed to learn that every dog of the breed is directly descended from a terrier owned by a milkman in Elsfield, near Oxford. Jack Russell bought the dog and developed the breed from it. Its name? Trump.

Our simplified intuitions about cause and effect fail, yet again, because the exact same causes will have different effects at different times. Making matters more complex, the precise sequence matters, from the order of mutations that cause cancer to the order of choices we make. In our gardens of forking paths, it doesn't just matter which path we take, but when we take it.

We too often imagine that we can simply ignore the "noise," the flukes, the contingent uncertainty produced by our beliefs, where something happens, who's involved, or when it takes place. But we can't. Even our best experts routinely get it wrong. And that yields a disconcerting fact: we do not understand ourselves. The question then is this: Can we?

CHAPTER 11

THE EMPEROR'S NEW EQUATIONS

Why rocket science is easier than understanding human society

Imagine you're a king or queen, sitting in your palace, inviting sooth-sayers to share their wisdom with you at court. Two oracles approach. Both claim to have specialist knowledge about the future. The first proclaims that she can accurately predict a trend that will happen in six months. Then, the second oracle kneels before you and states with supreme confidence that she can predict, with certainty, an event that will take place on Saturday, April 26, in the year 3,000. Whom should you trust more?

The impulse is to go for the shorter time scale. Much can change in 975 years. But it depends on what's being predicted, which source of uncertainty each oracle is trying to tame. This becomes clear if I reveal that the first prediction is that American economic growth will be above 3 percent in six months, while the second prediction is that a total eclipse will occur on Saturday, April 26, 3000. I'd be willing to bet on the eclipse, but not the growth rate.

We often use the phrase "It's not rocket science." But, as I'll try to convince you—and, yes, I admit this sounds bonkers at first—it makes more sense to say "It's not social science" to refer to an extremely difficult problem. Geniuses are working on both kinds of problems.

But rocket scientists would admit that predicting the broadly stable behavior of planets and moons is a piece of cake compared to making correct long-term predictions within the complex systems of 8 billion intertwined humans.*

Nonetheless, much of our world is shaped by our flawed understanding of how humanity works. We allocate budgets and set tax rates based on economic forecasts that are rarely accurate beyond short periods. We go to war—or not—based on subjective risk assessments, which are then proven catastrophically wrong. Businesses sometimes invest billions based on speculative predictions of trends.

So far, we've seen that the world works in ways that are different from how we imagine it. That false image of reality persists because it is reflected back at us in flawed social research. Most of our modern oracles in economics, political science, and sociology entrench our storybook version of reality—the tidy myths that write out the important flukes of life as mere "noise." Much of our understanding of ourselves starts from the incorrect assumption that regular, linear patterns of cause and effect are stable across time and space. Our search for understanding is a "Does X cause Y?" search, which systematically downgrades the role of chance and complexity. But if the storybook version of reality used in most research is misleading, how can we present reality in a way that captures the contingent accidents and takes them seriously as drivers of change?

"All models are wrong, but some are useful," noted the statistician George Box. Too often, we've forgotten that lesson, conflating map and territory, wrongly imagining that our simplistic representations of the world accurately depict it. How many times have you read some

---

* Hyperion, a moon of Saturn, has a chaotic rotation. It's impossible to predict how the moon will be spinning in the future. The planets technically have chaotic orbits, too, but those only matter over long time scales (probably over millions of years).

version of "a new forecast says" or "a recent study discovered that" and accepted it at face value without examining the underlying assumptions or methodology? Social research is our best tool to navigate an uncertain world. It's often tremendously helpful. But if we want to avoid costly, sometimes catastrophic, mistakes, we need to have a more accurate recognition of what we can—and can't—understand about ourselves as we navigate a complex world swayed by the random, the arbitrary, and the accidental. It's time to be honest about how little we know with certainty. We need to take a brief dive into the world of social research and see how the sausage is made.

We can break down this problem into two parts, which I call the Easy Problem of Social Research and the Hard Problem of Social Research. The Easy Problem is derived from flawed methods. It can be—and should be—slayed. It's fixable. By contrast, the Hard Problem is probably unsolvable, as it's derived not from human error or bad methodology, but because some forms of uncertainty tied to human behavior are absolute and unresolvable.

Let's examine what's easy—and what's hard.

—

A decade ago, a prominent social psychologist, Daryl Bem, decided to test whether precognition or extrasensory perception (ESP) was real. Bem was no crackpot. He had studied physics at MIT, received his PhD from the University of Michigan, and taught at Harvard, Stanford, and Cornell. Using a standard research methodology, Bem conducted a series of experiments. In one setup, participants were shown two curtains on a screen, and they had to guess which curtain was hiding an erotic image behind it. Astonishingly, the participants guessed correctly more often than would've been predicted by random chance. Even more astonishingly, their predictive powers disappeared if the photos behind the curtains were not erotic. These results were verified using standard measures of statistical significance.

Bem had no compelling explanation for this apparently supernatural ability (nor any plausible theory for why participants were miraculously better at anticipating sexy images than nonsexy ones). But when Bem crunched the numbers, he confirmed his suspicion: some people could, as the title of his article suggested, "feel the future." Bem's 2011 research findings went through the standard peer review process and were published in one of the field's top journals, the *Journal of Personality and Social Psychology*. It made a big splash. The press lapped it up. Bem took a victory lap, appearing on high-profile TV shows.

But not everyone was convinced. Researchers Stuart Ritchie, Richard Wiseman, and Christopher French tried to replicate the results independently. When they conducted the same experiments, nobody in their studies could "feel the future." Here was compelling evidence that Bem's findings weren't as real as he suggested. However, when the trio tried to publish their challenge to Bem, they didn't find many takers. They were treading on old territory, they were told. Why repeat something that had already been studied? They finally got their paper sent out for peer review, the process by which research is anonymously evaluated by fellow academics. The first reviewer enthusiastically praised their work. The second reviewer rejected the paper, killing its chances at publication. The second reviewer's name? Daryl Bem.

Eventually, the new study—which challenged Bem's "discovery"—was published. It contributed to a long-overdue reckoning in social research, and particularly in social psychology, known as the "replication crisis." When researchers tried to repeat previous studies and experiments— including findings that had been widely accepted as conventional wisdom—they got different results. In one study from 2015, researchers attempted to replicate the findings of one hundred influential experiments published in prominent psychology journals. Only thirty-six passed the test. Bold claims were invalidated. Many things we thought we knew turned out to be wrong. This methodological earthquake shook our faith in accepted truths. It also raised an unnerving question: What else were we wrong about?

To prove a point about how broken the system of understanding ourselves had become, some researchers tried to get obviously untrue claims published. In one instance, researchers successfully produced seemingly statistically valid results proving that listening to the Beatles song "When I'm Sixty-Four" caused people to become younger. Not to feel younger. To *become* younger. Another study showed that women were more likely to vote for Barack Obama in 2008 if they were ovulating when they cast their ballot. These "findings" followed accepted methodologies and passed the standard statistical thresholds for publication. What was going on?

Social researchers are, unfortunately, sometimes guilty of using bad research methods or even deliberately gaming the system. This may seem like inside baseball, the esoteric concerns of someone, like me, who is professionally employed as a social scientist. But we all have a stake in understanding how social research is produced, warts and all, because it's often the information that our societies—and leaders—use to make decisions. Airing the dirty laundry of social research is useful as a corrective to our incorrect storybook version of reality, the imagined world in which X always causes Y and flukes don't matter. But understanding these flaws will also give you the intellectual tools to evaluate new "findings" with a healthy dose of skepticism.

I must now, I'm afraid, briefly bring us into the weeds. Bear with me, it's important to understand why we often get it wrong. Most studies conducted in political science, economics, sociology, psychology, and so on produce a quantitative metric known as a P value. I'll gloss over a lot of the mathematical detail here, but this is the measure that social researchers use as a shortcut to determine whether a finding might be "real"—or if it may be a study that discovers nothing, producing a "null result." When the P value is sufficiently low, researchers tend to interpret that as evidence that the finding *is* likely to be real, or, as it's formally known, *statistically significant*. The research community has largely agreed that the threshold for publication is a P value below 0.05. In practice, this often means that a study with a P value of 0.051, just above the threshold, won't be published, while the same study with a P value of 0.049, just below the threshold, likely will be. So, if that dreaded 0.051 number pops up, researchers can salvage the chance of getting published if they can creatively massage that P value down to 0.05 or 0.049.* After all, data can be sliced and diced in lots of different justifiable ways. Researchers might reasonably pick the option that yields the lower P value. Ronald Coase, a Nobel laureate in economics, put it thus: "If you torture data long enough, they will confess."

This threshold system embeds a terrible incentive into research production since publishing is tied to promotions, future grants, and career advancement. When researchers tweak their data analysis to produce a P value that's low enough for an article to be published, that's called *P-hacking*, and it's a scourge of modern research, one that causes us to misunderstand our world. But how widespread is it?

In one analysis of articles published in top journals, researchers found an enormous spike in the number of articles that had P values *just* below the threshold for publication, strong evidence that published research is being skewed by this system. The replication crisis, partially sparked by Bem's discredited ESP studies, blew the lid off P-hacking. Unfortunately, it didn't do much to stop it. When economists examined

---

* Some social scientists and statisticians, such as Jennifer Tackett and Andrew Gelman, have called for strict P value thresholds for statistical significance to be abandoned altogether. I agree with them. Gelman has also made the astute point that the reference point of a "null hypothesis"—that an intervention had no effect—is ridiculous because any intervention will have *some* effect.

data in twenty-five top economics journals many years *after* the replication crisis, they found that up to a quarter of results using certain kinds of research methods showed misleading data interpretations and potential evidence of P-hacking. That's a big proportion of research that affects how we see the world—and our place within it. These bogus studies, which often trace straightforward causes and effects, incorrectly reinforce the notion that we can write out society's flukes because reality—when contorted by P-hacking—does appear tidier and more ordered. X causes Y in a straightforward way, and we've got the low P value to prove it!

Bad research sometimes also sees the light of day due to an issue known as the file drawer problem. Think about it this way: If I ask you to flip a coin ten times, chances are about 5 percent that you'll end up with at least eight heads. If you flip a coin ten times in a row on twenty separate occasions, it's reasonably likely that you'll end up with at least eight heads on one of those twenty occasions. Now, imagine that you decide to repeat the ten sets of coin flips over and over *until* you got eight heads. When you finally do, you rush to tell an (easily impressed) friend your astonishing result: "I flipped a coin ten times and got eight heads! What a rare and interesting result!" To reinforce the friend's awe, you fail to mention how many times you tried, and failed, before that attempt.

Now, imagine the same logic, but with researchers trying to establish the legitimacy of ESP or precognition. Nineteen researchers conduct experiments and find nothing. No finding, no publication. They quietly take their findings and stick them in a file drawer, never to be seen again. Then, purely by random chance, the twentieth researcher "discovers" something astonishing that passes statistical benchmarks that are conventionally used in the field. Excitedly, she/he rushes to publish, and because it passes the statistical tests, it passes peer review and is published, with a big splash. The nineteen failed experiments are invisible because they never show up outside the file drawer. The one "successful" experiment is visible—and convinces people that an effect is real. That's the file drawer problem.

If you knew that nineteen out of twenty researchers had found no result, you'd question the "discovery," but those nineteen studies aren't published, are collecting dust in file drawers, so you're blind to their existence. Not only does the file drawer problem produce a pernicious form of *publication bias* that skews our understanding of reality by making it seem more ordered than it is, but it also creates strong incentives for researchers to focus on research that produces "positive" results of novel, intriguing findings, rather than the less rewarding but equally important tasks of showing no relationship between a cause and an effect, or of debunking bad research. Some researchers who made bold claims that later got debunked are still famous. Few have heard of those who do the debunking.

Unfortunately, bad research is just as influential as good research. A 2020 study found that research that failed to replicate (and is therefore likely to be bogus) is cited at the same rate as research that's been independently verified through a repeat study. These research flaws are often glaringly obvious. One study asked experts to read papers and then place bets on which research would and wouldn't be confirmed through replication tests. Overwhelmingly, their bets paid off. They could spot what was too good to be true a mile off. DARPA, the secretive American defense research agency, has even devoted resources to what some have called a "bullshit detector" for social research, with some success. But despite being reasonably easy to spot, plenty of bad research is still produced. And peer review—the mechanism of having scholars review one another's work to determine what merits publication—is, itself, a broken system. In one study, researchers deliberately planted severe flaws into research articles just to see how many would be caught by peer reviewers. Guess how many were? One in four.

These issues are layered on top of others that are more directly linked to our storybook version of reality. For example, an enormous body of research continues to imagine that we live in a linear world in which the size of a cause is proportionate to the size of its effect—the world mapped as though everything fits on a straight line. As we've seen, over and over, that's clearly the wrong way to understand our world. Yet many quantitative models in widespread use still imagine that world exists. Why? Because quantitative social science emerged mostly in the 1980s and 1990s, when computing power was expensive and less sophisticated. But because of arbitrary lock-in, that way of seeing the world stuck around—and continues to dominate most social research fields—even though we're now capable of much more sophisticated modeling.

Complexity science—and those who use the more sophisticated logic of complex adaptive systems to understand our world—sadly represents a tiny sliver of modern research production. We just pretend the world is one way when we know it's another way, and that causes us to make serious, avoidable errors in how we run society.

Now, some careless readers might take these critiques as a directive to throw the baby out with the bathwater—wrongly concluding that social research is pointless, meaningless, hopelessly flawed. It's not. We navigate our world much better than we did in the past because of important advances in the research fields that study ourselves. Social science graduate students are warned about the perils of P-hacking, and some journals are making wise efforts to address the file drawer problem. Transparency has substantially increased. Just because economists or political scientists get it wrong some of the time doesn't mean we should abandon economics and political science. Rather, we should work hard to solve the Easy Problem of Social Research. And it can be solved.

But what can't be solved, I fear, is the Hard Problem.

This is where everything gets pretty bewildering—and where it becomes clear that the seemingly random "noise" matters much more than we pretend. A few years ago, social scientists from Germany and the United Kingdom decided to try something novel. They would crowdsource research to try to answer a long-standing question that had divided both scholars and the public alike: As more immigrants arrive in a country, do voters become less supportive of the social safety net? Does an influx of immigrants create a backlash against social spending programs, such as unemployment benefits, from voters who see them as illegitimate "handouts"? That question is clearly important, but the evidence has so far been mixed. Some studies have said yes, while others have said no. What would happen, the researchers wondered, if they gave a bunch of researchers the same exact data and asked them the same question? Would they get the same answers?

Seventy-six research teams participated. There was no communication between them, so they couldn't compare notes or succumb to groupthink. Instead, they each took their own approach to decipher the hidden patterns in the numbers. When the study ended, the seventy-six teams had produced 1,253 mathematical models to estimate the effect of immigration on support for social welfare programs. None of the models were the same. Each research team took a slightly different approach.

What they found was extraordinary: a completely mixed result. A little more than half of the researchers found no clear link between immigration levels and public support for the social safety net. But the remaining teams were split—almost down the middle—with some finding that immigration eroded support for the social safety net, while others found the exact opposite. About a quarter of the models were saying yes, about a quarter were saying no, and half were saying "nothing to see here."

Trying to figure out what had happened, the researchers carefully examined each team's methodological decisions. But methodological choices could only explain about 5 percent of the variation in the findings. The other 95 percent was inexplicable dark matter. Nobody could explain it. The researchers drew a conclusion that matches the ethos of this book: "Even the most seemingly minute [methodological] decisions could drive results in different directions; and only awareness of these minutiae could lead to productive theoretical discussions or empirical tests of their legitimacy." The smallest decisions made a big difference. That creates unavoidable challenges that can't be wished away or solved with better math. Part of the Hard Problem is that we live within, as that paper's title suggested, a "universe of uncertainty."

Most of the time, seventy-six research teams aren't assigned to answer a specific question. It's almost always just one researcher, or a small group of them, working to tackle a question about our world. Imagine what would've happened if this question was asked of and answered by just one researcher or research team. An authoritative study might have been published showing that immigration decreases support for social spending, or one showing that immigration increases support for social spending. (This experiment shows that each finding would be about equally likely.) That lone study might have generated press coverage and changed public views on immigration. But it would be a toss-up whether the study said immigration was helpful or harmful to public support for social spending.

Now, imagine if the research was open-ended and each team could pick and choose whatever data it preferred rather than using the same data to answer the question. All bets would be off. But that's how research normally works. This is another part of the Hard Problem: we can't agree on what's going on even when we're working on the exact same question with the exact same data.

Unfortunately, that's not where the Hard Problem ends. What if the world we're trying to understand is, as Heraclitus reminded us, constantly changing? Take the study of dictatorships, for example. In the 1990s and 2000s, political scientists developed a concept called "authoritarian durability" to describe dictatorships. The idea was straightforward. Certain kinds of dictatorships survive for a long time, come what may. The theory made sense. The data backed it up. There were even palace poster boys for the theory, particularly in the Middle East—terrible tyrants such as Muammar Gaddafi of Libya, Ben Ali of Tunisia, and Hosni Mubarak of Egypt. Books were written about why their resilient regimes were so unshakable. Careers were made off those books. The concept became accepted wisdom. Dictators may be ruthless, but, by golly, they produce stability.

Then, in late 2010, a vegetable vendor in Tunisia lit himself on fire. Soon, the theory was seemingly obliterated. The poster boys were toppled, their palaces ransacked by angry mobs at the vanguard of revolutions. In a matter of months, Ben Ali fled into exile, Mubarak was arrested, and Gaddafi was killed. Authoritarian durability had apparently been badly wrong. Its chief proponents saw their stars fall and appeared to be deeply mistaken in their diagnosis of world affairs. But it had taken *everyone* by surprise, not just those in ivory towers. When I was working toward my doctorate, shortly before I traveled to conduct field research in Tunisia, I remember sitting in one professor's office and looking up at a poster she had hung on the wall to prove this point. It was a 2010 "political risk map" of the Middle East, created by people who were professionally employed to navigate risk and uncertainty. The safe, stable countries were shaded green. As I looked up at the map in early 2011, I noticed that every single green area on the map was currently on fire, in the midst of revolution or war.

Here's the crucial, unanswerable question: Was the original theory wrong, or *did the world change*?

It's plausible that Gaddafi and Mubarak were fragile all along, and we just misunderstood and overestimated them. But there's an alternative explanation: maybe the Arab Spring changed how Middle Eastern dictatorships function. What was once resilient became brittle. We accept these shifts in the physical world, the same way that water struck with a hammer absorbs a blow and mostly returns to its previous state, but freeze it, and the damage from a hammer strike becomes visible and lasting, etched into the ice. The water has changed, so the theory of its properties must change, too. Maybe the theory of Middle Eastern dictatorships was right, at least from the Cold War until around 2010, and then the world became a fundamentally different place.* Who knows? It's impossible to say for sure. Theories don't come with an expiry date.

However, when we conclude that social theories have gotten something wrong, many assume the theory was wrong all along. That's a mistake. Social theories aren't the same as those in chemistry. If cavemen could add baking soda and vinegar together, they'd get the same fizz as we do. Such enduring stability across time, space, and culture does not exist with social dynamics. Instead, a pattern of causes and effects may exist in one context for a time, until the social world changes and the pattern ceases to exist. In human society, some forms of causality shapeshift. Yet, we imagine that there is some Fixed Truth about ourselves that we're on the cusp of discovering, all while failing to recognize that the actual truth of our social systems is constantly morphing, shifting, eluding our understanding.

Everything gets even more baffling when you consider that we inhabit but one *possible world*. If you take the metaphor of the Garden of Forking Paths seriously—and you should—then our world is clearly the offshoot of countless potential paths that, but for a small tweak, we might have followed. But we have only one Earth to observe. That makes

---

* In the new research area of machine learning, a similar problem is often captured by the term *model drift*, but it hasn't been adequately addressed in most social research.

it impossible for us to know what's probable and what's improbable, particularly for rare, important events.

On September 10, 2001, for example, there was some unknowable probability that the attacks planned for the following day would succeed at killing a large number of people. Perhaps the terrorists had a 5 percent chance of pulling off the attack. Or, perhaps they had a 95 percent chance, almost a sure thing. But once 9/11 happened, we can't replay history and try to figure out which it was, because we only have a single data point: it happened.

Events with low probability sometimes happen, and so do events with high probability, but if an event only happens once, it's hard to tell whether the event was inevitable or a freak occurrence. You can keep flipping a coin to understand its properties, but you can't keep rerunning history. We simply can't know whether our world is a representative sample of all possible worlds, or if it's a crazy outlier, a one-in-a-billion bizarro reality. With just one Earth to observe, there are some things we may never know.

Let's return to Nate Silver's forecast in the 2016 presidential election, which predicted that Hillary Clinton had a 71.4 percent chance of victory. The models used by his website are an aggregation of polls, combined with "fundamentals" data that's included based on beliefs that Silver has about how elections tend to play out based on past patterns. Silver is a world-leading expert at estimating whether polls are accurately capturing public attitudes and then putting together a model based on that data combined with a rigorous set of assumptions. But he's no better than the rest of us at anticipating what's known as *epistemic uncertainty*, gazing into the future to predict highly contingent events (such as whether a foreign government will hack a political data server or whether a sex-offender politician's unrelated computer files will prompt FBI director James Comey to reopen a federal investigation days before the election). Yet, all of Silver's analysis has the veneer of hard science because it's incredibly sophisticated statistically, using thousands of simulations to prove his points. But there aren't thousands of elections. There's just one. It's inherently uncertain. We don't know whether the outcome we experienced—Trump winning—was an average outcome, an extreme outlier, or anything in between because we can't rerun history. You can find out that the underlying probability of flipping a heads in a coin toss is roughly 50 percent by simply flipping the coin over and over and observing the results. But can you tell whether a coin is fair or biased if all you have is a single flip that comes up tails? Obviously not, but for one-off events in a highly particular context, we too often try, and fail, to make that judgment.

When Clinton lost, Silver pointed to his model as a defense: 71.4 percent isn't 100 percent! There was nearly a 30 percent chance of Clinton losing in the model, so the model wasn't wrong—it was just something that would happen nearly a third of the time! If you say we were wrong, you don't understand math! This raises the obvious question: Could Nate Silver's model ever be "wrong" in that election? When the model predicts something with a low probability and it happens, then it's just the world that's being weird, not the model being incorrect. It's unfalsifiable, impossible to disprove. And when you can't disprove things, we get stuck in ruts—and our misconceptions about our world grow steadily worse.

—

Now, there's still a lingering question to address: If the old storybook worldview of ordered individualism, linear relationships, and big effects having big causes is so wrong, then why does it persist? Surely, if it was *that* wrong, it would have been replaced by something better and more accurate. Right?

To understand how science is supposed to work, consider the differences between basketball and rowing. Basketball teams with one exceptional star—the player who can score fifty points in a game—can win even if one of the players on the team is useless. That makes basketball, to borrow the term from Chris Anderson and David Sally, a *strong-link problem*. You can afford to have a weak link—so long as your strongest link is really strong. Spotify is another example of a strong-link problem. Millions and millions of terrible songs can be on Spotify and you'll still be happy, so long as it has the songs that you love best. The weak links—those terrible songs you never listen to—don't derail its effectiveness as a music platform. To improve a strong-link problem, you can ignore the bad stuff and focus on making the best stuff better.

Rowing is the exact opposite. Speed is a function of synchronization, balance, and timing. In a crew of eight rowers and one coxswain, if even one rower is a bit off, the boat will start to lurch side to side, the oars slapping the water and creating drag. The crew will lose. They're only as good as their *worst* athlete. That makes it a *weak-link problem*. Weak-link problems lurk everywhere. In the words of the psychologist Adam Mastroianni, "Food safety, for example, is a weak-link problem. You don't want to eat anything that will kill you. . . . A car engine is a weak-link problem: it doesn't matter how great your spark plugs are if your transmission is busted." To fix a weak-link problem, you can't focus on the best bits. You must eliminate the weakest links.

As Mastroianni points out, science is a strong-link problem. It's the best discoveries that change society, and it doesn't matter much if a bunch of bogus sludge clogs up low-level academic journals. Plenty of people had stupid ideas about how to split the atom. That didn't matter because all that was needed was one idea that worked.

In addition to being a strong-link problem, science is a realm of survival of the fittest. Science performs acid tests on theories. At some point they just don't work, and we can conclude that the theory has been falsified. Plenty of idiots still believe the earth is flat, but that doesn't affect our ability to engage in space exploration because it's the strong link, not the weak one, that matters. Science is therefore an engine of progress because it combines a strong-link problem with evolutionary pressures, which usually makes the strong links stronger over time. The weak ideas eventually die, relegated to the ash heap of scientific history. The strong ideas survive, driving human progress.

In principle, the same dynamics should apply to social theories. In practice, they don't. That, unfortunately, gives bad ideas staying power. In physics, even the smallest error is often enough for an idea to be rejected and replaced with something better. That's not remotely true in social theories. Recall that the IMF wasn't able to accurately predict recessions, yet the same economic models continue to dominate. Even theories with a strikingly bad track record—such as the notion that cutting taxes for the richest people in society leads to a major spike in economic growth—have an uncanny ability to persist for decades. It's difficult to falsify social theories. Getting it right some of the time is usually good enough for people to keep believing in the theory. That makes it harder to differentiate the gold from the garbage. As a result, the garbage isn't collected and taken away.

Even when a theory seems to fail, it's impossible to conclude that it has been falsified. Maybe that country was just an outlier. Maybe the economy dipped for another reason. Social complexity and ideology shield social research from the pruning of ever-stronger links that occurs in the natural sciences. The stubborn survival of incorrect social theories is also worsened because everyone *feels* like an expert on understanding society, which isn't true for quantum mechanics or nanotechnology. What should be a strong-link problem ends up getting distorted, and weak links can hold sway, even become the dominant paradigm. Few influential social theories are ever definitively disproven the same way as, say, the false belief that the sun rotates around the earth. As a result, we get a distorted view of reality reflected back at us anytime we read about how our societies are supposed to work. That fun-house mirror has a magic trick: it makes the flukes, the accidents, and the small, arbitrary changes seem invisible.

—

There's one more reason why our modern sages underestimate the importance of small, contingent tweaks as drivers of change. In the last several decades, social research has undergone a quantitative revolution. Our understanding of our world has become mathematized. This was made possible by a parallel revolution in computing, which made it far easier and cheaper to analyze large datasets and tease out patterns within them. To understand ourselves, we turned to regressions.

Quantification isn't, in itself, a bad thing.* Plenty of anti-quantitative intellectuals are reflexively suspicious of everything to do with math. I'm not one of them. Math governs everything. Our world is one of mathematical relationships, from the orbits of celestial bodies to the transcription errors of RNA within our cells. Everything, at its core, is math. You—and the networks of neurons inside your brain that are helping you make sense of this sentence—are determined by mathematical weights, constantly shifting, constantly updating. But sometimes, the equations that govern systems are so complex, so mind-bogglingly intricate, that trying to represent the underlying dynamics with mathematical precision is a fool's errand. It's theoretically possible, but utterly impractical.

---

* It can, however, produce problems when you believe that "the only things that are important are those that can be easily measured." This is now known as the McNamara fallacy, named after a U.S. secretary of defense during the Vietnam War, Robert McNamara. He insisted on measuring everything he could, and on paper the numbers showed the United States was winning the war—even as it lurched toward disastrous defeat.

One way of thinking about complexity is to ask, How long would the equation have to be to accurately depict what's going on? The evolutionary biologist David Krakauer explains, "Einstein could write down a beautiful equation like $E = mc^2$ that captures the equivalence between energy and mass and has all these beautiful implications for special relativity, in less than a line. But how would you write down an equation for a mouse?"

Krakauer's point isn't that an equation to describe a mouse doesn't exist, but rather that it would be unimaginably long. It's just too complex. So, too, is human society. But that hasn't stopped us from trying—and failing—to represent complex systems with simple, short equations. That's part of the reason why we're so often wrong. We often use pared-down linear equations to describe maddeningly complex nonlinear systems that can radically pivot on the tiniest detail. We're trying to describe a mouse in a few lines. It's impossible.

In 2005, the comedian Stephen Colbert coined a term that became widely used in American politics: *truthiness*. If a claim felt true, it was true, no matter the facts. Several years later, the economist Paul Romer riffed on Colbert's phrase to describe what he saw as a major flaw in economics research: *mathiness*. Romer argued that modern economics was using math to obscure rather than illuminate, to hide flawed assumptions and flimsy results behind the impenetrable wall of symbols and seemingly rigorous figures.

Modern attempts to understand ourselves too often end up producing equations that are nonsensical, the mathiness that Romer warned about. I suspect that's partly why, these days, I often look at increasingly sophisticated quantitative research in social science journals and shake my head. Imagine a civil war has broken out in your country. You wonder to yourself, "Will my friend Peter decide to grab a gun and join the rebel movement?" Wouldn't it be nice if there were an easy way to figure out whether someone will take up arms? Well, look no further. One piece of recent scholarship provides the formula for whether someone joins a rebel militia:

$$E\left[\frac{\mathbf{1}_{\{\theta<\theta_2^m\}}}{1-a+a\Pr(x_j<x_2^m)}\middle|x_i=x_2^m, \theta\geq\theta_1^m\right]$$

$$=\int_{\theta_1^m}^{\theta_2^m}\frac{1}{1-a+a\Pr(x_j<x_2^m|\theta)}\frac{\text{pdf}(\theta|x_2^m)}{\Pr(\theta>\theta_1^m|x_2^m)}d\theta$$

$$=\int_{\theta_1^m}^{\theta_2^m}\frac{1}{1-a+aF\left(\frac{x_2^m-\theta}{\sigma}\right)}\frac{f\left(\frac{x_2^m-\theta}{\sigma}\right)g(\theta)}{\int_{\theta_1^m}^{\infty}f\left(\frac{x_2^m-\theta}{\sigma}\right)g(\theta)d\theta}d\theta \quad (\text{let }g(\theta)\text{ be the prior pdf of }\theta)$$

$$=\frac{\int_{\theta_1^m}^{\theta_2^m}\frac{f\left(\frac{x_2^m-\theta}{\sigma}\right)}{1-a+aF\left(\frac{x_2^m-\theta}{\sigma}\right)}d\theta}{\int_{\theta_1^m}^{\infty}f\left(\frac{x_2^m-\theta}{\sigma}\right)d\theta} \quad (g(\theta)=1\text{ for uniform}).$$

Glad that's cleared up.

Rather than the emperor's new clothes, these are the emperor's new equations. They're clearly absurd, but nobody dares say so. In such equations, the flukes of life are dismissed as the "error term," to be written out and ignored. It's not just flawed, hubristic logic, it also engenders a fundamentally convergent worldview, in which the "noise" within the details are irrelevant because what matters are "signals"—large shifts in obvious variables that are identifiable, measurable, and countable. Even worse, when researchers notice a few unusual data points, some will "clean" the data by eliminating pesky outliers. The logic is straightforward: if you want to show a clear pattern, you can't let the equation be swayed by one unusual thing that happened once. In pursuit of regular findings within an irregular world, purge whatever doesn't fit. Detect the signal, delete the noise.

But that's madness. Because of self-organized criticality and the nature of social cascades, those outliers are often the most important bits of the data. It's akin to proclaiming the *Titanic*'s maiden voyage a success because 99.8 percent of the journey proceeded without a hitch or that Abraham Lincoln enjoyed most of the play. Nonetheless, outliers in data are sometimes deleted in the hopes of producing a neater, tidier equation, reflecting back at us the convergent, orderly world we think we're looking at in the first place.

This problem is compounded because the quantification of social research has meant that few contemporary social researchers come face-to-face with the human dynamics they're trying to understand.* If you study actual people and why they do things, the nature of intertwined complexity hits you over the head. In sterile, stripped-down data, it doesn't. Imagine going to a talk by an expert on elephant behavior who has never observed an elephant. It would be ludicrous. But for those who study humans, that detached aloofness has become the norm, not the exception.

—

"Now, wait a minute," you might be objecting. "Data is king. Looking at one elephant is all well and good, but what you really need to understand is *the herd.*" Sometimes, that's true. But the problem is this: for the most part, we don't understand the human herd, either. Understanding ourselves is most useful if we can use the insights we glean to solve problems and forge a better world. That's what social research is for—to make our world better. To achieve that lofty goal, we need to be able to predict what will happen if we lower tax rates or invade a country or try to rehabilitate, rather than punish, criminals. Yet, astonishingly, social science basically doesn't even try to make such predictions. Mark

---

* The political scientist Katherine Cramer was one of the few to anticipate Donald Trump's rise in 2016. Rather than doing data analysis on polls, she drove around Wisconsin and spoke to voters across the state. She captured the fury of rural voters in ways that weren't being captured within "harder" data.

Verhagen of the University of Oxford examined the top academic journals in a variety of disciplines. Over a decade in the *American Economic Review*, only 12 articles out of 2,414 tried to make predictions. In the *American Political Science Review*, that figure was 4 out of 743. And in the *American Journal of Sociology*, there were zero—count 'em—zero articles out of 394 that tried to make predictions.

Instead, social researchers chase what I call the Holy Grail of Causality. This is an admirable goal because we all know that correlation isn't causation, and disaster lurks when you conflate the two. But like the mythical Holy Grail, the Holy Grail of Causality proves elusive. We so badly crave clear evidence that one X causes one Y, and so long as we continue our quest for the Holy Grail of Causality within our storybook reality, we convince ourselves we might just find it. But in a complex world defined by tipping points, feedback loops, increasing returns, lock-in, emergence, and self-organized criticality, the search is going to be long and mostly futile. It's important to try to figure out which causes are most important, even if they're not the sole cause of an outcome. But that's a question not of pure causality, but rather of usefulness. Once we start chasing usefulness instead of the Holy Grail of Causality, we'd be better off doing what science tends to do best: putting rival theories through an acid test to see which ones survive— by predicting outcomes. Prediction for the sake of it isn't useful, but it can transform our lives and our societies if it allows us to get even marginally better at improving outcomes and avoiding disaster.

How good are we at predicting social outcomes? The answer lies with the Fragile Families Challenge. Roughly five thousand families were studied, each with a child born to unmarried parents. The purpose was to try to figure out how predictable our life trajectories can be. Data was collected about the same children at various snapshots in their lives: at ages one, three, five, nine, fifteen, and twenty-two. The collected data was exceptionally detailed, not just with quantitative metrics, but also with repeated interviews with the children. But here was the brilliant bit: after the data from the children who had turned fifteen was collected, it wasn't released. Instead, the researchers held a competition, in which they gave competing teams of scientists access to the data from the children at ages one, three, five, and nine. The challenge was to see who could best predict life outcomes for the children now that they were fifteen years old. Because the researchers already had the real-world outcomes, they could see how well the teams had done relative to reality. The teams used machine learning, the most powerful data analysis tool ever invented, and took their best shot.

The results took the researchers completely by surprise. They had assumed that some of the teams would be comically wrong, but figured that at least a few would have nailed it. Instead, the teams were *all* bad. On virtually every metric, even the best teams were about as good as a model that just used random guessing based on simple averages. That provides two lessons. First, if we want to get better at understanding ourselves, we need to make (bad) predictions, so that we can learn from those failures and develop new tools to iteratively make better predictions. Because of its surprising result, the Fragile Families Challenge will be a major catalyst for innovation in social research. We will get better at it, and new tools will overcome many challenges derived from the Easy Problem.

But the second lesson is this: our lives and the future of society are *really* hard to predict. By comparison, rocket science is easy. That's why the Hard Problem will continue to survive, blocking humans from ever fully understanding ourselves. In our complex world, some uncertainty cannot be slayed. No matter how hard we try, the flukes of life will continue to mystify us.

CHAPTER 12

COULD IT BE OTHERWISE?

*Are our lives scripted from the start, or do we
have the freedom to choose our futures?*

We must finally confront the elephant in the room, as I've carefully concealed it so far, trunk and all. I've argued that small, contingent flukes shape our lives—and that everything would turn out radically differently *if* small changes were made to our world. But I've ignored a crucial question: Is it possible to make small changes? Or are our lives and our world on a fixed trajectory that we're powerless to alter? Put more bluntly, do we have free will or are our lives scripted?

To most people, those are bizarre, even absurd questions. Of course things could be different! You could stop reading this book right now, or stand up and dance a *Fluke*-inspired jig, or spontaneously burn down your house. Each act would change your trajectory in some unknown way. But if you did any of those things, what caused them? We often speak of thoughts without considering what, precisely, we mean. How can we describe this mystical property we possess? Is it somehow independent of the causal web that drives every other aspect of change in our world? It's time to take a closer look.

Let's return to the question that launched our journey together: "If you could rewind your life to the very beginning and then press play, would everything turn out the same?" The question hinges on possible sources of variation in our world. Within the garden we call home, what causes our paths to fork? There are, I suspect, six main ways that most people would answer the "Would everything turn out the same?" question:

1. No, everything would be different because human choices are idiosyncratic. There are plenty of times when I've thought of doing something differently, and if my life were repeated, I might have made different decisions. (Let's call this the "I could have done otherwise" answer.)

2. No, everything would be different because God (or gods) sometimes intervenes to change things. (The "divine intervention" answer.)

3. No, the world would be at least a bit different because quantum mechanics proves that some things—at least at the smallest levels of atomic and subatomic particles—are truly random. Random processes, when repeated, produce different outcomes. (This answer isn't widespread among nonscientists, but let's call this the "quantum flukes" answer.)

4. Yes, everything would be the same because a supernatural being (God or gods) directs everything—and the universe unfolds according to that fixed divine script. (The "God decides everything" answer.)

5. Yes, everything would be basically the same because even though there would be small changes in the replayed life, the small stuff gets washed out and doesn't matter much. (The "everything happens for a reason" answer.)

6. Yes, everything would be identical because the world follows the natural laws of physics, and everything that happens is caused by what happened previously, in an unbroken chain of causes and effects. (The "deterministic universe" answer.)

This book has already provided a detailed refutation of the convergent storybook "everything happens for a reason" answer, so I won't press the point further. Nor will I debate the "divine intervention" or "God decides everything" answers. I don't believe either is true, but if a supernatural being does exist, we won't discover that with logical proofs. (It's also possible to believe in some form of a supernatural being and choose one of the other answers.) But for those who believe, it's a matter of faith—and faith, by definition, cannot be defeated by rational, scientific argument.

Within the realm of possibilities rooted in reason and direct evidence, that leaves us three options: the "I could have done otherwise" answer; the "quantum flukes" answer; and the "deterministic universe" answer. Put differently, any changes in a replayed tape of our lives would come either from unbridled free will or from quantum weirdness. Alternatively, the tape cannot be changed, no matter how many times it's replayed. Which view is correct?

The first question we need to answer is, Is our world *deterministic* or *indeterministic*? There's no third option. It must be one or the other. Those who say that replaying the tape of our life from the beginning would produce an identical result are determinists.* Those who say a replay could turn out differently are indeterminists.

If the world is deterministic, then everything is, in effect, scripted. Determinism is the notion that change is simply a function of initial

---

* This assumes that nothing is different—that the starting point (or initial conditions) of the replayed tape is exactly identical.

conditions (the way things are at a certain snapshot in time) and the natural laws of the universe. Everything that happens is directly and completely caused by that which came before it, a nonstop chain reaction of endless causes and effects, unfolding according to physics.

We accept determinism in many aspects of our lives. For example, if you strike a billiard ball and it knocks into another ball at the right angle, with the right amount of force, the laws of physics fully determine where both balls will end up. If you've struck the first ball perfectly, then you can have confidence that the second ball will end up going into the pocket. There's no magic, the trajectory isn't random, and the balls have no choice about where they will end up. Where the ball is now is determined by where the ball was a split second ago, combined with any physical forces acting on it. It's just physics. The state of the universe at every snapshot of time is determined by *antecedent causes*, or, in plain language, by what came before. The past determined the present and the present will determine the future. Everything links together, stretching back infinitely.

But if the world is fully deterministic—meaning that everything that happens is completely caused by what happened previously—then where does it end? What happened this instant was determined by what happened an instant earlier. Today was determined by yesterday. What happened on May 7, 1642, was determined by what happened on May 6, 1642, and that was determined by what happened on May 5, 1642, on and on and on.

Eventually, the stunning logical conclusion of a deterministic universe is that everything that happens was fully determined by the initial conditions and the laws of physics all the way back to the very beginning of the universe. The exact state of particles in the instant after the big bang, 13.7 billion years ago, determined the state of the universe in the next instant, which determined what happened in the next instant, on and on, endlessly, until the present moment. If causes and effects are fully determined in an unbroken chain of events, that means that if you brushed your teeth at 8:07 this morning or if your dog barked after seeing a squirrel in the yard, then that was fully and irrevocably determined by the initial conditions of the universe 13.7 billion years ago during the big bang. Everything was set in motion way back then, and our existence is akin to the most complex game of billiards ever played, with countless trillions of atoms colliding endlessly. If that's true, then everything in our lives is governed by the deterministic forces of physics. It couldn't have been otherwise—because physics doesn't allow for magical causes and effects. Weird, yes, but quite possibly true.

"Wait a minute!" you might object. "You've just devoted eleven chapters to telling me about a bunch of small, contingent changes and how if they'd been different, everything would be different. How does that fit in with some scripted universe where nothing *can* be different?"

Let's return to the *Sliding Doors* film, in which the viewer sees Gwyneth Paltrow's character miss her train in one scene, only to squeeze on board just in time in the next clip. The film imagines how different her life would be from that one seemingly meaningless change. Determinism says that only one outcome is possible given the exact state of the world at the time of the attempt—Paltrow's character was always going to make the train or miss it—but that doesn't negate the value in speculating as to what might have happened if the other world had come to pass. For a determinist, then, examining that which is impossible is nonetheless valuable. We understand our world better when we do something that no other species can do so effectively—explore that profound question "What if?"

Think about it this way: Determinism means that there's no way that the asteroid that killed the dinosaurs could have hit the earth one second later—it was on a fixed trajectory dictated by gravity and the other laws of the universe. But *if* it had, our world would be unrecognizably different. Now, imagine that humans are just more complex, living versions of that asteroid, our thoughts, actions, and behavior derived from physical processes. If that's true, then whether we can change the script or not, it's always useful to imagine how minuscule tweaks could alter the plot, even in scenes that will never be written.

In a deterministic system, small details still make a big difference. For example, a grain of sand on the billiard table, in just the right place, could divert the trajectory of the balls. Moving the grain of sand by even a millimeter might mean that the ball ricochets, narrowly missing the pocket. The rest of the game can be drastically changed by a nearly invisible speck. The laws of physics still govern what happens (there's still no supernatural mystery about why the ball behaved as it did), but a tiny change—a fluke in a grain of sand—can alter everything that follows. We grasp this intuitively when we think about taking a time machine and the risks of minuscule tweaks to the past, but somehow seem immune to the same deterministic logic when it's our present.

Determinism doesn't mean that we can predict the future. Chaos theory shows that seemingly insignificant tweaks to the initial conditions in a deterministic system can produce wildly different results over time. Our lives could therefore be both deterministic and utterly unpredictable. The question isn't whether we can anticipate what will happen (we can't), but rather whether everything is caused by what came before. There are no magical properties that make rain clouds— it's all physics, caused by what came before—but because the system is so complex, we can only reliably predict the weather a few days in advance. After two weeks or so, all bets are off, even for the world's best supercomputer. Determinism combined with chaos theory says that we can't change the script, but *if we could*, then even one microscopic change to the plot or the characters—even a butterfly flapping its wings as it flits across the stage—could alter everything that follows in the rest of the play.

"Wait a minute!" you might angrily object, yet again. (Do you need a hug?) "I routinely disprove this idea of some 'fixed trajectory.' I've learned from my mistakes in the past! I've decided to lose weight and now I go to the gym three times a week!" This is a common mistake people make when first encountering determinism, conflating the notion of things being causally determined with things being static. Determinism claims that the interlocking pattern of causes and effects is fixed and inevitable, but that doesn't mean that your nature or your behavior is fixed. If you, a smoker, watch a documentary that shows images of lungs riddled by cancer, you may decide to stop smoking. That fits perfectly with deterministic thinking, which would explain that the complex chain of causes and effects in the past led inexorably to the moment in which you watched that documentary. Why did you watch it? Because your friend recommended it to you. Why did she recommend it to you? Because she lost a friend to lung cancer. Why did that friend die of lung cancer? Every explanation goes on and on, back and back, an unbroken infinite regress of causes and effects that culminated, inevitably, in you watching that film. Likewise, it was equally inevitable that your brain—made of neurons, chemicals, hormones, and so forth—would react to that documentary by deciding to quit smoking, or not. The physical state of your brain determined what would happen if you received a new input (the documentary). When you did receive that new input, the output was already determined, a physical reaction in your brain that produced the experience of a mental decision.

The debate isn't about whether self-improvement or self-destruction is possible (of course it is), but rather where the *origin* of the self-improvement or self-destruction comes from. Determinists argue that complex interactions in the physical world govern the way that you decide to act. There are no disembodied thoughts that are independent of the physical matter that composes you. Instead, decisions come from the physical matter within your brain and body, which is shaped by what came before—your genes, your experiences, your interactions with your environment, your joys and traumas encoded into neural networks in your brain, even by the bacteria living in your gut and what you ate for breakfast this morning. It all fits together in a causal chain to produce fully determined outcomes, as fixed as a chemical reaction. In determinism, nothing that happens is *uncaused*.

Indeterminism, by contrast, suggests that the script can change. If you rewound your life to the very beginning and pressed play, starting with the exact same initial conditions, things could unfold differently. Multiple possible futures could flow from an identical starting point. We're not stuck on a fixed trajectory. But that leaves a bit of a mystery: What could cause the deviations from that trajectory if everything is caused by that which came before it?

Humans have answered that question differently throughout history. Early pre-Socratic philosophers, such as Heraclitus, proposed a deterministic universe as early as twenty-six hundred years ago. In Eastern philosophy, some concepts such as the Buddhist idea of *pratītyasamut-pāda*, often translated as "dependent origination," or the Ājīvika school of Indian philosophy, incorporated similar echoes of determinism in their ideas about how the universe works.

However, whenever determinism was proposed, some in the ancient world objected vehemently. "If you accept that we live in a deterministic universe," they warned, "then you'll have to abandon the notion of free will!" Eventually, some got around this roadblock with a convenient idea called an atomic "swerve." Roughly twenty-three hundred years ago, the Greek philosopher Epicurus tried to salvage free will within a deterministic worldview by proposing that atoms occasionally deviate randomly from their expected course. No scientific mechanism was proposed for this swerve, but it provided a convenient way to soften the philosophical blow of a deterministic universe. If some things were random, then the world was comfortingly uncertain, perhaps leaving a bit of wiggle room for free will.

But the seemingly magical swerve didn't convince everyone. In the first century BC, the Roman poet Lucretius highlighted the lingering problem in his treatise *De Rarum Natura*, or *On the Nature of Things*.

If ev'r all motions are colinked
And from the old ever arise the new . . .
Whence this free will for creatures o'er the lands,
Whence is it wrested from the fates?

The great thinkers of natural science, philosophy, and theology grappled with this enduring problem for the next two thousand years, with divergent views about determinism, the role of God, and the degree to which human characters within a divine script were free to alter the storyline. Some developed ideas about *theological determinism*, which implied that determinism was true, but that the script was written and directed exclusively by God. Calvinists, for example, elaborated a theory of predestination. In the words of John Calvin himself, "All events whatsoever are governed by the secret counsel of God. . . . Nothing happens but what [God] has knowingly and willingly decreed." Others continued to insist that free will was both real and meaningful. God may have created the universe, but sins are freely chosen, scripted neither by divine law nor the laws of physics.

Then, in 1687, Isaac Newton's *Principia* was published, sparking a scientific revolution that forever changed how we think our world works. Newtonian physics or Newtonian mechanics—which accurately explains how many objects behave in the universe most of the time—is deterministic. It dominated scientific thinking about change for centuries, leading to thought experiments such as Laplace's demon, and a belief in a clockwork universe. But Newton's laws don't explain everything. In the last century, three major challenges to Newtonian physics have been discovered. His laws don't apply well to the very small (which requires

227

quantum physics), the very fast (which requires special relativity), or the very large (which requires general relativity).

Quantum mechanics most warrants our attention. I won't go into the technical details here (if you're interested, read up on the double-slit experiment, Schrödinger's equation, Heisenberg's uncertainty principle, quantum superposition, or wave function collapse). But scientific research shows that the very smallest particles behave in strange ways. While these baffling behaviors have been thoroughly documented, checked, and rechecked through rigorous experiments, there are fierce disagreements about what the results mean. Some scientists have given up on interpreting any larger meaning or philosophical truths from quantum effects—a camp known as the "shut up and calculate" thinkers. But the dominant interpretation of quantum mechanics is known as the Copenhagen interpretation. It remains contested because, like all interpretations of quantum mechanics, it's riddled with several unresolved problems.

Here's the crucial bit for us: the Copenhagen interpretation implies that at the tiniest levels of matter, some aspects of our world are completely random, governed not by determinism, but by probabilities. The interpretation implies that some changes at the subatomic level are unlike anything else in the known universe. They are genuinely uncaused—meaning true randomness reigns. To an extent, quantum mechanics was a bit like a scientifically rigorous resurrection of the swerve that Epicurus proposed more than two millennia ago. This interpretation gave rise to a scientific paradigm that concluded the world is indeterministic, not because we can change things, but because things change randomly by their very nature. We might call this camp the *quantum indeterminists.* To them, the world isn't scripted or on a fixed trajectory. However, that variation doesn't come from us, but because of subatomic strangeness, the baffling behavior of the tiniest building blocks of matter. Replaying the tape of life would lead to divergent outcomes only because the random behavior of subatomic particles will never repeat in exactly the same way twice. If true, our world is governed—at the smallest levels at least—by genuine randomness.

Some interpretations of quantum effects remain deterministic (such as Bohmian mechanics, the many-worlds interpretation, or superdeterminism). The debate is unresolved. Nobody *really* knows what's going on! However, what's broadly agreed on within much of the scientific community is that one of these two propositions is correct:

1. Determinism is true.

2. The world is indeterministic, but only due to quantum weirdness.

You might notice that a certain proposition is missing from these options: the notion that we, alone, can be independent authors who change our own scripts. Where's free will in this scientific consensus?

———

The experience of free will is universal. Humans can't escape certain sensations no matter how hard we try. But when you check those sensations a bit more carefully, the certainty begins to flake away. When I consider where "I" am—in a metaphysical rather than a geographic sense—it's logically clear to me that I am, quite clearly, somewhere inside my body. But if my entire body is "me," then getting a haircut or cutting my fingernails would change something fundamental about who I am, and that seems like a strange way of viewing ourselves. Instead, the sensation of existence, of navigating the world, makes me feel that the real "me" is lurking somewhere behind my eyes, as though everything from my limbs to my liver is simply a minion of Brian HQ, with the real "me" as a disembodied CEO perched somewhere within my brain toward the front of my skull.

This sensation is so universal and comes so naturally to us that a widely held seventeenth-century scientific theory about the origins of human life suggested that each sperm cell contained a microscopic fully formed human, now known as a homunculus, who was believed to grow into a person. That theory—preformationism—lingered on for two centuries before being disproven. It reflects our desire to imagine an eternal executive—a deciding soul—within each of us, an irreducible essence who controls everything, freely thinking, freely choosing.

Since most people don't debate determinism and free will over a beer (hats off to you if you do—we'd enjoy a pub trip together), few have carefully contemplated how to reconcile the sensation of free will with truths discovered by modern science. Clearly, no homunculus is pulling levers in our skulls, but it's tempting to imagine that the brain performs the same function, the same miniaturized CEO who just happens to be a bit wrinkled, dressed in pink and gray. Yet, swapping out the mental image of a disembodied shrunken version of ourselves for 86 billion unromantic neurons somehow feels like a downgrade. Worse, it leads to an uncomfortable question that we cannot answer to our satisfaction: Am "I" just a physical being, the sterile aggregation of chemicals and lumps of matter?

This line of questioning brings us, inevitably, to the same conundrum that once stared down Descartes. Where, physically, is our mind, or our soul? His answer was that those mystical entities were nonphysical—that our brains are composed of physical matter but our minds are not, a concept known as *dualism*. Mental processes can exist separately from the physical body, and our bodies cannot think.

But as we began to unlock the secrets of the world with science, it became clear that the idea proposed by Descartes would violate every known law about the way the universe works. Everything has a physical basis, which means that your thoughts, memories, impulses, whims, and indeed your will all reside within you, tangible entities composed of matter, their properties produced by the emergent interactions of countless complex neural networks.

Once we accept the physical basis of our minds—which we must if we are to adhere to the basic principles of scientific reason—then an immediate and worrying conundrum moseys into view, like an inconvenient and uninvited guest. If there's no homunculus directing things, and if our thoughts, desires, and wills are all physically housed within us, then are we just the by-product of a relentless stream of chemical interactions that we are powerless to change? We like to think we're calling the shots, somehow miraculously independent of the stuff that forms our brains and bodies. But we've got a problem: free will, at least in the sense of human minds as independent agents operating separately from the physical composition of our brains, quickly runs up against quite a few stubborn laws of physics.

If Helen of Troy was the face that launched a thousand ships, the debate over free will has launched a thousand definitions. Philosophers contort the concept beyond recognition, twisting both what it means to be "free" and what it means to have a "will." Nobody who debates these ideas professionally can agree on what either word means. But for most people, the concept is relatively straightforward, and it means that you, and you alone, can choose what to do. Crucially, you have an overriding sense that at any given moment you could do something different—that your choice is not scripted for you beforehand. You may not be a homunculus pulling levers within your skull, but you feel equally unshackled. You're free to keep reading, or to slam the book shut, or to toss it out the nearest window, clobbering an unsuspecting bystander below. This common conception of free will, that at any given moment we are free to choose, completely separately from the deterministic physical reactions going on in our brains, suggests that we have the power to "do otherwise." That comforting notion is known as *libertarian free will.**

Our feeling of possessing libertarian free will is central to the experience of being human. It leads to a common argument: we feel as if we have free will, therefore we must. This is terrible logic. Perceptions do not make reality. To us, the earth doesn't "feel" like a giant round ball hurtling through space around a burning ball of gas that allows us to live in its warmth, but it is. As we've already seen with the Fitness Beats Truth theorem, our brains have repeatedly evolved to deceive us. The magician produced by our minds is a master of illusions. What we feel is not what there is. The laws of physics don't care about your feelings.

If you are a rational thinker who believes in science, then anything that happens must either be caused or uncaused. There are only two options. If something is caused, then it is the necessary product of what came before—things can't be caused by something that hasn't yet happened. If you throw a brick at a window and it shatters, the window couldn't have been broken by the shards of glass. Similarly, in this view, our thoughts are caused by the arrangement and functioning of our neurons and the rest of our bodies, which is caused by a whole series of complex factors: DNA transcription; mutations; chemicals; the neurological encoding of our upbringing, past experiences, and memories into brain networks; and so on. We independently control none of that. (Good luck trying to stop cell division with your thoughts.)

So, if we are to rescue libertarian free will from the jaws of physics, then we must propose scientific heresy: that human brain matter has a unique magical property, replicated nowhere else in the known universe. That's why some philosophers disparagingly refer to libertarian free

---

* This has nothing to do with libertarian political views, but rather is derived from the notion that we have the liberty to do otherwise from that which we choose to do at any given moment.

will as the "ghost in the machine" argument—the idea that within our brains is some otherworldly, supernatural substance that is completely independent and totally different from every other type of matter in the universe, allowing us to make decisions. Are we somehow able to produce thoughts—nonphysical thoughts with the power to reshape physical matter—conjured from the ether? We may furrow our brows as much as we like, yet how this might work remains unclear.

If libertarian free will does exist, it would violate everything we know about the way the universe works, as it would require us to be, in the words of the philosopher Daniel C. Dennett, "spectral puppeteers" who are able to control our brains from the outside. The physicist Sabine Hossenfelder refers to libertarian free will as "logically incoherent nonsense" for anyone who "knows anything about physics." Most neuroscientists, the people who study the brain most closely, are also overwhelmingly skeptical, if not downright dismissive, of this conception of free will. It requires, to put it bluntly, a belief in metaphysical magic.

If we are to accept that our thoughts, feelings, desires, preferences, and wills are the by-product of physical matter, then we have to question what we mean when we say "free will." Perhaps it just means that our behavior is internally caused. Consider whether you like this book. I hope that you do, and you surely hoped you would, too, or you wouldn't have started to read it. But as you've read, you have reacted to it. Your reaction lies somewhere on a spectrum between those who have started accosting random passersby to tell them how great it is, and those who are contemplating when would be the most opportune time to burn it on a satisfyingly large bonfire. Now, here's the question: Could you *choose* to react differently? If you hate the book, could you choose to love it? (Please try before posting a review.) You could tell yourself that you do or twist yourself into mental knots trying to persuade yourself that you should, but ultimately your reaction is determined by antecedent causes, coded into the physical state of your brain and body, shaped by the laws of physics. But might you still have free will even if your gut reaction isn't strictly "up to you"?

"Absolutely!" say the *compatibilists* (the name refers to the idea that free will and determinism are compatible ideas). These thinkers readily admit that your thoughts and preferences and desires are likely to be physically caused by "background causes," that which came before. Nobody puts a gun to your head and forces you to order a cheese rather than a pepperoni pizza, but your choice will be determined by your taste buds, how long it's been since you had cheese or pepperoni pizza, the way the neurons in your brain responded in the past while eating each type of pizza, whether you had recently been to a hog farm and it upset you (or not), whether you were given cheese or pepperoni pizza as a child, whether you were born with a certain allergy, and so on. Each of those experiences gets translated into a physical structure in your brain, which affects your future decisions. If you pick pepperoni pizza, then it logically follows that choice was always going to be the outcome in that moment—it was inevitable, given your physical state. There's no scenario in which you, in that exact moment, with your body in that exact state, and your neurons arranged exactly as they were, could have picked cheese pizza instead. When we speak of cravings, we don't imagine that a choice is involved. But what is a choice between pepperoni and cheese pizza if not just a less intense form of a craving with an equally physical basis?

This idea becomes even clearer if we switch from hunger to thirst. You can decide to drink water, but do you choose to want to drink water in the first place? Do you sit down, reflect, and then say, "I choose to feel thirsty!"? Your body decides for you. When you then decide to drink water, you're responding to your body, and the complex interactions within it. But what's true of thirst is true of everything else. There's no mystical transformation from a thought about a bodily need to one about a desire, a want, or a preference. Yet, people continue to discuss their thoughts as though a disembodied wizard-like homunculus is in their heads—the real "them"—who's calling the shots.

When I was eight years old, my parents sat me down to watch the four-hour-long epic film *Gettysburg*, a fictionalized depiction of the 1863 American Civil War battle, complete with star performances by Martin Sheen and Jeff Daniels. They showed me the movie because our family was about to go on a road trip from Minnesota to the East Coast, which would include a stop at the Gettysburg battlefield. I was a nerdy kid (which, I'm sure, comes as a total shock to you), and I was mesmerized by the film, then transfixed by the visit to the battlefield. Something happened in my brain that created that reaction, which I can't explain.

When I returned home, I shunned my Nintendo and quickly devoured dozens of books about the Civil War—an entire bookcase of those books is still in my childhood bedroom—reasonably bizarre behavior for a second-grader. But thousands of pages couldn't quench my thirst. I wanted to know everything there was to know about the moral justice of the war, about Antietam and Shiloh, about Stonewall Jackson and Joseph Hooker.* I begged my parents for subscriptions to not one, but two Civil War magazines—*America's Civil War* and the *Civil War Times*. I even pleaded with them to let me become a Civil War reenactor, to let me dress up on weekends as a child soldier in the Union Army. (Thankfully, my parents did not let me commit social suicide and got me the magazines for my birthday, but rightly drew the line at reenactment.)

---

* Joseph Hooker was a relative of mine, on my maternal side. The term *hooker* was used for a prostitute before him, so it's not true as is often claimed that the term originated because of him, but the word's usage stuck when his troops, centered in Washington, DC, frequented a red-light district that became known as Hooker's Division. It's yet another case of linguistic lock-in. My grandma called Hooker the "black sheep" of the family.

Why did I become so obsessed? I have no idea. Nobody in my family was interested in it. I didn't wake up one day and actively choose to be an eight-year-old Civil War aficionado, accosting the mailman to see if he had the latest edition of the *Civil War Times*. I just had an obsession that I couldn't explain. Through a complex mix of genes, experiences, upbringing, parental decisions, innate nerdiness, social influences, and thoughts and chemical reactions produced by the billions of interconnected neurons within my brain, I was hooked. I was then free to follow my newfound passion—and I did. So, is that free will?

Some say yes, but of a slightly diminished kind. We are free to want what we want, they say, but we cannot will what we will. We are free because we can pursue our preferences, even if we can't independently choose our preferences. To a compatibilist, my Civil War fixation was a form of free will because I decided to pursue what I found interesting, free from coercion (except for my parents urging me to dial it back just a little so the other kids didn't think I was a total weirdo).

Compatibilists sometimes point to aspects of human cognition that do appear to be unique among living beings. The philosopher Harry Frankfurt has argued that we have a form of free will because we have, in his phrasing, "second order desires." Drug addicts may pursue what they want (the first order desire—drugs), but they may wish that they didn't want to crave drugs (the second order desire—to no longer be addicted). Your mouth waters when you see a bar of chocolate before bed, but you might wish you didn't have that reaction. Compare humans to most other living beings, and it's less clear that they have second order desires. My border collie, Zorro, is obsessed with his Frisbee. Does he ever wish that he were less obsessed with it? (Zorro is, I modestly note, a canine genius, but I doubt he's ever acting on anything other than first order desires.) Frankfurt's observation is both interesting and persuasive, but it doesn't solve the underlying problem. Where do the second order desires come from? From our brains interacting with other people, objects, and beings as we navigate our social and cultural environment. That means our thoughts are still subject to the laws of physics, following an unbroken series of causes and effects, just like everything else. We're back to square one.

If you think the compatibilist line of thinking is a cop-out—a redefinition of free will into a watered-down version that isn't *really* free will—then you're likely to be a *hard determinist*. Hard determinists reject compatibilism on the grounds that it's just trying to salvage free will through wordplay, a linguistic contortion hoping to twist us up in philosophical knots until we forget what *free will* really means. The neuroscientist Sam Harris argues that the logic of compatibilists is akin to saying, "A puppet is free as long as he loves his strings." Or, as he memorably describes it, it's as though the compatibilists are pointing at Sicily, but proclaiming that they've discovered Atlantis. Redefining the concept of free will doesn't save it, Harris insists. It's just wishful thinking.

I don't believe in free will, though I acknowledge that these questions are mind-bending, baffling, and mysterious. We don't understand consciousness, so it's plausible that some new discovery will change how we answer this question. In discovery, never say never. But if libertarian free will is indeed what we have, then pretty much everything we know about science would have to be wrong. Compatibilist conceptions of free will aren't at odds with science so much as they're redefinitions of what it means to be free.

In the face of this bewilderment, some have tried to use quantum mechanics as a bit of unexplained scaffolding to prop up free will. That argument is nonsensical. Yes, some aspects of our world may be irreducibly random. But if your choices deviate from the script of antecedent causes—that which came before—only due to randomness, well, are you any more free? Nope. Your behavior being dictated by nature's random-number generator isn't freedom. No matter how much we water it down, free will won't sprout from quantum dice.

Nonetheless, an ineffable something does seem to be within us. We, as humans, do not feel like a well-dressed pile of cells. We love and hate. We reason. We are brought to tears by literature, inspired by heroism, swayed by beauty. We are ever-striving beings. Some of us would sacrifice ourselves in pursuit of an idea, or to save a loved one, without hesitation. It is tempting, therefore, to rebel against the sterile claims of science. "To hell with these logic games! I know what free will is—and I've got it. Don't try to tell me I'm some form of a meat computer!" These are understandable sentiments, and scientists would be foolish not to acknowledge how much we don't understand about our mysterious existence. All I can do is present the pieces of the puzzle as I see them, and how they might fit together.

So, take your pick. Solve the puzzle your own way. But after reading this section, with your brain and body in exactly the state they're currently in, I'm afraid it's probably inevitable which solution you'll choose. That choice, free as it feels, was likely affected by everything that came before you, infinitely stretching back into the mists of time.

———

A world devoid of libertarian free will has some potentially unsettling implications. Some of the moral implications, for example, are used as counterarguments against the concept itself. "If we don't have libertarian free will, then our framework of morality doesn't make sense!" you might object. I disagree, but even if that claim were true, the argument is a bad one. I wish cancer didn't exist, but that wish doesn't negate its existence. Nonetheless, the moral implications of rejecting libertarian free will are worth considering. To help unpack them, let's consider a murderer.

Charles Whitman grew up as a polite Boy Scout with a newspaper route and an extraordinarily high IQ. As an undergraduate in the 1960s, he studied mechanical engineering at the University of Texas at Austin.

By the age of twenty, he had married his sweetheart, the happy couple having a promising life ahead of them.

Then, at 6:45 p.m. on July 31, 1966, Whitman sat down to type a chilling note. "I do not quite understand what it is that compels me to type this letter. . . . I do not really understand myself these days. . . . However, lately (I cannot recall when it started) I have been a victim of many unusual and irrational thoughts." He wrote of intense headaches and included a strange request—to have an autopsy performed on his body after he died to see if his actions were affected by anything abnormal in his brain.

A few hours later, he drove to his mother's house and killed her. He then drove home and murdered his beloved wife, stabbing her five times. He left notes expressing despair and remorse for both murders. The next morning, he went to the University of Texas campus, climbed to the top of the campus clock tower, and opened fire. He killed four-teen people before he was killed by law enforcement officers. After Whitman died, medical examiners performed an autopsy. They found a tumor in his brain, which appeared to be pressing on his amygdala, a key area of the brain for emotions and decision-making.

Does that change your view of Whitman?

For many, the answer is yes. It undercuts our certainty in his malicious intent—that he, and he alone, chose to murder people. Suddenly, when the tumor enters the picture, our intuition about his maliciousness wavers, and we begin to see him less as a monster and more as an unwilling victim of cancerous cells. Most of us have a sense that he is less morally responsible because he wasn't fully in control of his actions and choices.

But if libertarian free will is a delusion, nothing more than a neuro-logical magician's conjuring trick, then can we ever feel that someone is morally responsible for his or her actions? If our thoughts come from our neurons, and we can't actively control our neurons with some magical material we call our minds, then the way we think and the actions our thoughts produce are not so different from thoughts and actions swayed by a tumor. One act is swayed by malignant tissue, another act swayed by healthy tissue, but does that make them morally different? We can't control healthy tissue within our brains any more than we can control cancerous cells. If we can accept that I couldn't choose to be interested in the Civil War, but rather my thoughts and fascination were the inevitable result of neurological and biological processes according to the laws of physics, then why would it be any different for choices that had moral weight?

We don't choose our genes, our parents, our childhood experiences, or the physical composition of our brains, yet those factors clearly determine our future behaviors. Does it make sense to blame people for their actions—or to praise them for their achievements? If not, that's incredibly disconcerting, as it seems to let "evil" people off the hook. It's a difficult notion to stomach, and it raises an even more problematic question: How could we justify punishing criminals if they had no free choice?*

The justifications for criminal punishment fall into three main categories. Some think that punishment is for retribution, an eye for an eye—punishment for the sake of it. Others see it as a tool of deterrence, locking up criminals to prevent future crimes. A third group sees punishment as a means to rehabilitation, turning a criminal back into a productive member of society. If morally responsible free will doesn't exist, then punishment for the sake of punishment makes no sense. But the other two justifications remain applicable. Even if murderers don't have free will, they still need to be taken off the streets to reduce harm to society. Punishing them will still deter future crimes, and rehabilitation is still intrinsically valuable. Criminals would still therefore need to face

---

* Some compatibilists, such as Daniel C. Dennett, argue that free will under their definition also implies moral responsibility. Others disagree. Like so many issues in philosophy, it's unresolved.

punishment, but the logic behind it would put less of an emphasis on condemning them as monsters who freely made awful choices.

We already have a precedent for this kind of pragmatism in an unfair society that creates winners and losers through no fault of their own. While intelligence is difficult to define, most of us willingly accept that some people have greater natural intellectual aptitudes than others, irrespective of education levels. But smart people don't choose to be smart and less intelligent people don't choose to be less intelligent. We mostly accept that it's a complex mix of nature and nurture, but nobody could reasonably claim that children with a high IQ and wonderful, supportive homes that allowed them to develop to their full potential somehow independently "earned" their intelligence. Nonetheless, society has made pragmatic judgments that we would all be better off if the head of cancer research at Oxford or Harvard is someone who was fortunate enough to be born intelligent and have that intelligence nurtured rather than someone who wasn't. It's nonsensical to morally praise Einstein for being a genius. But that means it's just as nonsensical to morally condemn a psychopath with a damaged amygdala if he truly couldn't have done otherwise.

We should celebrate Einstein because creating a pantheon of intellectual heroes has pragmatic value. It inspires us, bolstering our natural impulse for striving. Similarly, we can and should continue to condemn people who behave in awful ways because that still serves a function, even if it wasn't, technically speaking, their "fault" in the simplistic way we usually think about blame. As Harris puts it, "Viewing human beings as natural phenomena need not damage our system of criminal justice. If we could incarcerate earthquakes and hurricanes for their crimes, we would build prisons for them as well. . . . Clearly, we can respond intelligently to the threat posed by dangerous people without lying to ourselves about the ultimate origins of human behavior."

I suspect he's right. But it would be foolish to imagine that rival viewpoints are without merit. As neuroscience research progresses at its breakneck pace, these will be the great philosophical debates of our time.

Strangely, these debates rarely rage within mainstream social research. You might think that free will, determinism, and indeterminism would be central concepts for people trying to understand why things happen in human society. But outside of psychology, or the niche subfield of the philosophy of social science, it's basically an intellectual wasteland. It's rarely discussed. I was taught about determinism for about an hour in grad school, then it disappeared from my professional life forever. Appropriately, the reason for its glaring absence is contingent, hinging on a historical moment that caused determinism to become enshrined as a dirty word for sociologists, economists, and political scientists.

Pernicious strains of determinism with vile social agendas emerged in the late nineteenth and early twentieth centuries. As discussed previously in "The Lottery of Earth" chapter, environmental or geographical determinism was misused to justify a series of despicable ideologies, including racism and colonialism. Moreover, eugenicists used biological determinism, the false notion that we are exclusively the product of our genes, to justify a junk pseudoscience that aimed to "prove" white supremacy. Understandably, a major backlash occurred within social science against any form of argumentation that involved even a whiff of deterministic logic. But in rightly targeting the vile ideologies that had co-opted determinism, the backlash destroyed any belief within social science that the world follows *any* deterministic processes, even though it clearly does.

As a result, entire fields that seek to understand why changes happen in our social world have rejected deterministic arguments not for rational reasons, but for moral ones. Twentieth-century critics of determinism argued that determinism "had dangerous moral and political consequences," which could provide an "alibi for evading responsibility and blame." This led most social science to operate under a logically incoherent set of beliefs, including a highly influential theory called structuration, which explicitly argues that humans have libertarian free will, "in the sense that the individual could, at any phase in a given sequence of conduct, have acted differently."*

This is the "magic" that philosophers and physicists have warned about. Yet, so much emphasis has been put on freely made individual choices as the main drivers of change in modern society that the word *determinism* has become an insult. Calling a theory "deterministic" is one of the harshest social science attacks, a shorthand that aims to discredit ideas as both absurd and morally repugnant. The "ghost in the machine" continues to haunt how we understand ourselves and our world.

But we shouldn't shy away from ideas that challenge how we think about our lives and how we behave. We should vigorously debate these concepts, not just dismiss them because they're unsettling. Turning on the light to examine something that lurks in the darkness is better than pretending it's not there.

—

To me, determinism is awe-inspiring. Our present moment is woven together with infinite threads that stretch back billions of years. Try to pull on one thread, hoping to just change one microscopic corner of the tapestry, and the entire fabric would begin to unravel. Pull one thread, change the entire image. Tweak one strand from the past, and you likely wouldn't exist, or perhaps you'd have a different partner, or different children. But for a different tiny change, you might also have avoided that horrific heartbreak, or the loss of a loved one, or close friend. This leads to a deeply moving conclusion. Our best and worst moments are

---

* Structuration and similar theories operate under the assumption that what we do is a mix of *structure* (the norms, rules, and cultures we live within) and *agency* (our libertarian free will).

inextricably linked. The happiest experiences of your life are part of the same thread in which you suffered the most crushing despair. One couldn't follow without the other. That may sound strange, but I obviously wouldn't exist if my great-grandfather's first wife hadn't murdered her family, so my most joyous moments are unavoidably tethered to that horrific tragedy. In a literal sense, my most euphoric moments couldn't exist without their suffering. That doesn't mean that we should celebrate suffering, but that future elation will emerge directly or indirectly from seemingly senseless suffering can be a consoling truth that blunts our worst moments of pain. Conversely, my joyous moments will, in some way, lead inexorably to someone else's agony, or my own. That's just the way it works. For good or ill, I find this mind-bendingly beautiful, providing the most vivid sense of interconnection between all beings, intertwined across space and time.

If you consider yourself an isolated individual who's completely in control—Lord of All the Beasts of the Earth and Fishes of the Sea—well, then the loss of libertarian free will is a crushing blow. But if you think of yourself as a constituent part of a greater whole, a sentient, complex being that is constantly causing and being caused by the unity of an interconnected world stretching back well beyond your most distant ancestors, then acknowledging the deterministic tapestry can feel exhilarating.

If someone else existed in your place, the world would be different. Because you exist, you will have an impact on the world, some good, some bad, but all part of the tapestry. You matter, down to the littlest, most insignificant decisions you have made or will ever make. Your words, your actions, even your thoughts and feelings, will have ripple effects that emanate widely, beyond what you'll ever see or realize, even well beyond your lifetime. The decisions you make now, whether chosen by a libertarian ghost or not, will partly determine which future humans will exist, and also which world they will inhabit, thousands of years into the future. That is, in a word, incredible. What you do matters—all of it, every little bit. That may not be free will as most of us conceive of it, but I'd say that's certainly a kind of will that's worth having.

Is it important whether you feel, deep within your bones, that you could have behaved differently? For me, it's sufficient to know that I can freely pursue my desires. Is it really so terrible to imagine that your actions and your thoughts—which will always feel like your own—have been caused not by a phantomlike presence or a homunculus, but instead by a potluck mix of all that you've experienced, your brain chemistry, and everyone and everything that came before you?

You are the contingent culmination of the entirety of cosmic history. Everything had to be exactly as it was for you to exist, just as you are, in this precise moment, in this exact world. That leads us to a simple, wondrous truth: we all are the living manifestation of 13.7 billion years of flukes.

Perhaps we can finally accept that we will never be able to fully understand our own existence. Nonetheless, Kurt Vonnegut gives us good advice on how to live fully within that uncertainty: "A purpose of human life, no matter who is controlling it, is to love whoever is around to be loved."

CHAPTER 13

WHY EVERYTHING
WE DO MATTERS

The upside of uncertainty in our chaotic, intertwined world

Our journey together, alas, nears its end. We have now glimpsed a world that is entirely unlike what our intuitions and perceptions try to tell us, reinforced by conventional wisdom, stuffed into straitjacket models. This new world may bewilder us, but at least it's closer to the truth. Our storybook notions of why things happen are a lie. Our perceptions evolved to deceive us. Reality is entirely interconnected, constantly changing, ever swayed even by the minuscule and the minute. That means that our trajectories, as we wade through the rivers of our Heraclitean world, are contingent on a near-infinite number of factors. If we change anything, we change everything. These truths lead inexorably to a mystifying revelation: the world is uncertain, unexplainable, and uncontrollable.

But what are we to *do* with that information? How are we to live?

As the essayist Maria Popova reminds us, "To live wonder-smitten with reality is the gladdest way to live." How many of us, trapped scurrying on the hamster wheel of modern life, have become unsmitten? It's time to let go of those false idols of mastery and control, and to marvel at the beauty that lies within uncertainty, if you only know where to look.

Perhaps our modern malaise is derived from an obsession with trying to control an uncontrollable world, an extension of a flawed worldview that traps us in an impossible quest for certainty. That quest always ends in disappointment. The way we now live is entangled with the way we misunderstand the world, regarding the inevitable flukes of an interconnected world as mere curiosities and coincidences rather than the green shoots of an elegant, complex garden displaying its unknowable majesty. When our economic and political models of reality reduce a breathtaking world full of the richness of fractals and Fibonacci spirals into sterile, fixed linear equations that can be solved with a mere handful of easily measured variables, our vision of ourselves and our surroundings becomes duller. Life itself, in that futile longing for control, can morph into a solve-for-X slog, where we constantly feel that we are just one hidden factor—one product or one promotion—away from what we really want, which, when we buy it or achieve it, turns out to be yet another unsatisfying mirage.

Yet, we continue to worship at the Altar of Progress in the Church of Control. Most of our waking lives are devoted to achieving some undefinable human progress—Can we hit the Q3 target?—which will allow us to tame an ever-greater wedge of the world. But when we try to distill every waking effort into a struggle for ratcheting optimization, it's the essence of being human that's dissolved away, leaving only a residue of clockwork, atomized inner barrenness. We toil in a quixotic frenzy, to squeeze the last cold drop of efficiency from corporate strategies, life hacks, and to-do lists, a drive-thru strategy to living. Do more, even if you enjoy each bit less. Life's victories have become, to many, eliminating moments of slow, quiet reverence and replacing them with hyperproductive multitasking as we chase Sisyphean goals that will never be enough to satiate us. It feels, to many of us, like a checklist existence. But our greatest moments are often the least efficient, those fleeting experiences in which our desires to achieve are put on hold, and the prize is just a moment of ecstatic being.

This is the paradox of twenty-first-century life: staggering prosperity seems to be tethered to surging rates of alienation, despair, and existential precariousness. Humans have constructed the most sophisticated civilizations ever to grace the planet, but countless millions need to medicate themselves to cope with living within them. We can control more of the world than the ancients could have imagined, scraping minerals out of the earth, powering them with a flow of electrons we can direct or disrupt, conjuring up images on our screens of wizards and aliens and superheroes that once existed only in fanciful minds. Now, we're even starting to be able to *invent* other minds, capable of producing their own art and literature. Where has it got us? On every measurable metric, we're better off than ever before, but many of us feel worse off for it.

This is a despair of our own making, according to the German sociologist Hartmut Rosa, not because of technology, but because of a futile yearning to make the world controllable. The categorial imperative of late modernity, Rosa writes, is straightforward but bleak: "Always act in such a way that your share of the world is increased." Relationships become a means to an end, reducing a magically networked existence into mere "networking." The writer and former nun Karen Armstrong shares this uneasiness, noting that when people visit museums, they no longer simply absorb being next to an object with world-historical implications. Rather, they take a photograph with their phones and move on, seeking "to own it in some way, as though it does not become real to them until they have a virtual copy." But that aspiration for control is misguided, Rosa argues, for "it is only in encountering the uncontrollable that we really experience the world. Only then do we feel touched, moved, alive." Even in life's planned celebrations, we most remember the unplanned flourishes.

Nonetheless, we devour the lies of hucksters who tell us that true control is merely one self-help book away from our grasp. Not only is the storybook version of reality real, they insist, but *you* are the main character within it. You, alone, can shape the plot—if you'd only tap into a magical wellspring of positive thoughts.

Take, for example, Rhonda Byrne's *The Secret*. It has sold 30 million copies and been translated into more than fifty languages. Byrne insists that the misfortune of scant possessions and poverty is a mental state, waiting to be vanquished by the enlightened thinker. "The only reason any person does not have enough money is because they are blocking money from coming to them with their thoughts," she claims. The X of positive thinking causes the Y of wealth. If only all the poor, huddled masses of Negative Nancies and Debbie Downers could afford her book! If they could, they would learn astonishing lessons, including the notion that "thoughts are sending out that magnetic signal that is drawing the parallel back to you." (Never mind that magnets attract their opposite, not their parallel.) What a shame that enslaved people two centuries ago didn't just imagine themselves differently! Their chains were but manacles in their minds. In Byrne's mumbo jumbo, victims of terrible misfortune only have themselves to blame.

This is nonsense. People in Hiroshima didn't choose to be vaporized with a new weapon they didn't know existed, nor did anyone in Kyoto choose to be rescued by the sentimentality of a long-forgotten holiday-maker. Henry Stimson didn't decide to be born knowing that one day he would play God in Japan. Claude Monet didn't paint to save a man's life with a tie inspired by Monet's artwork during a fateful September day seventy-five years after his death, nor did Joseph Lott decide to survive with an assertion of control when he received the gift of a Monet tie. Lott, like all of us who are currently alive, just happened to be at the right place at the right time. These are not freak moments of unusual powerlessness in which unlucky people became the plaything of the Fates, but rather glimpses into the way the world really works. Countless distant decisions, accidents—happy and not—separated by space and time, come together in ways that we could never anticipate, and our lives change because of them. It can be comforting to accept what we truly are: a cosmic fluke, networked atoms infused with consciousness, drifting on a sea of uncertainty.

We don't have to control everything. It's okay.

The problem isn't just that Byrne and her fellow opportunists are selling pseudoscientific nonsense such as *The Secret*, but that they're selling a road map to the impossible, a guide to taming an untamable universe. It also entrenches the corrosive idea that any despair you confront can be solved with more money, more control, more individual action. Byrne's lies obliterate the intertwined nature of reality, suggesting that you alone determine your destiny. The only reason to look inward, it's suggested, is so that you can conquer more of the outward world, acquiring it like the museum photograph. The worst excesses of the self-help industry, particularly with books such as *The Secret*, is too often the self-obsessed narcissist's guide to the universe, in which everything in existence can be beckoned to you if you just use the right words or thoughts to call it to your servitude. Even if the world worked that way (it doesn't), research has established that humans tend to get stuck on a *hedonic treadmill*, in which we race and race as fast as we can toward the things that we think will make us happy—usually stuff and status—but in the end we find ourselves in the same place, right where we started.

This isn't to say that we should be stoics constantly chanting the Serenity Prayer, retreating from the injustices of the world, or accepting misfortune without trying to change our lot in life. Striving is part of what it means to be human. Instead, it's simply to insist that the way we view the world matters, and too many of us have been sold a lie. You can't control the world by chanting incantations or summoning riches with your thoughts. Putting your faith in faux oracles will lead to constant disappointment.

But it's not just that worship within the Church of Control makes us miserable. Paradoxically, misguided attempts to assert control make the world *less* controllable—and in dangerous ways. Mao's disastrous Four Pests campaign in China—in which the dictator tried to tame nature to his whims and instead wiped out millions of people due to famine—is but one example of the hubris that has backfired against us. Complexity science, as we have seen, establishes the risks of living on the "edge of chaos," in which a system teeters on the precipice of a tipping point, the moment when Black Swans become most likely to blindside us. Yet, what do we do? We race toward the edge, hoping to slay every last bit of slack within our social systems, prostrating ourselves before the God of Efficiency. In recent years, we've fallen off the cliff repeatedly with human-made calamities, amplified by fully optimized systems with no room for error, yet we stick to the same gospel, no matter the toll.

As a result, the world—which was already an uncertain jamboree of accidents and flukes—has become even more uncertain. That kind of uncertainty, in which lives and livelihoods teeter on a knife's edge of our own making, laces catastrophic risk into our societies. We should learn our lesson, build more slack into our systems, and trade perfect efficiency for better resilience. It's a better, sturdier way to live.

But strange as it seems, there are good kinds of uncertainty—and they make us human. Consider this: If you could know, with absolute certainty, everything that would happen in your life, from a spreadsheet of impending heartaches to a calendar that would mark the precise moment of your earthly end, would that knowledge beckon to you?

A world without lived mystery would be a cold, disembodied one, in which we drift through life never surprised, never pausing to contemplate how nature spun us into its endlessly intricate web, never overwhelmed with an existential sense of awe. We would be living zombies, with numb brains, stuck in a world of vast, calculable emptiness. Modernity is a collective mission to destroy the unknown, but we would be lost without it.

As a species, we delude ourselves when we imagine that we would prefer a certain world that we could fully control. In truth, we crave a healthy balance between order and disorder, fulfilled by our world of contingent convergence. The physicist Alan Lightman notes, "We love the structure of Western classical music, as well as the free-wheeling runs or improvised rhythms of jazz. We are drawn to the symmetry of a snowflake, but we also revel in the amorphous shape of a high-riding cloud. . . . We might respect those who manage to live sensibly and lead upright lives. But we also esteem the mavericks who break the mould, and we celebrate the wild, the unbridled and the unpredictable in ourselves." Life would be boring and monotonous if everything were structured and ordered, but pure disorder would destroy us.

Nietzsche wrote that this tension comes from the human impulses for both the Apollonian and Dionysian. Both were sons of Zeus, but Apollo represented order, logic, and reason, while Dionysus is said to be an irrational agent of chaos who loves to party and dance. To fully live, we need both.

Many of us feel that we have too little of the Dionysian, so we try to shoehorn a little bit more into our lives. Too often, it proves as futile as the insomniac trying to force themself to fall asleep. Within the misguided mentality of the Church of Control, Dionysian moments are to be engineered, not discovered. Everything, even joy, can be turned into a metric. Did you really go on that walk in the wilderness if your Fitbit didn't register your step count? How many of you are looking at these words because you've put "read *Fluke*" on your to-do list? But if every goal leads to yet another one, and that one leads to another one, are we not just always striving for an unattainable vista that never arrives? How many actions do we take in modern life that are not *for* something else?

Embracing the beauty of uncertainty means a bit less emphasis on how your individual action in the present can produce an optimized future, and a bit more emphasis on celebrating the present that has been created for you, the symphony of our lives that is being played by an orchestra of trillions of individual beings hitting their respective notes across billions of years, culminating in this utterly unique, contingent moment.

It's humbling to recognize that you're not the conductor of the symphony but are rather one vibrating string within it. That truth situates us within something vast and unknown. We can't know where we are going, or why we're here (if there is any reason). It leads to three of the most important words in existence: *I don't know*. Wislawa Szymborska, the Nobel Prize–winning poet and writer, cherishes that phrase. "It's small," she says, "but it flies on mighty wings. . . . If Isaac Newton had never said to himself, 'I don't know,' the apples in his little orchard might have dropped to the ground like hailstones and at best he would have stooped to pick them up and gobble them with gusto."

The good society is one in which we accept the uncertain and embrace the unknown. To do so, we must make sure that each of our daily lives is full of exploration, simple pleasures, and pleasant surprises—flukes—and moments where the anxious futures embedded in to-do lists are obliterated in our minds, at least for a time, by a feeling of joy in the present moment. Aristotle wrote not of fleeting happiness, but of lasting *eudaemonia*, or flourishing. To erect the framework for flourishing, we need a reliable superstructure that provides for our basic needs, a bulwark against a sense of precarious survival. What we don't need is a society that regularly gets upended by major systemwide shocks that jerk us in undesirable directions, ripping us out of the present to worry about our existential future. We've engineered a society that is, in too many ways, the opposite of that good society, in which day-to-day life is overoptimized, overscheduled, and overplanned, while society itself is more prone to unwanted surprises, of catastrophic upheaval and destructive disorder. We've invented an upside-down world where Starbucks will remain unchanging, while rivers dry up and democracies collapse. We'd be better off with daily serendipity but stable structures.

But if we can draw our societies back from the edge of chaos, how can we live better individual lives within them? What are the lessons we can draw from our new, slightly bewildering worldview? Yet again, evolution can teach us something: that experimentation will bring us closer to Aristotle's eudaemonia.

—

For many, despair in modernity is derived from a feeling of power-lessness, even a crippling sense of pointlessness. If you're a warehouse employee staring down the prospect of being replaced by a robotic arm and having bathroom breaks tracked by digital surveillance, it's hard to get overwhelmed by a sense of cosmic meaning. "I don't have any effect on the world!" or "None of this matters!" are the refrains of modern misery. Yet, one of the beautiful implications of accepting the intertwined, contingent way the world *really* works is that everyone—and everything that person does in a lifetime—matters. Many of our ripple effects will be hidden to us, as with the Stimsons' vacation in 1926. The truth of this fresh worldview provides a more potent message than any self-help book can imagine: we may control nothing, but we influence *everything*.

All of us matter, though some of us will influence events within our lifetimes in more or less profound and visible ways. But if we want to maximize the chance that our actions will matter even more, then the best pathway comes from one of the finest innovations our species has ever evolved: cooperation. Humans who work together create change together.

How should we live within this world of potent influence? Humans, like all creatures, face a trade-off between two strategies for interacting with the world: *explore* versus *exploit*. To explore is, by definition, to wander, to not know where you're going. To exploit is to race toward a known destination. The trade-off between them has been an area of intense research within mathematics, particularly relating to a hypothetical puzzle known as the multiarmed bandit problem. The core idea, however, doesn't require any numbers. Trying a new restaurant that you've never been to before after you happened upon it is an explore strategy. Going to the same restaurant you've been to a hundred times before because you know it's your favorite is an example of an exploit strategy.

These ideas are related to what's known as a *local maximum* versus a *global maximum*. Imagine you're a mountain climber, and your biggest goal in life is to reach the highest possible elevation. You're based in the Alps, so you wander around for a bit, pick out the highest peak, and climb it with a sense of smug satisfaction. *Job done,* you think to yourself. Then, you meet another Alps-based mountain climber, who tells you that he's climbed much higher. For when he summited the highest peak in the Alps, he kept exploring, wandering until he arrived in the Himalayas, where he climbed Everest. The Alps climber reached the local maximum, unaware that a global maximum was waiting to be conquered. The lesson is that exploiting too soon—before you've explored far enough—means you get stuck always climbing the local maximum, unaware of better possibilities.

In this way of thinking, achieving the global maximum is always the best. But that's not always true. Maybe the Alps are good enough. Sometimes, all we need is the local maximum. (If it's not broke, why fix it?) Unless you're a foodie, constantly exploring new restaurants might leave you perpetually unsatisfied, craving that one dish you already know you love. Other times, if the system itself is uncertain, trying to get to the highest point can be a mistake—particularly when it's near a cliff. When the landscape can change in an instant, from a fluke or a Black Swan, then the logic of local and global maxima end up on shaky ground. In ever-changing terrain, it's sometimes useful to turn to the wisdom of randomized experimentation.

Through random tinkering, evolution has forged ingenious solutions to complex problems, the likes of which are far better than what we, as self-reflective, intentional, and intelligent beings, could ever come up with. In biology, this is known as Orgel's second rule: evolution is cleverer than you are. If life had not been built on exploration built on mutation, selection, and genetic drift, then we would still be stuck as archaebacteria 3.7 billion years later. The unthinking, unreflective engine of relentless experimentation within life has given rise to the most astonishing diversity of body plans, survival strategies, even consciousness, carved out of trial and error. Explore, then exploit, then explore, then exploit. To explore effectively, sometimes you must fully embrace uncertainty. Rather than trying to engineer better solutions deliberately, the wisdom of evolution is unleashed by turning to randomized solutions to tackle problems that can't be solved by "smarter thinking."

One intriguing example comes from the Kantu people, who live in tropical forests on the island of Borneo. The Kantu cultivate rice and rubber. The crops are completely different. The rice crop is fickle. Because the Kantu farm it in areas with poor soil, minor fluctuations—pests, rainwater, floods, or drought—can cause the same field to be bountiful one year, barren the next. Because of that sensitivity, the "best" place to cultivate the rice can't be predicted. By contrast, rubber is a sure thing. So long as the Kantu follow good farming techniques, the rubber crop will be bountiful, year after year. For the Kantu, the rubber follows well-defined patterns, repeating from one year to the next. By contrast, rice cultivation is fundamentally uncertain and can't be controlled by the Kantu. But despite that irreducible uncertainty, the Kantu must still decide where they should plant the rice.

They have developed an unusual strategy: look for divine signs in the movement of sacred birds. Out of hundreds of birds on Borneo, the Kantu determine where to plant rice based on the movements and calls of seven species: the white-rumped shama, the rufous piculet, the scarlet-rumped trogon, the Diard's trogon, the banded kingfisher, the maroon woodpecker, and the crested jay. The Kantu believe the birds can guide them. Interpreting the omens from the birds is an art, depending on the order in which they show up, which calls they make, and the position of the human observer relative to the birds. It's so complex as to be effectively random. At first glance, randomness seems like a poor strategy for deciding where to plant the food you need to survive.

But when researchers studied the Kantu, they found something astonishing: their crop failures were substantially less common compared to those of other communities. The reason was simple: in an uncertain, ever-changing environment, putting all your eggs in one basket that you think you understand is a bad idea, even if that basket has reliably been a safe place for your eggs in the past. Other communities that tried to control the environment by optimizing based exclusively on past results courted disaster. Minor fluctuations changed the growing environment and caused all their crops to fail in the same way. Meanwhile, the Kantu had found, by superstitious accident, a highly effective way to diversify their agricultural portfolio. They did so not by trying to squeeze the last drop of efficiency out of farming based on a flawed theory that would afford them absolute control, but rather by randomizing the process as a means of coping with unavoidable uncertainty. (The Kantu embody the wise advice that my grandfather once gave me on how to have a successful life: "Avoid catastrophe.")

In our world, some of the challenges we face are "rubber problems" and others are "rice problems." Some closed systems are remarkably stable—rubber problems—in which the best strategy is to get better and better, optimizing to the limit, because the global maximum is fixed and you just need to climb it. But when you come up against an open, complex system, full of feedback loops, tipping points, and irreducible uncertainty—rice problems—well, you better make sure that you're constantly experimenting because otherwise ruin may find you. For rice problems, it's easy to get seduced into thinking that you've found the global maximum, only to then fall off a cliff. Once you factor that cataclysmic uncertainty into the equation, the optimal solution over time may be a bit farther down the mountain, where it's still pretty high up, but not quite so precarious.

We rarely demarcate rubber problems from rice problems. Take, for example, how data analytics have been used to revolutionize baseball, the so-called *moneyballing* of the game (the name refers to the book *Moneyball* by Michael Lewis, later turned into a film starring Brad Pitt). It details how data analytics have transformed professional baseball, replacing intuitions and folk superstitions with hard-nosed, data-driven calculations. In closed, noncomplex systems (such as a heavily regulated sports competition), those calculations are extremely effective at predicting outcomes. In baseball, the only metric that matters is whether you win. Moneyballing helped teams win. The data nerds took over the corner offices. Baseball, treated like a rubber problem, became far more optimized.

But there was a problem. The analytics were so effective that the game became boring. Pitchers knew exactly where to throw the ball to minimize the chance of a batter making contact. Strikeouts—which are dull to watch and kill the prospect of an exciting rally—increased. Baseball became more like two spreadsheets of convergent probabilities battling it out on a diamond. The sport was optimizing for the wrong thing. Sports are interesting precisely because they're action-packed uncertainty. Instead, the action became slower, more methodical, sterile. Baseball's fan base shrunk. Major League Baseball finally reversed course and changed the rules for the 2023 season to "de-moneyball" the game, aiming to generate more on-field action. The suits had solved the rubber problem. But fans wanted baseball to be more of a rice problem, swayed by a bit more randomness, the superstition of rally caps, not the cold data of Monte Carlo simulations.

This saga was merely a matter of sporting preference, so the consequences of that miscalculation were hardly dire. But you get lulled into disaster—both as an individual and as a society—if you mistake rice problems for rubber ones, moneyballing everything, only to be wiped out by an uncertain event you could never have anticipated. Much more of our world is governed by rice problems than we believe, and that means that the best solution is often to be found through a healthy dose of randomized experimentation producing diverse solutions, with slack built in, before we turn to exploit mode.

Many of our seemingly less intelligent animal counterparts already live by these principles. Just over a decade ago, researchers attached tracking devices to a series of fish, sharks, and other marine creatures to see how they moved around the sea. Using more than 13 million data points, they began to map where the creatures went and compare those movements to mathematical formulas. Astonishingly, their paths from shallow seas to deep oceans followed two equations for random motion: Lévy walks and Brownian motion. A Lévy walk is characterized by lots of little movements in various directions, followed, every so often, by a big movement in one direction. Brownian motion, by contrast, is just a series of small movements within the same area. When sharks didn't know where to find their next meal, they entered explore mode—Lévy walks. But when they stumbled upon a tasty school of fish, they switched to Brownian motion, exploiting the supply of nearby food.*

This isn't a good strategy for grocery shopping. So, how might this approach help in human society? Consider how we allocate research funding. It's impossible to know where research will lead when it

---

* Recently, Jimena Berni, a researcher at the Brighton and Sussex Medical School in southern England, has led experiments in which she used genetic wizardry to raise fruit fly larva with deactivated brains. Even without functioning brains, the fruit fly larva displayed an explore/exploit pattern that matched Lévy walks, raising the possibility that these patterns have evolved—a mathematical instinct for navigating an uncertain world.

starts, and it's also impossible to anticipate what future problems will need to be solved. Research is, by its nature, a task of exploration. The destination is unknown. But organizations that offer research grants often want to see evidence of exploitation: "Tell us the destination if you want the money!" Studies have shown that research grant proposals that promise the moon—a tangible discovery, with obvious and immediate impact—are more likely to get funding. They don't necessarily deliver that impact more often. And we are often saved by exploration with no obvious application.

In the mid-1990s, Katalin Karikó believed her work had promise, so she applied, over and over, for grants. She struck out each time, rejection after rejection. Venture capitalists also deemed her ideas a waste of money. After these repeated failures, her university gave her an ultimatum: quit or face demotion. Karikó persisted. We should be thankful she did. Her work, on mRNA, would soon save countless millions of lives, as it was the basis of the most effective coronavirus vaccines during the COVID-19 pandemic. It wasn't useful—until all of a sudden, the world changed, and it became the most useful scientific discovery in existence. She won a Nobel Prize.

To decide who gets grant money (and in other similar decisions of irreducible uncertainty), we may be better off first setting a threshold to make sure that the proposals are serious and thoughtful. But beyond that threshold, some grant allocations should be made randomly. If we were certain what the next breakthrough would be, or what the next challenge would be, then it would be time to follow a strategy of exploiting knowledge. But since that certain world doesn't exist, we should sometimes use the power of randomness to explore the unknown.

The lesson is that, sometimes, life's best flukes come *not* from ever-more-precise analytics of a seemingly stable past, but in exploring a fresh, uncertain future—sometimes even aimlessly. In closed systems with objective metrics that are geared toward problem-solving (such as deciding where to allocate health-care spending in this financial year), by all means, moneyball everything. But for the rice problems of life—the areas of unavoidable uncertainty—then treating them like a rubber problem can at worst be disastrous, and at best suck the joy out of life's awe-inspiring wonder.

These lessons are too often ignored in a culture obsessed with productivity, efficiency, and control. If there's no obvious output (or *deliverable*, to choose my least favorite dystopian word), then what's the point? But exploration also requires letting your thoughts drift without purpose. Millions now treat undirected contemplation as a waste of time, a frivolity to be life hacked out of your goal-driven schedule. A drive or commute must be filled with radio, chatter, mindless games, music, or podcasts—but rarely silence. Even thirty empty seconds while waiting in line at the grocery store beckons many of us to our smartphones. (To these charges, I, too, plead guilty.) In one recent study, when participants were left alone for between six and eleven minutes in a room that was empty except for a device that could give them a painful electric shock, many opted to shock themselves rather than to sit alone with their thoughts. One man shocked himself 190 times in less than ten minutes.

What happens when we give up a bit of control and let ourselves drift and explore a bit more without direction? We know—with clear evidence—that moments of diversion, in which idleness envelops us, and our minds linger away from directed action, are often moments of brilliance. These moments often provide us with insights in a phenomenon that the poet John Keats once called "negative capability," when mankind "is capable of being in uncertainties, mysteries, doubts." This is a verified phenomenon. In scholarly language, it's sometimes referred to as leisure-time invention, in which intellectual lightning strikes only when our minds turn their gaze away from a problem. Galileo's discovery that a pendulum could be used to measure time, which paved the way for later clocks, was said to have emerged in a quiet moment of intently watching a chandelier suspended from a cathedral ceiling swing back and forth. Einstein said that many of his most important insights emerged while he was playing the violin. And the Wright brothers imagined their flying machine during a relaxing picnic while watching buzzards.

The French mathematician Henri Poincaré, one of the greatest thinkers of the last two centuries, swore by the magic that happens when you don't try to assert control. For fifteen days, he toiled with a problem, sitting at his desk, scratching out possible solutions with his quill, to no avail. The harder he worked, the more frustrated he became. But then, "one evening," he explains, "contrary to my custom, I drank black coffee and could not sleep." Once he stopped trying to tame the problem with concerted action, Poincaré marveled at what came next: "Ideas arose in crowds; I felt them collide until pairs interlocked." By the next morning, the solutions flowed out of him: "I had only to write out the results." By chasing control, we trap ourselves. By letting go just a little, we may liberate not only ourselves, but our best ideas.

Poincaré, fittingly, is the mathematician who paved the way for chaos theory, which would later become known by the image of an intertwined world, in which hurricanes could be swirled into existence by a single butterfly flapping its wings.

The butterfly offers us a poetic end to our saga. In North America, the monarch butterfly, that charming orange-and-black insect, overwinters in the highlands of the Mexican state of Michoacán. In the spring, a new generation is born, and they begin their long journey north. But the journey, which stretches for three thousand miles each way, is far too long for any individual monarch to complete. Instead, the migration is an interconnected journey, each life started where the parents stopped, each butterfly part of an endless relay across generations. Every butterfly is shaped by history, their lives emerging from a chrysalis that was created at a specific time and place by decisions accumulating from long-dead ancestors. They, like us, produce unknown ripple effects with their lives. They may cause hurricanes or, more likely, provide a profound moment of beauty and wonder to a child who pauses to gaze at them flitting across a meadow.

We are like those butterflies, and they are like us, part of a chaotic, networked unity we call existence. "When we try to pick out anything by itself," the naturalist John Muir once said, "we find it hitched to everything else in the Universe." We are each hitched to one another, which yields a profound gift: that everything we do matters, including whatever you decide to do now, when you close this book, and go out to explore that wonderful, maddening, infinitely complex world that we call home.

ACKNOWLEDGMENTS

As with all humans, every good idea my brain ever produced has come, in part, from someone else's good idea, so there are many people to thank. But in writing acknowledgments for this particular book I have two problems.

First, my argument makes clear that writing *Fluke* was only made possible by precisely everyone and everything that came before me, including my cruelest ancestors and even a series of wormlike creatures that thankfully didn't get squished hundreds of millions of years before they evolved into humans. I literally couldn't have done it without you.

Second, if I'm right that the world is deterministic, everyone who helped me was always going to—and they didn't really have much free choice in the matter.

Nonetheless, my atoms are arranged neatly together on this weird and wonderful planet, and that's a good thing because I get to share it with some exceptional beings.

My editor at Scribner, Rick Horgan, believed in me and this outlandish idea for a book. Rick has the useful characteristic of always being right, including when he correctly discerned that the first draft was twenty thousand words too long and needed a rather savage haircut. *Fluke* was drastically improved by his wisdom. Joe Zigmond, my editor at John Murray in the UK, encouraged me to never shy away from the big questions and to write what I thought was true, even if it could be strange or unsettling. Anthony Mattero, my agent, offers sage advice and always has my back, which is often what a writer needs most. Caspian Dennis, agent and gentleman of Britain, offered enthusiastic backing and guidance when the idea for this book was germinating. (I already thanked them by turning each of them into fleas in a thought experiment in chapter 9.)

Richard Lenski and Zachary Blount, who have unlocked the mysteries of evolution in a lab in central Michigan, were generous with their time and wisdom. They profoundly shaped my ideas about change. Mark Pagel was extremely kind, helpful, and patient with me, correcting some of my flawed ideas about speciation and evolutionary biology. Sabine Hossenfelder and Sean Carroll helped me understand some of the weirder realms of physics. Jerome Buhl taught me about locusts. Nick Lane helped me understand the origins of mitochondria. Clint Ballinger, an unsung titan in his field, helped me understand the influence of geography on human trajectories.

Charlotte Yung, Nikhil Chauhan, and Sophie Wüpping provided indispensable early research assistance, helping my ideas take shape.

Marcel Dirsus and David Landry offered thoughtful feedback for years. They're wonderful friends. Alex Teytelboym helped me temper some of my harsher views about social science and did something all good friends must: tell you when you're wrong.

My parents gave me the two greatest gifts anyone can receive: existence and an endless supply of love and support.

Ellie has transformed how I see the world and reinforced in me a clear sense that life is best lived when accompanied by curiosity, wonder, awe, and exploration. If there are multiple universes, I am prone to Panglossian optimism: with Ellie, this is surely the best one.

ACKNOWLEDGMENTS

Finally, thanks are due to Zorro, my rambunctious young border collie. I came up with many of the ideas in *Fluke* while walking him, and he reminds me of something easily forgotten in modern life: to just enjoy every moment we have. Hidden in each sentence of this book are one or two throws of his favorite Frisbee, without which I couldn't have gotten a single word on the page.

ENDNOTES

CHAPTER 1:
INTRODUCTION

1 Miyako Hotel: O. Cary, "The Sparing of Kyoto—Mr. Stimson's 'Pet City,'" *Japan Quarterly* 22 (4) (1975): 337, https://www.proquest.com/scholarly -journals/sparing-kyoto-mr-stimsons-pet-city/docview/1304279553 /se-2. See also J. M. Kelly, "Why Did Henry Stimson Spare Kyoto from the Bomb? Confusion in Postwar Historiography," *Journal of American–East Asian Relations* 19 (2) (2012): 183–203.

2 agreed on a target: "Summary of Target Committee Meetings on 10 May and 11 May 1945," top-secret memo of the United States Target Commit- tee, 12 May 1945, https://nsarchive2.gwu.edu/NSAEBB/NSAEBB162/6 .pdf.

2 four hundred aircraft engines: Alex Wellerstein, "The Kyoto Miscon- ception," *Restricted Data: The Nuclear Secrecy Blog*, 8 August 2014.

2 railway yards: Ibid.

3 "I don't want Kyoto bombed": "The Interim Committee," Atomic Heritage Foundation, 5 June 2014.

3 "and that was Kyoto": Kelly, "Why Did Henry Stimson Spare?"

3 met with President Truman twice: B. J. Bernstein. "The Atomic Bomb- ings Reconsidered," *Foreign Affairs* 74 (1) (1995): 135–52, https://doi .org/10.2307/20047025.

3 "pet city": Cary, "Sparing of Kyoto," 337.

4 cloud cover: Alex Wellerstein, "Nagasaki: The Last Bomb," *New Yorker*, 7 August 2015.

4   "Kokura's luck": Alex Wellerstein, "The Luck of Kokura," *Restricted Data: The Nuclear Secrecy Blog*, 22 August 2014.

6   "The Garden of Forking Paths": J. L. Borges, "The Garden of Forking Paths," in *Collected Fictions* (New York: Penguin Books, 1962).

7   *amor fati*: *The Stanford Encyclopedia of Philosophy*, s.v. "Friedrich Nietzsche," 17 March 2017, https://plato.stanford.edu/entries/nietzsche/.

8   "Terrible Act of Insane Woman": "Terrible Act of Insane Woman," *Manitoba Free Press*, 17 June 1905.

9   "us the lucky ones": Richard Dawkins, *Unweaving the Rainbow: Science, Delusion and the Appetite for Wonder* (London: Houghton Mifflin, 1998).

10 *Back to Methuselah*: Michael Holroyd, *Bernard Shaw: The One-Volume Definitive Edition* (New York: Random House, 1997).

13 "every constellation": Hannah Arendt, *The Human Condition* (Chicago: University of Chicago Press, 1958).

14 "infrared pulse": R. Black, *The Last Days of the Dinosaurs: An Asteroid, Extinction and the Beginning of Our World* (Cheltenham, UK: History Press, 2022).

14 broiled chicken: Ibid.

14 resourceful diggers: Martha Henriques, "How Mammals Won the Dinosaurs' World," *BBC Future*, 15 August 2022.

14 asteroid came from oscillations: Lisa Randall, *Dark Matter and the Dinosaurs: The Astounding Interconnectedness of the Universe* (New York: Random House, 2017).

15 PAX6 gene: W. J. Gehring, "The Evolution of Vision," *Wiley Interdisciplinary Reviews: Developmental Biology* 3 (1) (2014): 1–40.

15 squid eyes: A. Ogura, K. Ikeo, and T. Gojobori, "Comparative Analysis of Gene Expression for Convergent Evolution of Camera Eye between Octopus and Human," *Genome Research* 14 (8) (2004): 1555–61.

16 "bends toward justice": Dr. Martin Luther King Jr., "Remaining Awake through a Great Revolution," speech given at the National Cathedral, 31 March 1968.

17 secrets of plants: Tomoko Y. Steen, "Always an Eccentric? A Brief Biography of Motoo Kimura," *Journal of Genetics* 75 (1) (1996): 19–25.

17   food poisoning: Ibid.

17   meaningless, neutral changes: M. Kimura, *The Neutral Theory of Molecular Evolution* (Cambridge: Cambridge University Press, 1983).

CHAPTER 2:

CHANGING ANYTHING CHANGES EVERYTHING

20   Ivan from North Macedonia: Michelle Butterfield, "Tourist Survives 18 Hours at Sea by Clinging to Soccer Ball off Greece," *Global News Canada*, 14 July 2022.

21   "garment of destiny": Martin Luther King Jr., "Letter from a Birmingham Jail," 16 April 1963.

23   Laplace's demon: R. Hahan and R. Hahn, *Pierre-Simon Laplace, 1749–1827: A Determined Scientist* (Cambridge, MA: Harvard University Press, 2005).

23   "before its eyes": David P. Feldman, "Newton, Laplace, and Determinism," in *Chaos and Fractals: An Elementary Introduction* (Oxford: Oxford University Press, 2012; online ed., Oxford: Oxford Academic, 17 December 2013).

24   "upper air section": "The *Bulletin* Interviews Professor Edward Lorenz," *MIT Bulletin* 45 (2) (April 1996).

24   LGP-30 computer: James Gleick, *Chaos: Making a New Science* (New York: Viking Books, 1987).

26   *chaos theory:* Edward Lorenz, *The Essence of Chaos* (Seattle: University of Washington Press, 1995).

26   "infinitely the most important": Arthur Conan Doyle, *The Adventures of Sherlock Holmes: Collins Classics* (Glasgow, Scotland: William Collins, 2016).

26   six or seven times: Michael Berry, "The Electron at the End of the Universe," in *A Passion for Science*, by L. Wolpert and A. Richards (Oxford: Oxford University Press, 1988).

26   "wrong planet": Pema Chödrön, *Living Beautifully with Uncertainty and Change* (Boulder, CO: Shambhala, 2012).

28   Black Swans: Nassim Nicholas Taleb, *The Black Swan: The Impact of the Highly Improbable* (New York: Random House, 2007).

28   same river twice: D. J. Allan, "The Problem of Cratylus," *American Journal of Philology* 75 (3) (1954): 271–87. See also G. S. Kirk, "Natural Change in Heraclitus," *Mind* 60 (237) (1951): 35–42.

29   "sight of my life": F. Turner, "Earthrise: How Man First Saw the Earth," *Technology and Culture* 51 (1) (2010): 272–74.

29   "burned in the heavens about me": Ezzy Pearson, "The Overview Effect and Apollo," *BBC: Sky at Night Magazine*, 23 March 2023.

29   overview effect: N. Kanas, "Spirituality, Humanism, and the Overview Effect during Manned Space Missions," *Acta Astronautica* 166 (2020): 525–28. See also D. B. Yaden et al., "The Overview Effect: Awe and Self-Transcendent Experience in Space Flight," *Psychology of Consciousness: Theory, Research, and Practice* 3 (1) (2016).

30   *control nothing, but influence everything*: This is an adapted version of a quote often used by Professor Scott E. Page, an expert on complex adaptive systems at the University of Michigan.

30   YouTube stars: Chloe Taylor, "Kids Now Dream of Being Professional YouTubers rather than Astronauts, Study Finds," CNBC, 19 July 2019.

31   plainly we came *out* of it: Alan Watts, *The Book: On the Taboo against Knowing Who You Are* (New York: Pantheon Books, 1966).

32   *atomistic* and the *relational*: J. Baggini, *How the World Thinks: A Global History of Philosophy* (London: Granta Books, 2018).

32   "aggregate of individuals": Elizabeth Wolgast, "Primitive Reactions," *Philosophical Investigations* 17 (4) (1994): 587–603.

33   "man of the forest": See Roland Ennos, *The Wood Age: How Wood Shaped the Whole of Human History* (New York: Harper Collins, 2021).

33   *Brahman*: H. Chaudhuri, "The Concept of Brahman in Hindu Philosophy," *Philosophy East and West* 4 (1) (1954): 47–66.

33   "integration of all life": E. Salmón, "Kincentric Ecology: Indigenous Perceptions of the Human-Nature Relationship," *Ecological Applications* 10 (5) (2000): 1327–32.

33 "present everywhere in everything": Karen Armstrong, *Sacred Nature: How We Can Recover Our Bond with the Natural World* (London: Bodley Head, 2022). See also Karen Armstrong, *A History of God* (New York: Vintage, 1999).

33 "Mechanicks and Geometry": S. D. Snobelen, "Newton's Theology," in *Encyclopedia of Early Modern Philosophy and the Sciences*, ed. D. Jalobeanu and C. T. Wolfe (New York: Springer, 2022), https://doi.org/10.1007/978-3-319-31069-5_106.

35 *reductionism:* A. Rosenberg, "Reductionism in a Historical Science," *Philosophy of Science* 68 (2) (2001): 135–63; and P. J. Verschuren, "Holism versus Reductionism in Modern Social Science Research," *Quality and Quantity* 35 (2001): 389–405.

35 *holobiont:* See, for example, R. Guerrero, L. Margulis, and M. Berlanga, "Symbiogenesis: The Holobiont as a Unit of Evolution," *International Microbiology* 16 (3) (2013): 133–43.

35 "stars in our galaxy": Merlin Sheldrake, *Entangled Life: How Fungi Make Our Worlds, Change Our Minds and Shape Our Futures* (New York: Vintage, 2021).

35 affect our biological clocks: G. Mazzoccoli et al., "The Circadian Clock, the Immune System, and Viral Infections: The Intricate Relationship between Biological Time and Host-Virus Interaction," *Pathogens* 9 (2) (2020).

35 parasites alter our thoughts: See, for example, Erik Stokstad, "A Parasite Makes Wolves More Likely to Become Pack Leaders," *Science* 24 (November 2022).

35 mood disorders: A. Minuti et al., "The Complex Relationship between Gut Microbiota Dysregulation and Mood Disorders: A Narrative Review," *Current Research in Neurobiology* 3 (2022).

36 easily demarcated individuals: Derek Parfit, *Reasons and Persons* (Oxford: Oxford University Press, 1984). See also David Shoemaker, "Personal Identity and Ethics," in *The Stanford Encyclopedia of Philosophy*, ed. Edward N. Zalta (Stanford, CA: Metaphysics Research Lab, Fall 2021).

37 "like a glass tunnel": Parfit, *Reasons and Persons*.

CHAPTER 3:
EVERYTHING DOESN'T HAPPEN FOR A REASON

39   ended up inside it: L. Margulis, "Symbiotic Theory of the Origin of Eukaryotic Organelles: Criteria for Proof," *Symposia of the Society for Experimental Biology* 29 (January1975): 21–38; and Nick Lane, *Power, Sex, and Suicide: Mitochondria and the Meaning of Life* (Oxford: Oxford University Press, 2005).

40   unexpected microbial merger: Ed Yong, "The Unique Merger That Made You (and Ewe and Yew)," *Nautilus* 3 (February 2014).

40   evolution of placenta: K. Imakawa et al., "Endogenous Retroviruses and Placental Evolution, Development, and Diversity," *Cells* 11 (15) (2022): 2458; and E. B. Chuong, "Retroviruses Facilitate the Rapid Evolution of the Mammalian Placenta," *BioEssays: News and Reviews in Molecular, Cellular and Developmental Biology* 35 (10) (2013): 853–61.

41   freak mutation: P. Martin et al., "The Enigmatic Marmorkrebs (Marbled Crayfish) Is the Parthenogenetic Form of *Procambarus fallax*," *Contributions to Zoology* 79 (3) (2010): 107–18.

41   German pet shop: Immanuel Jotham, "Mutant Crayfish Learned to Clone Itself in a German Pet Store and Is Now Taking over Europe," *International Business Times*, 2 June 2018; and Carl Zimmer, "This Mutant Crayfish Clones Itself, and It's Taking over Europe," *New York Times*, 5 February 2018.

41   supply of delicious nutrition: Kate Connolly, " 'We Started Eating Them': What Do You Do with an Invasive Army of Crayfish Clones?," *Guardian*, 17 January 2022.

41   prey on freshwater snails: Ibid.

41   new source of nourishment: Rowan Moore Gerety, "Invasion of the Crayfish Clones: Q&A with Ranja Andriantsoa," *Mongabay*, 27 January 2021.

42   twenty times larger than another: Michael Blastland, *The Hidden Half: How the World Conceals Its Secrets* (London: Atlantic Books, 2019).

42 "because it got that way": D'Arcy Thompson, *On Growth and Form* (Cambridge: Cambridge University Press, 1917).

43 talent mattered, but so did luck: A. Pluchino, A. E. Biondo, and A. Rapisarda, "Talent versus Luck: The Role of Randomness in Success and Failure," *Advances in Complex Systems* 21 (03) (2018).

44 "narrative fallacy": Nassim Nicholas Taleb, *The Black Swan: The Impact of the Highly Improbable* (New York: Random House, 2007).

44 "hindsight bias": See, for example, Duncan Watts, *Everything Is Obvious Once You Know the Answer: How Common Sense Fails* (London: Atlantic Books, 2012).

44 happily accept randomness: D. L. Krantz, "Taming Chance: Social Science and Everyday Narratives," *Psychological Inquiry* 9 (2) (1998): 87–94.

45 "love of poetry": Claire Wilson, "Nature, Nurture, Luck: Why You Are More Than Just Genes and Upbringing," *New Scientist*, 21 September 2022.

45 random discrepancies in their neural wiring: A.-Y. Smith Matthew et al., "Idiosyncratic Learning Performance in Flies," *Biology Letters* 18 (2022).

48 Bishop James Ussher: William R. Brice, "Bishop Ussher, John Lightfoot and the Age of Creation," *Journal of Geological Education* 30 (1982): 18–24.

49 "evolution by jerks": Jonathan Rée, "Evolution by Jerks," *New Humanist*, 31 May 2007.

50 "evolutionary one-offs": Jonathan Losos, *Improbable Destinies: How Predictable Is Evolution?* (New York: Penguin, 2017).

50 "preparation by artificial means": This remark was made by the zoologist George Shaw in 1799. Ibrahim Sawal, "The Platypus: What Nature's Weirdest Mammal Says about Our Origins," *New Scientist*, 5 May 2021.

50 "a promiscuous intercourse": This remark was made in 1793 by John Hunter. Natalie Zarrelli, "Why 19th-Century Naturalists Didn't Believe in the Platypus," *Atlas Obscura* 21 (April 2016).

50 movie theater lobby in the jungle: L. K. Greene et al., "Reproductive Endocrine Patterns and Volatile Urinary Compounds of *Arctictis*

binturong: Discovering Why Bearcats Smell like Popcorn," *Science of Nature* 103 (2016): 1–11.

50 "crab-like form": See, for example, G. Scholtz, "Evolution of Crabs: History and Deconstruction of a Prime Example of Convergence," *Contributions to Zoology* 83 (2) (2014): 87–105.

50 insects, bats, birds, and pterosaurs: For more on the evolution of flight, see Richard Dawkins, *Flights of Fancy: Defying Gravity by Design and Evolution* (New York: Apollo Books, 2021).

51 triggered by a single event: C. Venditti, A. Meade, and M. Pagel, "Phylogenies Reveal New Interpretation of Speciation and the Red Queen," *Nature* 463 (7279) (2010): 349–52.

52 elegant in its simplicity: See, for example, R. E. Lenski et al., "Long-Term Experimental Evolution in *Escherichia coli*. I. Adaptation and Divergence during 2,000 Generations," *American Naturalist* 138 (6) (1991): 1315–41.

52 lasts for 26.9 years: R. J. Wang et al., "Human Generation Times across the Past 250,000 Years," *Science Advances* 9 (1) (2023).

54 thaw the bacteria back out: Interviews with Richard Lenski and Zachary Blount, East Lansing, MI, 16 May 2022.

54 "like flasks of water": Zachary Blount, "Replaying Evolution," *American Scientist* 105 (3) (May–June 2017).

55 "thought it was a lab error": Email interview with Tim Cooper, 21 July 2022.

55 "'when in doubt, throw it out'": Interview with Richard Lenski, East Lansing, MI, 16 May 2022.

55 seemingly meaningless errors: See, for example, Z. D. Blount, C. Z. Borland, and R. E. Lenski, "Historical Contingency and the Evolution of a Key Innovation in an Experimental Population of *Escherichia coli*," *Proceedings of the National Academy of Sciences* 105 (23) (2008): 7899–906.

56 "lemony dessert": See, for example, Stephanie Bucklin, "A Conductor of Evolution's Subtle Symphony," *Quanta*, 3 November 2016.

57 Cournot contingency: I. Ermakoff, "Contingency and Randomness: A Modal Approach," in *Research Handbook on Analytical Sociology*, ed.

Gianluca Manzo (Northampton, MA: Edward Elgar Publishing, 2021), 264–85.

58   "a miserly accountant": Richard Dawkins, *The God Delusion* (New York: Bantam Press, 2006).

58   *genetic drift*: See, for example, M. Lynch et al., "Genetic Drift, Selection and the Evolution of the Mutation Rate," *Nature Reviews Genetics* 17 (11) (2016): 704–14.

58   northern elephant seals: A. R. Hoelzel, "Impact of Population Bottlenecks on Genetic Variation and the Importance of Life-History: A Case Study of the Northern Elephant Seal," *Biological Journal of the Linnean Society* 68 (1–2) (1999): 23–39.

59   just forty people: J. Hawks et al., "Population Bottlenecks and Pleistocene Human Evolution," *Molecular Biology and Evolution* 17 (1) (2000): 2–22.

59   potential human gene pool: The science on these questions remains unsettled, and the Toba volcano theory is contested. See, for example, S. H. Ambrose, "Late Pleistocene Human Population Bottlenecks, Volcanic Winter, and Differentiation of Modern Humans," *Journal of Human Evolution* 34 (6) (1998): 623–51.

59   river in Cameroon: See, for example, A. Auton et al., "A Fine-Scale Chimpanzee Genetic Map from Population Sequencing," *Science* 336 (6078) (2012): 193–98. See also "Chimps Show Much Greater Genetic Diversity Than Humans," University of Oxford, 2 March 2012, https://www.ox.ac.uk/news/2012-03-02-chimps-show-much-greater-genetic-diversity-humans.

60   250 individuals: N. J. Fagundes et al., "Statistical Evaluation of Alternative Models of Human Evolution," *Proceedings of the National Academy of Sciences* 104 (45) (2007): 17614–19.

60   Tristan de Cunha: N. Zamel et al., "Asthma on Tristan da Cunha: Looking for the Genetic Link," *American Journal of Respiratory and Critical Care Medicine* 153 (6) (1996): 1902–6. See also H. Soodyall et al., "Genealogy and Genes: Tracing the Founding Fathers of Tristan da Cunha," *European Journal of Human Genetics* 11 (9) (2003): 705–9.

60   now-extinct dodo: The nearest living relative of the dodo is the Nicobar

pigeon (*Caloenas nicobarica*). "How Did the Dodo Evolve?," University of Oxford, Museum of Natural History, https://oumnh.ox.ac.uk/learn-how-did-dodo-evolve.

60 "good enough" solutions: See Daniel S. Milo, *Good Enough: The Tolerance for Mediocrity in Nature and Society* (Cambridge, MA: Harvard University Press, 2019).

62 net benefit to London's economy: S. Larcom, F. Rauch, and T. Willems, "The Benefits of Forced Experimentation: Striking Evidence from the London Underground Network," *Quarterly Journal of Economics* 132 (4) (2017): 2019–55.

62 imitation and trial and error: This paragraph was largely inspired by a conversation between Richard Dawkins and the physicist Sean Carroll on the latter's *Mindscape* podcast. "Richard Dawkins on Flight and Other Achievements," 2 May 2022, https://podcasts.apple.com/us/podcast/richard-dawkins-on-flight-and-other-evolutionary/id1406534739?i=1000559344259.

62 small iterative changes: See, for example, S. J. Sober and M. S. Brainard, "Vocal Learning Is Constrained by the Statistics of Sensorimotor Experience," *Proceedings of the National Academy of Sciences* 109 (51) (2012): 21099–103.

62 a documentary featuring rare footage: *The Beatles: Get Back*, directed by Peter Jackson (Apple Corps/Wingnut Films, 2021).

62 adjust to the broken piano: The economist Tim Harford has popularized this story, writing about it in his book *Adapt* and also discussing it on his *Cautionary Tales* podcast.

CHAPTER 4:
WHY OUR BRAINS DISTORT REALITY

65 Fitness Beats Truth theorem: Donald D. Hoffman, *The Case against Reality: How Evolution Hid the Truth from Our Eyes* (London: Penguin, 2019).

66   "manifest image": Wilfrid Sellers, *Science, Perception and Reality* (New York: Humanities Press, 1963).

67   "organisms, not angels": Steven Pinker, *How the Mind Works* (New York: Penguin, 1999).

67   "more robust and efficient": See J. Sakai, "How Synaptic Pruning Shapes Neural Wiring during Development and, Possibly, in Disease," *Proceedings of the National Academy of Sciences* 117 (28) (2020): 16096–99.

68   "We see emotion": For a discussion of Wittgenstein on emotion, see D. Harris, "Of Somethings and Nothings: Wittgenstein on Emotion," *International Philosophical Quarterly* 51 (1) (2011): 73–84.

68   red-green color-blind: M. Siniscalchi et al., "Are Dogs Red-Green Colour Blind?," *Royal Society Open Science* 4 (11) (2017): 170869.

68   Dolphins and whales: Jeff Hecht, "Colour Blind," *New Scientist*, 25 April 2001.

69   insects and reptiles: For an overview of animal color vision, see Laura Kelley, "Inside the Colourful World of Animal Vision," *Conversation*, 7 November 2014.

69   New World monkeys: Ibid.

69   cDa29: G. Jordan and J. Mollon, "Tetrachromacy: The Mysterious Case of Extraordinary Color Vision," *Current Opinion in Behavioral Sciences* 30 (2019): 130–34.

69   peacock mantis shrimp: Ed Yong, "Nature's Most Amazing Eyes Just Got a Bit Weirder," *National Geographic*, 3 July 2014.

70   offshoots of the fig primates: N. J. Dominy, J. C. Svenning, and W. H. Li, "Historical Contingency in the Evolution of Primate Color Vision," *Journal of Human Evolution* 44 (1) (2003): 25–45.

70   pattern detection machines: M. P. Mattson, "Superior Pattern Processing Is the Essence of the Evolved Human Brain," *Frontiers in Neuroscience*, 2014, 265.

70   Frigg's Distaff: Simon J. Cropper et al., "Why People across the World see Constellations, Not Just Stars," *Aeon Psyche*, 17 August 2022.

70   to infer cause and effect: A. J. Woods et al., "Space, Time, and Causality in the Human Brain," *Neuroimage* 92 (2014): 285–97.

71 philosopher Daniel Dennett argues: Daniel C. Dennett, *From Bacteria to Bach and Back: The Evolution of Minds* (New York: Penguin, 2018).

71 shapes moving haphazardly: F. Heider and M. Simmel, "An Experimental Study of Apparent Behavior," *American Journal of Psychology* 57 (2) (1944): 243–59.

72 signs of superstitious belief: This is contested. See, for example, W. Rendu et al., "Evidence Supporting an Intentional Neanderthal Burial at La Chapelle-aux-Saints," *Proceedings of the National Academy of Sciences* 111 (1) (2014): 81–86.

72 skull of a rhinoceros: Richard Gray, "Cave Fires and Rhino Skull Used in Neanderthal Burial Rituals," *New Scientist*, 28 September 2016.

72 noticed a horseshoe: This story is likely apocryphal. "Miscellany," *Lapham's Quarterly*, https://www.laphamsquarterly.org/magic-shows/miscellany/niels-bohrs-lucky-horseshoe.

72 heart-shaped amulets: For a discussion of superstition on World War I, see Owen Davies, *A Supernatural War: Magic, Divination, and Faith during the First World War* (Oxford: Oxford University Press, 2018). See also Malcolm Gaskill, "Ministry of Apparitions," *London Review of Books* 41 (13) (July 2019).

73 followed a Poisson distribution: Aatish Bhatia, "What Does Randomness Look Like?," *Wired*, 21 December 2012.

73 "which button to press": Theodore Zeldin, "Stratagems of Ignorance," *London Review of Books*, 5 January 1989. See also Judith Devlin, *The Superstitious Mind: French Peasants and the Supernatural in the Nineteenth Century* (New Haven, CT: Yale University Press, 1987).

73 a "storytelling animal": Jonathan Gottschall, *The Storytelling Animal: How Stories Make Us Human* (New York: Mariner Books, 2013).

73 "puncture mark in her throat": P. D. James, *Talking about Detective Fiction* (London: Faber & Faber, 2010).

74 "And He went away": Kurt Vonnegut, *Cat's Cradle* (New York: Penguin Classics, 2008).

74 the Interpreter: For an overview of split-brain research, see M. S. Gazza-niga, "Forty-Five Years of Split-Brain Research and Still Going Strong," *Nature Reviews Neuroscience* 6 (8) (2005): 653–59.

75 children in China: A. Schachner et al., "Is the Bias for Function-Based Explanations Culturally Universal? Children from China Endorse Tele-ological Explanations of Natural Phenomena," *Journal of Experimental Child Psychology* 157 (2017): 29–48.

76 apophenia: See, for example, S. Fyfe et al., "Apophenia, Theory of Mind and Schizotypy: Perceiving Meaning and Intentionality in Randomness," *Cortex* 44 (10) (2008): 1316–25.

76 "hot hand fallacy": P. Ayton and I. Fischer, "The Hot Hand Fallacy and the Gambler's Fallacy: Two Faces of Subjective Randomness?," *Memory & Cognition* 32 (2004): 1369–78.

77 "cannot deal with Chaos": Suzanne Langer, *Philosophy in a New Key: A Study in the Symbolism of Reason, Rite, and Art* (Cambridge, MA: Harvard University Press, 1996).

78 "attempting to insert the aedeagus": Robert Krulwich, "The Love That Dared Not Speak Its Name, of a Beetle for a Beer Bottle," NPR, 19 June 2013.

78 evolutionary traps: M. A. Schlaepfer, M. C. Runge, and P. W. Sherman, "Ecological and Evolutionary Traps," *Trends in Ecology & Evolution* 17 (10) (2002): 474–80.

CHAPTER 5:
THE HUMAN SWARM

81 3.5 trillion insects: Jackie Mead, "The Locust That Ate the American West," *Mental Floss*, 2 May 2022.

81 "seething, crawling mass": Alexandra M. Wagner, "Grasshoppered: America's Response to the 1874 Rocky Mountain Locust Invasion," *Nebraska History* 89 (2008): 154–67.

81 "cutting and snipping": Caroline Fraser, "Laura Ingalls Wilder and One of the Greatest Natural Disasters in American History," *LitHub*, 5 December 2017.

81 "a spray of hoar frost": Wagner, "Grasshoppered."

82 proposed a bounty: "Bounty for Grasshoppers," *New York Times*, 10 August 1876.

82 John the Baptist–style: "Locust Eating," *New York Times*, 19 August 1875.

82 "like an army": Fraser, "Laura Ingalls Wilder."

83 *edge of chaos:* See, for example, C. G. Langton, "Computation at the Edge of Chaos: Phase Transitions and Emergent Computation," *Physica D: Nonlinear Phenomena* 42 (1–3) (1990): 12–37.

83 all about density: J. Buhl et al., "From Disorder to Order in Marching Locusts," *Science* 312 (5778) (2006): 1402–6.

83 gather together in small groups: Helmut Satz, *The Rules of the Flock: Self-Organization and Swarm Structure in Animal Societies* (Oxford: Oxford University Press, 2020), https://academic.oup.com/book/40568.

84 "fairly firm tipping point": Email interview with Jerome Buhl, 27 July 2022.

86 anonymized cell phone data: C. Song et al., "Limits of Predictability in Human Mobility," *Science* 327 (5968) (2010): 1018–21.

86 Beau Brummell: Ian Kelly, *Beau Brummell: The Ultimate Dandy* (London: Hodder & Stoughton, 2005).

88 directed acyclic graphs: See, for example, G. W. Imbens, "Potential Outcome and Directed Acyclic Graph Approaches to Causality: Relevance for Empirical Practice in Economics," *Journal of Economic Literature* 58 (4) (2020): 1129–79.

88 called complexity science: See, for example, M. M. Waldrop, *Complexity: The Emerging Science at the Edge of Order and Chaos* (New York: Simon & Schuster, 1992).

90 that *adapt* to one another: See, for example, "Understanding Complexity," lecture series by Scott E. Page, professor at the University of Michigan.

91 *decentralized* and *self-organized*: See, for example, Melanie Mitchell, *Complexity: A Guided Tour* (Oxford: Oxford University Press, 2011); or J. H. Miller and Scott E. Page, *Complex Adaptive Systems: An Introduction to Computational Models of Social Life* (Princeton, NJ: Princeton University Press, 2009).

91 *basins of attraction:* See, for example, G. Ellison, "Basins of Attraction, Long-Run Stochastic Stability, and the Speed of Step-by-Step Evolution," *Review of Economic Studies* 67 (1) (2000): 17–45.

94 unexpected trophic cascade: Brodie Farquhar, "Wolf Reintroduction Changes Ecosystem in Yellowstone," Yellowstone National Park, 30 June 2021, https://www.yellowstonepark.com/things-to-do/wildlife /wolf-reintroduction-changes-ecosystem/.

94 entire ecosystem adjusted: W. J. Ripple and R. L. Beschta, "Trophic Cascades in Yellowstone: The First 15 Years after Wolf Reintroduction," *Biological Conservation* 145 (1) (2012): 205–13.

95 *critical slowing down:* M. Scheffer et al., "Generic Indicators of Ecological Resilience: Inferring the Chance of a Critical Transition," *Annual Review of Ecology, Evolution, and Systematics* 46 (2015): 145–67.

96 nature's early-warning system: Natalie Wolchover, "Nature's Critical Warning System," *Quanta*, 18 November 2015.

96 *self-organized criticality:* P. Bak, C. Tang, and K. Wiesenfeld, "Self-Organized Criticality," *Physical Review A* 38 (1) (1988): 364.

96 disturbance the size of a human hand: J. Buhl et al., "Group Structure in Locust Migratory Bands," *Behavioral Ecology and Sociobiology* 65 (2) (2011): 265–73.

97 55 million people dead: The death estimates vary widely, but it was likely in the tens of millions. See, for example, Judith Rae Shapiro, *Mao's War against Nature: Politics and the Environment in Revolutionary China* (Cambridge: Cambridge University Press, 2001).

97 highly optimized tolerance: J. M. Carlson and J. Doyle, "Highly Optimized Tolerance: A Mechanism for Power Laws in Designed Systems," *Physical Review E* 60 (2) (1999): 1412.

99 startling the "loader": Greg Watson, "Could Franz Ferdinand Welbeck Gun Accident Have Halted WWI?," BBC News, 25 November 2013. The Welbeck Abbey archives also have photos and records of this fateful shoot.

99 Gräf & Stift double phaeton: Benjamin Preston, "The Car That Witnessed the Spark of World War I," *New York Times*, 10 July 2014.

99 bounced off the car: Mike Dash, "Curses! Archduke Franz Ferdinand and His Astounding Death Car," *Smithsonian Magazine*, 22 April 2013.

100 "I have often wondered": "Game Shoots at Welbeck before 1914," Welbeck Abbey archives, https://www.welbeck.co.uk/assets/files/Game%20Shoots%20at%20Welbeck.pdf.

100 A-III-118: See, for example, Rebecca Taylor, "'A II II 18': Franz Ferdinand's Prophetic Number Plate," *Sky News*, 11 November 2018.

101 "TV pickups": See, for example, "9 of the Biggest TV Moments in UK Electricity History," *Drax*, 1 August 2022, https://www.drax.com/power-generation/9-of-the-biggest-tv-moments-in-uk-electricity-history/.

102 "decoupled" from the national system: Natalie Wolchover, "Treading Softly in a Connected World," *Quanta*, 18 March 2013.

103 "mutual accessibility of ideas": Felipe Fernández-Armesto, *A Foot in the River: Why Our Lives Change—and the Limits of Evolution* (Oxford: Oxford University Press, 2015).

103 measured in milliseconds: See, for example, Michael Lewis, *Flashboys* (New York: Penguin, 2015).

103 wiped out in a few minutes: Andy Verity and Eleanor Lawrie, "Hound of Hounslow: Who Is Navinder Sarao, the 'Flash Crash Trader'?," BBC News, 28 January 2020.

CHAPTER 6:
HERACLITUS RULES

106 a divination machine: See, for example, R. Wilhelm and C. F. Baynes, *The I Ching* (Princeton, NJ: Princeton University Press, 1950).

106 knucklebones of hooved animals: For a discussion of the history of probability, see Peter Bernstein, *Against the Gods: The Remarkable Story of Risk* (Hoboken, NJ: Wiley, 1998); and James Franklin, *The Science of Conjecture: Evidence and Probability before Pascal* (Baltimore, MD: John Hopkins University Press, 2015).

106 maritime republic of Genoa: See Karla Mallette, "How 12th-Century Genoese Merchants Invented the Idea of Risk," *Aeon Psyche*, 2 November 2021.

106 "what happened for the most part": See, for example, Dorothea Frede, "Necessity, Chance, and 'What Happened for the Most Part' in Aristotle's Poetics," in *Essays on Aristotle's Poetics*, ed. A. Oksenberg Rorty (Princeton, NJ: Princeton University Press, 1992), 197–219.

107 through the upward stem: See Bernstein, *Against the Gods*.

107 interrupted game: Franklin, *Science of Conjecture*; and R. Campe, *The Game of Probability: Literature and Calculation from Pascal to Kleist* (Redwood City, CA: Stanford University Press, 2013).

108 mortality in London: See, for example, D. V. Glass, "John Graunt and His Natural and Political Observations," *Proceedings of the Royal Society of London* 159 (974) (1963): 2–37.

108 "resemblance betwixt those objects": See David Hume, *The Philosophical Works of David Hume* (Outlook Verlag, 2020).

110 *hard problem of consciousness:* D. J. Chalmers, "Facing Up to the Problem of Consciousness," *Journal of Consciousness Studies* 2 (3) (1995): 200–219.

110 "1.4 kilogram lump": Oliver Burkeman, "Why Can't the World's Greatest Minds Solve the Mystery of Consciousness?," *Guardian*, 21 January 2015.

110 "fill a few holes": "A Few Holes to Fill," *Nature Physics* 4 (2008): 257.

110 collapse into a single position: For an overview of key concepts in quantum physics, see Michael G. Raymer, *Quantum Physics: What Everyone Needs to Know* (Oxford: Oxford University Press, 2017); and Sean Carroll, *Something Deeply Hidden: Quantum Worlds and the Emergence of Spacetime* (New York: Penguin, 2019).

ENDNOTES

111 "sherry were consumed": Sean Carroll, "Splitting the Universe," *Aeon*, 11 September 2019.

111 "long enough to reproduce": Zachary Blount made this comment to me while reading an early draft of *Fluke*.

112 the *Economist* analyzed: "A Mean Feat," *Economist*, 9 January 2016.

112 eighty-four thousand miles per hour: See, for example, Dimitra Kessenides, "The Mission to Sample a Comet Going 84,000 Miles per Hour—and Return," Bloomberg, 26 July 2018.

113 Frank Knight challenged: Frank Knight, *Risk, Uncertainty and Profit* (Boston: Houghton Mifflin, 1921).

114 "detracts from good decision-making": Interview with Sir Mervyn King, *Octavian Report*, https://octavianreport.com/article/mervyn-king-on -radical-uncertainty/.

115 deliberately bias the results: This is sometimes called wet bias, and it's discussed in Nate Silver, *The Signal and the Noise: The Art and Science of Prediction* (New York: Penguin, 2013).

116 Nate Silver forecasted: "Who Will Win the Presidency?," FiveThirtyEight, 8 November 2016, https://projects.fivethirtyeight.com/2016-election -forecast/.

117 Ian Hacking explains: Ian Hacking, *The Emergence of Probability: A Philosophical Study of Early Ideas about Probability Induction and Sta- tistical Inference* (Cambridge: Cambridge University Press, 2006); Ian Hacking, *An Introduction to Probability and Inductive Logic* (Cambridge: Cambridge University Press, 2002); and Ian Hacking, *The Taming of Chance* (Cambridge: Cambridge University Press, 1990).

118 "the possible outcomes are well defined": John Kay and Mervyn King, *Radical Uncertainty: Decision-Making for an Unknowable Future* (Wicklow, Ireland: Bridge Street Press, 2021).

120 Barack Obama's decision: Ibid., for a discussion at length.

123 "unknown unknowns": "DoD News Briefing—Secretary Rumsfeld and Gen. Myers," U.S. Department of Defense transcript, 12 February 2002, https://archive.ph/20180320091111/http://archive.defense.gov/Transcripts /Transcript.aspx.

126　"complex is unusable": Paul Valéry, *Notre destin et les lettres* (Conférencia, 1937).

126　*decision theory:* See, for example, Martin Peterson, *An Introduction to Decision Theory* (Cambridge: Cambridge University Press, 2017).

CHAPTER 7:
THE STORYTELLING ANIMAL

129　"set the entire Middle East ablaze": Gershom Gorenberg, *The End of Days: Fundamentalism and the Struggle for the Temple Mount* (New York: Simon & Schuster, 2001). See also Serge Schmemann, "A Red Heifer, or Not? Rabbi Wonders," *New York Times*, 14 June 1997.

130　before being arrested: See, for example, "Arms Cache Reportedly Meant to Blow Up Dome of the Rock," Associated Press, 30 August 1990.

130　"red heifer without defect": See Lawrence Wright, "Forcing the End," *New Yorker*, 12 July 1998.

131　2022 broadcast: Temple Talk Radio is available at the Temple Institute website, https://templeinstitute.org/.

131　looking for either a yellow one: D. M. Freidenreich, "The Use of Islamic Sources in Saadiah Gaon's Tafsīr of the Torah," *Jewish Quarterly Review* 93 (3) (2003): 353–95.

132　"Come on, this is serious!": Gerd Gigerenzer, *Rationality for Mortals: How People Cope with Uncertainty* (Oxford: Oxford University Press, 2010).

132　the Circumcellions: B. D. Shaw, "Who Were the Circumcellions?," in *Vandals, Romans and Berbers*, ed. Andrew Merrills (Abingdon, Oxfordshire, UK: Routledge, 2017), 243–74.

132　ornate marble tombs: I've conducted field research in Madagascar eight times since 2012, seeing these tombs regularly on the outskirts of the capital city, Antananarivo.

133　*bounded rational choice theory:* See, for example, B. D. Jones, "Bounded Rationality," *Annual Review of Political Science* 2 (1) (1999): 297–321.

134　Once every four years: K. D. Wald and C. Wilcox, "Getting Religion:

Has Political Science Rediscovered the Faith Factor?," *American Political Science Review* 100 (4) (2006): 523–29; and K. D. Wald, A. L. Silverman, and K. S. Fridy, "Making Sense of Religion in Political Life," *Annual Review of Political Science* 8 (2005): 121–43.

134   a rate of about 1.3 percent: S. Kettell, "Has Political Science Ignored Religion?," *PS: Political Science & Politics* 45 (1) (2012): 93–100.

134   Eighty-four percent: Conrad Hackett and David McClendon, "Christians Remain World's Largest Religious Group, but They Are Declining in Europe," Pew Research, 5 April 2017.

134   study of ninety-five countries: B. Gershman, "Witchcraft Beliefs around the World: An Exploratory Analysis," *PLOS One* 17 (11) (2022).

136   "Storytelling was the solution": Antonio Damasio, *Descartes' Error: Emotion, Reason and the Human Brain* (New York: Vintage, 2006).

136   traditional Bengali story: Rukmini Bhaya Nair, *Translation, Text and Theory: The Paradigm of India* (Thousand Oaks, CA: Sage Publications, 2008).

136   "hate and live by narrative": Quoted in F. W. Mayer, *Narrative Politics: Stories and Collective Action* (Oxford: Oxford University Press, 2014).

137   information is retained: R. A. Mar et al., "Memory and Comprehension of Narrative versus Expository Texts: A Meta-Analysis," *Psychonomic Bulletin & Review* 28 (2021): 732–49.

137   "It is addicted to meaning": Jonathan Gottschall, *The Story Paradox: How Our Love of Storytelling Builds Societies and Tears Them Down* (New York: Basic Books, 2021).

137   learn to swim before they walk: Carrie Arnold, "Watchers of the Earth," *Aeon*, 13 April 2017.

137   buzzing of cicadas: Rebecca Leung, "Sea Gypsies Saw Signs in the Waves," CBS News, 18 March 2005.

137   warns them of *laboon*: Susan Smillie, "Tsunami, 10 Years On: The Sea Nomads Who Survived the Devastation," *Guardian*, 10 December 2014.

138   "epidemics of popular narratives": Robert Shiller, *Narrative Economics: How Stories Go Viral and Drive Major Economic Events* (Princeton, NJ: Princeton University Press, 2021).

139 most human stories could be graphed: Vonnegut gave a lecture on this topic at Case Western Reserve University in 2004. It was the subject of his master's thesis at the University of Chicago, which rejected it. The lecture is available online at https://www.youtube.com/watch?v=oP3c1h8v2ZQ.

140 Nielsen TV ratings: Gottschall, *Story Paradox*.

140 "slips on a banana peel": Ibid.

141 *there is no story*: Ibid.

CHAPTER 8:

THE LOTTERY OF EARTH

143 Britain was cut off: Michael Marshall, "Tiny Island Survived Tsunami That Helped Separate Britain and Europe," *New Scientist*, 1 December 2020.

144 1.2 million trees: Stephen J. Thorne, "The Royal Navy's War on Trees," *Legion Magazine*, 15 February 2022.

144 "Statesmen plotted to obtain them": W. R. Carlton, "New England Masts and the King's Navy," *New England Quarterly* 12 (1) (1939): 4–18.

144 saving grace of the Royal Navy: S. E. Roberts, "Pines, Profits, and Popular Politics: Responses to the White Pine Acts in the Colonial Connecticut River Valley," *New England Quarterly* 83 (1) (2010): 73–101.

144 more than twenty-four inches: Carlton, "New England Masts."

144 "broad arrow" shape: Emily Cataneo, "Where Are the Last of Maine's Historic King Pines?," *Atlas Obscura*, 1 July 2021.

145 Pine Tree Riot: See, for example, Andrew Vietze, *White Pine: American History and the Tree That Made a Nation* (Essex, CT: Globe Pequot, 2017).

146 "interlock with ones in the bark": Roland Ennos, *The Wood Age: How Wood Shaped the Whole of Human History* (New York: HarperCollins, 2022).

146 "backing to car tires": Ibid.

146 "from the set of *Tarzan*": Lewis Dartnell, *Origins: How the Earth Shaped History* (New York: Vintage, 2020).

146 African apes eventually became us: Mark Maslin, "How a Changing Landscape and Climate Shaped Early Humans," *Conversation*, 7 November 2013.

146 "amplifier lakes": See, for example, M. H. Trauth et al., "Human Evolution in a Variable Environment: The Amplifier Lakes of Eastern Africa," *Quaternary Science Reviews* 29 (23–24) (2010): 2981–88.

147 periods of extreme climate volatility: Dartnell, *Origins*.

147 did not sprout randomly: Ibid., for a discussion at length, with maps.

149 Iron Age settlers: Beaumont James, *Winchester from Prehistory to the Present* (Cheltenham, Gloucestershire, UK: History Press, 2006).

150 the wheel was little used: R. Knauerhase, "The Economic Development of Saudi Arabia: An Overview," *Current History* 72 (423) (1977): 6–34.

150 "greedy, uncouth, and warlike": W. A. Rickett, *Guanzi: Political, Economic, and Philosophical Essays from Early China*, vol. 159 (Princeton, NJ: Princeton University Press, 1998).

150 Ibn Khaldun: See, for example, C. El Hamel, " 'Race,' Slavery and Islam in Maghribi Mediterranean Thought: The Question of the Haratin in Morocco," *Journal of North African Studies* 7 (3) (2002): 29–52.

151 largely culled from social theories: One of the main opponents of what he calls "neo-environmental determinism" is Andrew Sluyter. See, for example, his "Neo-environmental Determinism, Intellectual Damage Control, and Nature/Society Science," *Antipode* 35 (4) (2003): 813–17.

152 east/west pattern: One empirical test of the theory is available in D. Laitin and A. Robinson, "The Continental Axis Theory Revisited," *APSA 2011 Annual Meeting Paper*. See also P. Turchin, J. M. Adams, and T. D. Hall, "East-West Orientation of Historical Empires and Modern States," *Journal of World-Systems Research*, 2006, 219–29.

153 "F**k Jared Diamond": D. Correia, "F**k Jared Diamond," *Capitalism Nature Socialism* 24 (4) (2013): 1–6.

153 excuse for intellectual laziness: "Geographic Determinism," http://www.jareddiamond.org/Jared_Diamond/Geographic_determinism.html.

153 Clint Ballinger has pointed out: Clint Ballinger, "Why Geographic

Factors Are Necessary in Development Studies," MPRA paper, https://
mpra.ub.uni-muenchen.de/29750/1/mpra_paper_29750.pdf. See also
Clint Ballinger, "Initial Conditions as Exogenous Factors in Spatial
Explanation" (DPhil thesis, University of Cambridge, May 2008). The
main critique of the geographic determinism argument comes from one
of the most influential social science papers of the twenty-first century:
D. Acemoglu, S. Johnson, and J. A. Robinson, "Reversal of Fortune:
Geography and Institutions in the Making of the Modern World Income
Distribution," *Quarterly Journal of Economics* 117 (4) (2002): 1231–94.
That finding has been convincingly challenged in S. Bandyopadhyay
and E. Green, "The Reversal of Fortune Thesis Reconsidered," *Journal
of Development Studies* 48 (7) (2012): 817–31; and in Ballinger, "Initial
Conditions."

156 became a rich dark soil: G. R. Webster and J. Bowman, "Quantitatively
Delineating the Black Belt Geographic Region," *Southeastern Geographer*
48 (1) (2008): 3–18.

156 forced them to live and toil: See, for example, Allen Tullos, "The Black
Belt," *Southern Spaces*, 19 April 2004.

156 prone to malaria: This is discussed at length in Jonathan Kennedy,
Pathogenesis: How Germs Made History (London: Torva, 2023).

157 Donald Trump's defeat: David Bressan, "How US Presidential Elections
Are Impacted by Geology," *Forbes*, 3 November 2020.

CHAPTER 9:
EVERYONE'S A BUTTERFLY

159 non-identity problem: For a good overview of Parfit's thinking and
the debate around the problem, see M. A. Roberts, "The Non-Identity
Problem," *The Stanford Encyclopedia of Philosophy*, ed. Edward N. Zalta
(Stanford, CA: Metaphysics Research Lab, 2 April 2019).

161 *New York Times Magazine:* For a discussion of the poll, see Matt Ford,
"The Ethics of Killing Baby Hitler," *Atlantic*, 24 October 2015.

161   said they weren't sure: The *New York Times Magazine* tweeted the results, https://twitter.com/NYTmag/status/657618681204244480?s=20.

162   makes Hitler's father infertile: Stephen Fry, *Making History* (London: Hutchinson, 1996).

162   British scholar E. H. Carr: For a discussion of Carr's views, and a rebuttal to them, see D. Nolan, "Why Historians (and Everyone Else) Should Care about Counterfactuals," *Philosophical Studies* 163 (2013): 317–35.

163   "unhistorical shit": See Henry Abelove and E. P. Thompson, *Visions of History* (Manchester, UK: Manchester University Press, 1986).

163   observes David Byrne: David Byrne, *A History of the World in Dingbats* (New York: Phaidon Press, 2022).

163   "mandate of heaven": See, for example, D. Zhao, "The Mandate of Heaven and Performance Legitimation in Historical and Contemporary China," *American Behavioral Scientist* 53 (3) (2009): 416–33.

163   divine right of kings: For a nuanced discussion on the subject, see G. Burgess, "The Divine Right of Kings Reconsidered," *English Historical Review* 107 (425) (1992): 837–61.

163   Great Man Theory: For a discussion of Carlyle's views and the debate around Great Man Theory, see William Fielding Ogburn, "The Great Man versus Social Forces," *Social Forces* 5 (2) (1926): 225–31; and the original discussion: T. Carlyle, *On Heroes, Hero-Worship, and the Heroic in History*, vol. 1 (Oakland: University of California Press, 1993).

164   Marc Bloch: For a discussion of Bloch's role in creating the *Annales* school, see G. Huppert, "Lucien Febvre and Marc Bloch: The Creation of the Annales," *French Review* 55 (4) (1982): 510–13.

165   to "do history": For an introduction to trends in historiography, I recommend M. Bentley, *Modern Historiography: An Introduction* (Abingdon, Oxfordshire, UK: Routledge, 2005).

165   useful thought experiment: This is adapted from D. Ruelle, *Chance and Chaos*, vol. 11 (Princeton, NJ: Princeton University Press, 1993). The exact details of the flea scenario are my own.

167   All will have a clear logic: See, for example, David Herbert Donald,

Why the North Won the Civil War (Golden Springs Publishing, 2015). The explanations given are economic, military, diplomatic, social, and political, but they are all broad factors.

167 next to a fencerow: For a detailed discussion of these contingent events, see C. B. Dew, "How Samuel E. Pittman Validated Lee's 'Lost Orders' prior to Antietam: A Historical Note," *Journal of Southern History* 70 (4) (2004): 865–70.

168 reversing the momentum: See, for example, James McPherson, *Ordeal by Fire: The Civil War and Reconstruction* (New York: McGraw-Hill, 1991). McPherson highlights how Antietam was a dramatic diplomatic turning point that also changed the nature and perception of the war.

170 Schemas are psychological tools: See, for example, J. L. Kuethe, "Social Schemas," *Journal of Abnormal and Social Psychology* 64 (1) (1962): 31.

171 "Englishman with a large mustache": Terry Alford, "The Spiritualist Who Warned Lincoln Was Also Booth's Drinking Buddy," *Smithsonian Magazine*, March 2015.

172 multiple discovery: See, for example, R. K. Merton, "Singletons and Multiples in Scientific Discovery: A Chapter in the Sociology of Science," *Proceedings of the American Philosophical Society* 105 (5) (1961): 470–86; and D. K. Simonton, "Multiple Discovery and Invention: Zeitgeist, Genius, or Chance?," *Journal of Personality and Social Psychology* 37 (9) (1979): 1603–16.

172 jettisoning flawed theories through falsification: Karl Popper, *The Logic of Scientific Discovery* (Abingdon, Oxfordshire, UK: Routledge, 2002). For a rival view, see Michael Strevens, *The Knowledge Machine: How an Unreasonable Idea Created Modern Science* (New York: Penguin, 2022).

172 *The Structure of Scientific Revolutions*: Thomas Kuhn, *The Structure of Scientific Revolutions: 50th Anniversary Edition* (Chicago: University of Chicago Press, 2012).

173 few scientists even took notice: U. Marvin, "The British Reception of Alfred Wegener's Continental Drift Hypothesis," *Earth Sciences History* 4 (2) (1985): 138–59.

173 Abraham Ortelius: J. Romm, "A New Forerunner for Continental Drift," *Nature* 367 (6462) (1994): 407–8.

173 Simpson wrote a strong rebuke: Joshua Rothman, "How Does Science Really Work," *New Yorker*, 28 September 2020.

175 "the soul of man dies in him": J. Taylor, *The Voyage of the* Beagle: *Darwin's Extraordinary Adventure in FitzrRoy's Famous Survey Ship* (London: Anova Books, 2008).

175 informal search: Peter J. Bowler, *Darwin Deleted: Imagining a World without Darwin* (Chicago: University of Chicago Press, 2013).

175 "my nose had spoken falsely": See, for example, Matt Simon, "Fantastically Wrong: The Silly Theory That Almost Kept Darwin from Going on His Famous Voyage," *Wired*, 21 January 2015. Darwin originally wrote in his autobiography about the shape of his nose and how it displeased FitzRoy.

175 Cleopatra's nose: For a discussion of J. B. Bury's views, see D. S. Goldstein, "JB Bury's Philosophy of History: A Reappraisal," *American Historical Review* 82 (4) (1977): 896–919.

177 Wallace was an outsider: For excellent accounts of Wallace's life, see James T. Costa, *Radical by Nature: The Revolutionary Life of Alfred Russell Wallace* (Princeton, NJ: Princeton University Press, 2023); and Peter Raby, *Alfred Russell Wallace: A Life* (London: Pimlico, 2002).

177 swear by phrenology: For a profile of Wallace's views, see Jonathan Rosen, "The Missing Link," *New Yorker*, 4 February 2007.

177 "brought out of the night air": This quote comes from a letter from Alfred Russell Wallace to the *Spiritual Magazine*, which was published on 1 February 1867. The letter is available at https://people.wku.edu/charles.smith/wallace/S126.htm.

177 "clairvoyance and phantoms": This quote is from a chapter ("The Opposition to Hypnotism and Psychical Research") that Wallace wrote in an 1898 book called *The Wonderful Century*. The chapter text is available at https://people.wku.edu/charles.smith/wallace/S726CH17.htm.

177 54 percent of Americans: J. D. Miller, "Public Acceptance of Evolution

in the United States, 1985–2020," *Public Understanding of Science* 31 (2) (2022): 223–38.

178 Francis Galton: His role in the eugenics movement is outlined in N. W. Gillham, *A Life of Sir Francis Galton: From African Exploration to the Birth of Eugenics* (Oxford: Oxford University Press, 2001).

178 Meteorological Office: J. Burton, "Robert FitzRoy and the Early History of the Meteorological Office," *British Journal for the History of Science* 19 (2) (1986): 147–76.

178 coined the word *forecast*: See, for example, R. Hamblyn, "Watchers of the Skies," *Times Literary Supplement* 5851 (2015): 13–14.

CHAPTER 10:

OF CLOCKS AND CALENDARS

181 Joseph Lott is alive: For details of this story, see Kathleen O'Brien, "A Simple Gift on 9/11 Saves the Life of an Office Worker Heading to the Twin Towers," *Insider Jersey*, 9 September 2011. Lott also told the story in vivid detail as part of a presentation to the Arlington Rotary Club on 9 September 2021, https://www.youtube.com/watch?v=JJbCUOcOwlw.

182 first plane hit the tower: For other similar stories of how timing affected 9/11 tragedies, see Garrett Graff, "On 9/11, Luck Meant Everything," *Atlantic*, September 10, 2019.

184 why and how cancers develop: C. A. Ortmann et al., "Effect of Mutation Order on Myeloproliferative Neoplasms," *New England Journal of Medicine* 372 (7) (2015): 601–12.

185 "Time passes faster": Carlo Rovelli, *The Order of Time* (New York: Penguin, 2019).

185 time dilation: See, for example, A. R. Smith and M. Ahmadi, "Quantum Clocks Observe Classical and Quantum Time Dilation," *Nature Communications* 11 (1) (2020): 5360.

185 extremely precise clocks: C. W. Chou et al., "Optical Clocks and Relativity," *Science*, 24 September 2010.

185 head is older than your feet: Nicholas Jackson, "Study: Your Head Is Older Than Your Feet," *Atlantic*, 24 September 2010.

186 304 days: See, for example, B. M. Allen, "The Early Roman Calendar," *Classical Journal* 43 (3) (1947): 163–68.

186 by the phases of the moon: For a more general history of calendars, see E. G. Richards, *Mapping Time: The Calendar and Its History* (Oxford: Oxford University Press, 2000).

186 Woden's day follows: For more on the origins of these names, see P. Shaw, "The Origins of the Theophoric Week in the Germanic Languages," *Early Medieval Europe* 15 (4) (2007): 386–401.

187 King Sargon I: H. Lewy and J. Lewy, "The Origin of the Week and the Oldest West Asiatic Calendar," *Hebrew Union College Annual* 17 (1942): 1–152c.

187 In the first century BC: For a history of timekeeping in this period, see I. Bultrighini and S. Stern, "The Seven-Day Week in the Roman Empire: Origins, Standardization, and Diffusion," in *Calendars in the Making: The Origins of Calendars from the Roman Empire to the Later Middle Ages*, ed. Sacha Stern (Boston: Brill, 2021), 10–79.

188 diurnal pattern: For an overview of these effects, see Daniel Pink, *When: The Scientific Secrets of Perfect Timing* (London: Canongate Books, 2019).

188 energetic tunes during work hours: M. Park et al., "Global Music Streaming Data Reveal Diurnal and Seasonal Patterns of Affective Preference," *Nature Human Behaviour* 3 (3) (2019): 230–36.

188 Jing Chen and Elizabeth Demers: J. Chen, E. Demers, and B. Lev, "Oh What a Beautiful Morning! Diurnal Influences on Executives and Analysts: Evidence from Conference Calls," *Management Science* 64 (12) (2018): 5899–924.

189 "snapshot" view: P. Pierson, "Not Just What, but When: Timing and Sequence in Political Processes," *Studies in American Political Development* 14 (1) (2000): 72–92.

191 "English spelling is ridiculous": Arika Okrent, "Typos, Tricks and Misprints," *Aeon*, 26 July 2021.

191 *poeple* or *poepul*: Ibid.

191 *increasing returns:* W. Brian Arthur, "Increasing Returns and the New World of Business," *Harvard Business Review*, July–August 1996.

192 within Victorian-era Britain: Michael Worboys, *The Invention of the Modern Dog: Breed and Blood in Victorian Britain* (Baltimore: Johns Hopkins University Press, 2022).

192 a Victorian parson: For details on the origins of Jack Russell terriers, see Michael Worboys, "Inventing Dog Breeds: Jack Russell Terriers," *Humanimalia* 10 (1) (2021): 44–73.

192 Great Collie Ear Trial: Worboys, *Invention of the Modern Dog.*

CHAPTER 11:
THE EMPEROR'S NEW EQUATIONS

196 Hyperion, a moon of Saturn: J. Wisdom, S. J. Peale, and F. Mignard, "The Chaotic Rotation of Hyperion," *Icarus* 58 (2) (1984): 137–52.

197 precognition or extrasensory perception: D. J. Bem, "Feeling the Future: Experimental Evidence for Anomalous Retroactive Influences on Cognition and Affect," *Journal of Personality and Social Psychology* 100 (3) (2011): 407.

198 conducted the same experiments: S. J. Ritchie, R. Wiseman, and C. C. French, "Failing the Future: Three Unsuccessful Attempts to Replicate Bem's 'Retroactive Facilitation of Recall' Effect," *PlOS One* 7 (3) (2012): e33423.

198 second reviewer's name?: Interview with Christopher French, London, 24 May 2023.

198 thirty-six passed the test: For more details on these and other replication tests, see Gary Smith, "How Shoddy Data Becomes Sensational Research," *Chronicle of Higher Education*, 6 June 2023.

199 caused people to become younger: J. P. Simmons, L. D. Nelson, and U. Simonsohn, "False-Positive Psychology: Undisclosed Flexibility in Data Collection and Analysis Allows Presenting Anything as Significant," *Psychological Science* 22 (11) (2011): 1359–66.

199 ovulating when they cast their ballot: K. M. Durante, A. Rae, and V. Griskevicius, "The Fluctuating Female Vote: Politics, Religion, and the Ovulatory Cycle," *Psychological Science* 24 (6) (2013): 1007–16.

199 P value: Andrew Gellman, "The Problems with P-values Are Not Just with P-values," https://stat.columbia.edu/~gelman/research/published/asa_pvalues.pdf.

200 abandoned altogether: B. B. McShane et al., "Abandon Statistical Significance," *American Statistician* 73 (1) (2019): 235–45.

200 "they will confess": Smith, "How Shoddy Data."

201 quarter of results: A. Brodeur, N. Cook, and A. G. Heyes, "Methods Matter: P-hacking and Causal Inference in Economics," IZA Discussion Paper no. 11796, 2018.

202 file drawer problem: For a scathing indictment of modern research methods, see J. P. Ioannidis, "Why Most Published Research Findings Are False," *PLOS Medicine* 2 (8) (2005). For a rosier view, see Matt Grossman, *How Social Science Got Better: Overcoming Bias with More Evidence, Diversity, and Self-Reflection* (Oxford: Oxford University Press, 2021).

202 cited at the same rate: Y. Yang, W. Youyou, and B. Uzzi, "Estimating the Deep Replicability of Scientific Findings Using Human and Artificial Intelligence," *Proceedings of the National Academy of Sciences* 117 (20) (2020): 10762–68.

202 "bullshit detector": Brian Resnick, "The Military Wants to Build a Bullshit Detector for Social Science Studies," *Vox*, 25 February 2019.

202 a broken system: For a critique of peer review that I largely agree with, see Adam Mastroianni, "The Rise and Fall of Peer Review," *Experimental History*, 13 December 2022.

202 planted severe flaws: F. Godlee, C. R. Gale, and C. N. Martyn, "Effect on the Quality of Peer Review of Blinding Reviewers and Asking Them to Sign Their Reports: A Randomized Controlled Trial," *JAMA* 280 (3) (1998): 237–40.

202 how many would be caught: S. Schroter et al., "What Errors Do Peer Reviewers Detect, and Does Training Improve Their Ability to Detect Them?," *Journal of the Royal Society of Medicine* 101 (10) (2008): 507–14.

204　They would crowdsource research: This whole section is about this study: N. Breznau et al., "Observing Many Researchers Using the Same Data and Hypothesis Reveals a Hidden Universe of Uncertainty," *Proceedings of the National Academy of Sciences* 119 (44) (2022).

206　"authoritarian durability": See, for example, Jason Brownlee, *Authoritarianism in an Age of Democratization* (Cambridge: Cambridge University Press, 2007).

206　lit himself on fire: See, for example, F. Kaboub, "The Making of the Tunisian Revolution," *Middle East Development Journal* 5 (1) (2013): 1350003-1.

207　*model drift*: See, for example, J. Gama et al., "Learning with Drift Detection," *Advances in Artificial Intelligence—SBIA 2004: 17th Brazilian Symposium on Artificial Intelligence, São Luis, Maranhão, Brazil, September 29–October 1, 2004, Proceedings* 17 (Heidelberg, Germany: Springer Berlin Heidelberg, 2004), 286–95.

208　*epistemic uncertainty*: See, for example, E. Hüllermeier and W. Waegeman, "Aleatoric and Epistemic Uncertainty in Machine Learning: An Introduction to Concepts and Methods," *Machine Learning* 110 (2021): 457–506.

208　sex-offender politician's: Adam Goldman and Alan Rappeport, "Emails in Anthony Weiner Inquiry Jolt Hillary Clinton's Campaign," *New York Times*, 28 October 2016.

209　Silver pointed to his model: For Silver's evaluation of his 2016 model, see Nate Silver, "The Real Story of 2016," FiveThirtyEight, 19 January 2017. See also Isaac Faber, "Why You Should Care about the Nate Silver vs. Nassim Taleb Twitter War," *Towards Data Science*, 17 December 2018.

210　*strong-link problem*: Chris Anderson and David Sally, *The Numbers Game: Why Everything You Know about Football Is Wrong* (New York: Penguin, 2014).

210　psychologist Adam Mastroianni: Adam Mastroianni, "Science Is a Strong-Link Problem," *Experimental History*, 11 April 2023.

212　McNamara fallacy: For an example of how it's avoided in medical research, see S. O'Mahony, "Medicine and the McNamara Fallacy," *Journal of the Royal College of Physicians of Edinburgh* 47 (3) (2017): 281–87.

213 "equation for a mouse?": This is from an interview of David Krakauer by Sam Harris for his *Making Sense* podcast. The transcript is at https://www.samharris.org/blog/complexity-stupidity.

213 *mathiness*: P. M. Romer, "Mathiness in the Theory of Economic Growth," *American Economic Review* 105 (5) (2015): 89–93.

215 she drove around Wisconsin: Katherine Cramer, *The Politics of Resentment: Rural Consciousness in Wisconsin and the Rise of Scott Walker* (Chicago: University of Chicago Press, 2016).

216 that tried to make predictions: M. D. Verhagen, "A Pragmatist's Guide to Using Prediction in the Social Sciences," *Socius* 8 (2022).

216 Fragile Families Challenge: M. J. Salganik et al., "Measuring the Predictability of Life Outcomes with a Scientific Mass Collaboration," *Proceedings of the National Academy of Sciences* 117 (15) (2020): 8398–403.

CHAPTER 12:
COULD IT BE OTHERWISE?

220 "would everything turn out the same?": This is an adapted version of the famous thought experiment by Stephen Jay Gould called "replaying the tape of life." For a nuanced discussion of it, see Z. D. Blount, R. E. Lenski, and J. B. Losos, "Contingency and Determinism in Evolution: Replaying Life's Tape," *Science* 362 (6415) (2018).

221 If the world is deterministic: Carl Hoefer, "Causal Determinism," in *The Stanford Encyclopedia of Philosophy*, ed. Edward N. Zalta (Stanford, CA: Metaphysics Research Lab, 21 January 2016).

223 *Sliding Doors*: This device is also used in other films, such as Krzysztof Kieslowski's *Blind Chance*. See also D. Bordwell, "Film Futures," *SubStance* 31 (1) (2002): 88–104.

226 proposed a deterministic universe: See, for example, Tim O'Keefe, "Ancient Theories of Freedom and Determinism," in Zalta, *Stanford*

Encyclopedia of Philosophy, 30 October 2020. See also T. Christidis, "Probabilistic Causality and Irreversibility: Heraclitus and Prigogine," in *Between Chance and Choice: Interdisciplinary Perspectives on Determinism*, ed. Harald Atmanspacher and Robert Bishop (Exeter, Devon, UK: Imprint Academic, 2002), 165–88.

226 Ājīvika school of Indian philosophy: See, for example, M. R. Dasti and E. F. Bryant, eds., *Free Will, Agency, and Selfhood in Indian Philosophy* (Oxford: Oxford University Press, 2014).

226 called an atomic "swerve": Susanne Bobzien, "Did Epicurus Discover the Free-Will Problem?," *Oxford Studies in Ancient Philosophy* 19 (2000): 287–337.

227 *On the Nature of Things*: A full English language translation is available at https://www.gutenberg.org/files/785/785-h/785-h.htm.

227 "knowingly and willingly decreed": This is a quote from Calvin's *Institutes of the Christian Religion*.

228 "shut up and calculate": D. Kaiser, "History: Shut Up and Calculate!," *Nature* 505 (7482) (2014): 153–55.

229 Bohmian mechanics: M. Esfeld et al., "The Ontology of Bohmian Mechanics," *British Journal for the Philosophy of Science*, 2014.

229 many-worlds interpretation: For a more accessible overview to key ideas in this interpretation, see Sean Carroll, *Something Deeply Hidden: Quantum Worlds and the Emergence of Spacetime* (London: Oneworld, 2021).

229 superdeterminism: At the moment, this is a reasonably fringe theory. The main proponent is the German theoretical physicist Sabine Hossenfelder. I interviewed her about the theory on 22 November 2022.

230 preformationism: See, for example, L. Van Speybroeck, D. De Waele, and G. Van De Vijver, "Theories in Early Embryology: Close Connections between Epigenesis, Preformationism, and Self-Organization," *Annals of the New York Academy of Sciences* 981 (1) (2002): 7–49.

232 *libertarian free will*: See, for example, Randolph Clarke, "Incompatibilist (Nondeterministic) Theories of Free Will," in Zalta, *Stanford Encyclopedia of Philosophy*, 18 August 2021.

233 "ghost in the machine": For further discussions on the scientific problems with libertarian free will, see Daniel C. Dennett, *Consciousness Explained* (New York: Penguin, 1993); and Sam Harris, *Free Will* (New York: Free Press, 2012).

233 "logically incoherent nonsense": "Does Superdeterminism Save Quantum Mechanics? Or Does It Kill Free Will and Destroy Science?," Sabine Hossenfelder's YouTube channel, https://www.youtube.com/watch?v=ytyjgIyegDI.

235 Hooker's Division: For discussion of the etymology, see J. Peter Maher, "The Unhappy Hookers: Origin of Hooker 'Prostitute,'" working paper, 2021, https://scholarsmine.mst.edu/cgi/viewcontent.cgi?article=1172&context=artlan_phil_facwork.

236 The philosopher Harry Frankfurt: H. G. Frankfurt, "Freedom of the Will and the Concept of a Person," in *What Is a Person?*, ed. M. F. Goodman (Totowa, NJ: Humana Press, 1988), 127–44.

237 they've discovered Atlantis: Sam Harris, "The Marionette's Lament: A Response to Daniel Dennett," *Sam Harris Blog*, 12 February 2014, https://www.samharris.org/blog/the-marionettes-lament.

238 Charles Whitman grew up as a polite Boy Scout: For more on this case, see G. M. Lavergne, *A Sniper in the Tower: The Charles Whitman Murders* (Denton: University of North Texas Press, 1997).

239 "unusual and irrational thoughts": The original letter can be found at http://alt.cimedia.com/statesman/specialreports/whitman/letter.pdf.

241 "Viewing human beings as natural phenomena": Harris, *Free Will*.

242 "dangerous moral and political consequences": Clint Ballinger, "Determinism and the Antiquated Deontology of the Social Sciences," working paper, https://philsci-archive.pitt.edu/8493/1/Determinism_and_the_Antiquated_Deontology_of_the_Social_Sciences.pdf.

243 structuration: Structuration theory is explained in A. Giddens, *Elements of the Theory of Structuration* (Abingdon, Oxfordshire, UK: Routledge, 1984).

243 "have acted differently": N. Pleasants, "Free Will, Determinism and the

'Problem' of Structure and Agency in the Social Sciences," *Philosophy of the Social Sciences* 49 (1) (2019): 3–30.

243 a shorthand that aims to discredit: See, for example, G. Duus-Otterström, "Almost Pregnant: On Probabilism and Its Moral Uses in the Social Sciences," *Philosophy of the Social Sciences* 39 (4) (2009): 572–94.

245 "whoever is around to be loved": Kurt Vonnegut, *Sirens of Titan* (Gateway, 1999).

CHAPTER 13:
WHY EVERYTHING WE DO MATTERS

247 "gladdest way to live": Maria Popova, "Octopus Blues and the Poetry of the Possible," *Marginalian*, June 2022, https://www.themarginalian .org/2022/06/02/octopus-poem/.

249 "share of the world is increased": Hartmut Rosa, *The Uncontrollability of the World* (Cambridge, UK: Polity, 2020).

249 "until they have a virtual copy": Karen Armstrong, *Sacred Nature: How We Can Recover Our Bond with the Natural World* (London: Bodley Head, 2022).

249 "touched, moved, alive": Rosa, *Uncontrollability of the World*.

250 magnets attract their opposite: For a detailed critique of *The Secret*, see Michael Shermer, "The (Other) Secret," *Scientific American*, June 2007.

253 "unbridled and the unpredictable in ourselves": Alan Lightman, "In Defence of Disorder," *Aeon*, 15 April 2019.

254 "it flies on mighty wings": Wislawa Szymborska, "The Poet and the World," Nobel Lecture, 7 December 1996, https://www.nobelprize.org /prizes/literature/1996/szymborska/lecture/.

254 *eudaemonia*: See, for example, E. L. Deci and R. M. Ryan, "Hedonia, Eudaimonia, and Well-Being: An Introduction," *Journal of Happiness Studies* 9 (2008): 1–11.

256 multiarmed bandit: See, for example, M. N. Katehakis and A. F. Veinott

Jr., "The Multi-armed Bandit Problem: Decomposition and Computation," *Mathematics of Operations Research* 12 (2) (1987): 262–68.

256 constantly exploring new restaurants: This point was made to me by my editor at Scribner, Rick Horgan, who lamented the insufferable tendency to try new restaurants when all he wants is to go back to the culinary greatest hits. When I reflected on my own behavior, I agreed. Sometimes, local maxima are good enough.

257 Orgel's second rule: Jack D. Dunitz and Gerald F. Joyce, "Leslie E. Orgel, 1927–2007," *National Academy of Sciences*, 2013, https://www.nasonline.org/publications/biographical-memoirs/memoir-pdfs/orgel-leslie.pdf.

257 The Kantu cultivate rice and rubber: This section is drawn from Michael R. Dove, *Bitter Shade: The Ecological Challenge of Human Consciousness* (New Haven, CT: Yale University Press, 2021). For a shorter summary of some of Dove's insights, see Michael Schulson, "How to Choose," *Aeon*, 14 July 2014.

259 *moneyballing* of the game: Michael Lewis, *Moneyball: The Art of Winning an Unfair Game* (New York: W. W. Norton, 2004).

260 moneyballing everything: Derek Thompson, "What Moneyball-for-Everything Has Done to American Culture," *Atlantic*, 30 October 2022.

260 13 million data points: N. E. Humphries et al., "Environmental Context Explains Lévy and Brownian Movement Patterns of Marine Predators," *Nature* 465 (7301) (2010): 1066–69.

260 fruit fly larva with deactivated brains: J. Berni et al., "Autonomous Circuitry for Substrate Exploration in Freely Moving *Drosophila* Larvae," *Current Biology* 22 (20) (2012): 1861–70.

261 Karikó persisted: See, for example, David Cox, "How mRNA Went from a Scientific Backwater to a Pandemic Crusher," *Wired*, 12 February 2020.

261 should be made randomly: For a discussion on how this might work, see L. Roumbanis, "Peer Review or Lottery? A Critical Analysis of Two Different Forms of Decision-Making Mechanisms for Allocation of Research Grants," *Science, Technology, & Human Values* 44 (6) (2019): 994–1019.

262   shocked himself 190 times: T. D. Wilson et al., "Just Think: The Challenges of the Disengaged Mind," *Science* 345 (6192) (2014): 75–77.

262   leisure-time invention: See, for example, L. N. Davis, J. D. Davis, and K. Hoisl, "Leisure Time Invention," *Organization Science* 24 (5) (2013): 1439–58.

263   "Ideas arose in crowds": For a discussion of this phenomenon and Poincaré's experience, see A. N. Katz, "Creativity and the Right Cerebral Hemisphere: Towards a Physiologically Based Theory of Creativity," *Journal of Creative Behavior* 12 (4) (1978): 253–64.

263   three thousand miles each way: For more on monarch butterfly migration, see S. Zhan et al., "The Monarch Butterfly Genome Yields Insights into Long-Distance Migration," *Cell* 147 (5) (2011): 1171–85; and S. M. Reppert and J. C. de Roode, "Demystifying Monarch Butterfly Migration," *Current Biology* 28 (17) (2018): R1009–R1022.

263   migration is an interconnected journey: For a poetic discussion of this phenomenon and how it offers a nice parable for our own lives, listen to Jad Abumrad's 2022 commencement address at the California Institute of Technology, https://soundcloud.com/brainpicker/jad-abumrad-caltech-commencement.

INDEX

INDEX

INDEX